Milton Friedman

Series Introduction

The *Major Conservative and Libertarian Thinkers* series aims to show that there is a rigorous, scholarly tradition of social and political thought that may be broadly described as "conservative," "libertarian," or some combination of the two.

The series aims to show that conservatism is not simply a reaction against contemporary events, nor a privileging of intuitive thought over deductive reasoning; libertarianism is not simply an apology for unfettered capitalism or an attempt to justify a misguided atomistic concept of the individual. Rather, the thinkers in this series have developed coherent intellectual positions that are grounded in empirical reality and also founded upon serious philosophical reflection on the relationship between the individual and society, how the social institutions necessary for a free society are to be established and maintained, and the implications of the limits to human knowledge and certainty.

Each volume in the series presents a thinker's ideas in an accessible and cogent manner to provide an indispensable work for students with varying degrees of familiarity with the topic as well as more advanced scholars.

The following 20 volumes that make up the entire *Major Conservative and Libertarian Thinkers* series are written by international scholars and experts:

The Salamanca School by Andre Azevedo Alves (LSE, UK) and José Manuel Moreira (Universidade de Aveiro, Portugal)
Thomas Hobbes by R. E. R. Bunce (Cambridge, UK)
John Locke by Eric Mack (Tulane, UK)
David Hume by Christopher J. Berry (Glasgow, UK)
Adam Smith by James Otteson (Yeshiva, US)
Edmund Burke by Dennis O'Keeffe (Buckingham, UK)
Alexis de Tocqueville by Alan S. Kahan (Paris, France)
Herbert Spencer by Alberto Mingardi (Istituto Bruno Leoni, Italy)

Ludwig von Mises by Richard Ebeling (Northwood, US)
Joseph A. Schumpeter by John Medearis (Riverside, California, US)
F. A. Hayek by Adam Tebble (UCL, UK)
Michael Oakeshott by Edmund Neill (Oxford, UK)
Karl Popper by Phil Parvin (Loughborough, UK)
Ayn Rand by Mimi Gladstein (Texas, US)
Milton Friedman by William Ruger (Texas State, US)
Russell Kirk by John Pafford (Northwood, US)
James M. Buchanan by John Meadowcroft (King's College London, UK)
The Modern Papacy by Samuel Gregg (Acton Institute, US)
Murray Rothbard by Gerard Casey (UCD, Ireland)
Robert Nozick by Ralf Bader (St Andrews, UK)

Of course, in any series of this nature, choices have to be made as to which thinkers to include and which to leave out. Two of the thinkers in the series—F. A. Hayek and James M. Buchanan—have written explicit statements rejecting the label "conservative." Similarly, other thinkers, such as David Hume and Karl Popper, may be more accurately described as classical liberals than either conservatives or libertarians. But these thinkers have been included because a full appreciation of this particular tradition of thought would be impossible without their inclusion; conservative and libertarian thought cannot be fully understood without some knowledge of the intellectual contributions of Hume, Hayek, Popper, and Buchanan, among others. While no list of conservative and libertarian thinkers can be perfect, then, it is hoped that the volumes in this series come as close as possible to providing a comprehensive account of the key contributors to this particular tradition.

John Meadowcroft
King's College London

Milton Friedman

William Ruger

Major Conservative and
Libertarian Thinkers

Series Editor: John Meadowcroft

B L O O M S B U R Y
NEW YORK • LONDON • NEW DELHI • SYDNEY

Bloomsbury Academic
An imprint of Bloomsbury Publishing Plc

1385 Broadway
New York
NY 10018
USA

50 Bedford Square
London
WC1B 3DP
UK

www.bloomsbury.com

Hardback edition first published in 2011 by the Continuum International Publishing Group Inc.

This paperback edition published by Bloomsbury Academic 2013

Library of Congress Cataloging-in-Publication Data
A catalog record for this book is available from the Library of Congress.

ISBN: HB: 978-0-8264-2351-1
PB: 978-1-4411-5831-4
ePub: 978-1-6235-6617-3

Typeset by Newgen Imaging Systems Pvt Ltd, Chennai, India
Printed and bound in the United States of America

To Jennifer, Caleb, and Mason—who waited for me

Contents

Series Editor's Preface

Milton Friedman was one of the most important twentieth-century advocates of libertarian and conservative ideas in academia and amongst the wider public. As a professional economist and teacher at the University of Chicago, Friedman made a critical contribution to the development of the free market and monetarist economics that challenged the dominant interventionist and Keynesian paradigm throughout the developed world. As a public intellectual, Friedman's books *Capitalism and Freedom* and *Free to Choose*, as well as his shorter popular writings and television programs, were crucial to the advance of public understanding of the role of the market in the promotion of human freedom and well-being.

In this outstanding volume, Dr William Ruger of Texas State University sets out Friedman's intellectual contribution to economic methodology and our understanding of a host of economic phenomena, including the relationship between consumption and income, the workings of flexible exchange rates, and the relationship between inflation and the supply of money in the economy. Dr Ruger also sets out Friedman's contribution to political theory, discussing Friedman's work on the relationship between economic and political freedom; the social responsibilities of business; and the proper relationship between the individual and the state, particularly in the context of conscription, drug prohibition, and discrimination.

By setting out Friedman's thought in a highly lucid and accessible manner, this volume makes a crucial contribution to the *Major Conservative and Libertarian Thinkers* series. It presents Friedman's intellectual contributions in the context of his life and the turbulent century in which he did most of his work. The book also considers the reception of Friedman's work and its likely long-term relevance. As such, this volume will prove invaluable to those relatively unfamiliar with Friedman's work as well as more advanced scholars.

John Meadowcroft
King's College London

Author's Preface

In 2007, Naomi Klein published *The Shock Doctrine: The Rise of Disaster Capitalism,* a scathing critique of global capitalism that placed Milton Friedman squarely in the crosshairs as the evil genius behind our current economic system. Klein, as one review stated, "essentially accuses Friedman of being the godfather of a Mafia-like gang, the Chicago Boys, who have exploited the public disorientation associated with catastrophes and political crises to impose an unwanted free-market ideology on much of the world" (Redburn 2007). Many other Americans, however, picture Friedman as the pleasant, grandfatherly, and unthreatening advocate of freedom and markets from whom they learned economics on PBS's *Free to Choose* documentary. But who is the real Milton Friedman and which, if either, of these depictions is more accurate? The objective of this book is to help the reader answer these questions and to describe and explain Friedman's life, thought, and works. It also explores how Friedman was received, his influence, and his contemporary relevance.

Unlike most scholars and lay persons who have taken an interest in or even admired (or despised) Milton Friedman's work, I became intrigued by this economist and public intellectual through his writings on methodology, on the draft (with which I agreed), and on corporate social responsibility (which I disagreed with and found quite frustrating). Though many people first encountered Friedman through his *Newsweek* column, his famous PBS series, or one of his popular books (*Capitalism and Freedom* or *Free to Choose*), my initial contact with Friedman, oddly enough, was in reading his seminal 1953 essay on methodology (after seeing it employed in Kenneth Waltz's masterpiece *Theory of International Politics*).

I should note that my work on this book was interrupted by a nearly year-long stint on active duty in the U.S. military during which I was deployed to Afghanistan. It was a very tough, long, and frequently frustrating experience. But it was ultimately a rewarding one, and I am proud to be a veteran of that continuing war. It may be amusing to some readers that I brought a backpack full of Friedman works with me, carrying them all the way from Texas to Utah to Las Vegas to Gulfport, MS, to Columbia, SC, to Kuwait to Afghanistan and back. Unfortunately, I had very few spare moments in which to do anything unconnected with the war, let alone read serious economics, so the books basically just gathered the "dust" that fills the air in Afghanistan and lined the "walls" of the shipping container Mike Liles and I called home. However, I could occasionally be found reading *A Monetary History of the United States* or *Capitalism and Freedom* during the few precious moments of downtime I had there. Once I learned two of my senior leaders had been economics majors, though, I would jokingly ask them, "WWFD?" (What Would Friedman Do?), and they would joke back in kind. Given Friedman's role in helping create the military we have today, in a strange way this was all fitting. For I was part of an All-Volunteer Force made up of men and women who freely chose to be what General William Westmoreland, during an exchange with Friedman, infamously called "mercenaries." I salute all of the fine volunteers/"mercenaries" with whom I had the pleasure to serve in Afghanistan, especially Michael Liles, Liam Corley, Karl Wick, LT Josh "Battle" Welle, LtCol Tyler Bosco, Maj Clay Turner, Doug England, TSgt Ed Colon, CDR James Scarcelli, BG Peter Zwack, and others who preferred not to be identified by name.

* * *

Many people helped me in various ways as I worked on this book.

John Meadowcroft, my patient editor and fellow scholar, deserves special gratitude for his assistance in seeing this through to the end. Jason Sorens and Sven Wilson, two friends and co-authors, exhibited much appreciated patience and support when this book took time away from my separate projects with them. They have also assisted by discussing ideas and offering suggestions, for this book and otherwise. Hans Eicholz has always been a real mensch, helping me better understand the world of classical liberalism and providing constant support.

Special thanks are due to economists Andrew Farrant, David Henderson, Josh Hendrickson, David Beckworth, and an anonymous reviewer. Their feedback and suggestions were quite useful and made this a better book than it would be otherwise. Andrew, in particular, went above and beyond the call of duty. Andy Knauer also merits my appreciation for helping with citation counts.

Thanks for various things are also due to Damon Linker, Marc Eisner, Claire Morgan, James Otteson, Tyler Cowen, Jeffrey Rogers Hummel, David Theroux, David Beito, Doug Den Uyl, Ted Carpenter, Jerry Muller, Marty Zupan, Barkley Rosser, Gary Becker, Dan Hammond, Dan McCarthy, the staff at FEE who tracked down an article for me, and Bob Art (I'm not sure my graduate school mentor would fully understand why I wrote this book, but he played a part in helping me be fit to do so).

I'd also like to thank my colleagues at Texas State University who have supported my eclectic research agenda and helped in one way or another while I wrote this, especially Vicki Brittain, Patricia Shields (who must be tired of hearing Friedman stories!), Ken Grasso, Bob Gorman, Arny Leder, Howard Balanoff, Sherri Mora, Omar Sanchez, and Paul DeHart. I would be remiss not to thank the staff at Texas State who supported me in various ways, including Coleen Rankin, Jenni Small, Jo Korthals, Michelle Williams (who fulfilled many, many ILL requests) and Margaret Vaverek.

I cannot possibly express how much I owe my wife Jennifer and our two boys Caleb and Mason. I could not have finished the book and survived my crazy life without their strong support and inspiration. Therefore, this book is appropriately dedicated to them. Thanks also to my parents and my brother Matt for their support.

William Ruger
Texas State University

Chapter 1

Intellectual Biography and Historical Context

On December 10, 1976, Milton Friedman was awarded the Nobel Prize in Economics. For most laureates, this is the crowning achievement of a long, distinguished, but mostly concluded career. Not so for Friedman. After receiving this award, he would live another 30 productive years during which he solidified his reputation as one of America's foremost public intellectuals. Moreover, with what was called his "characteristic gall," Friedman himself downplayed the award, stating at the time that the Nobel was "not the pinnacle of my career." He argued that "the true test of a scholar's work is the judgment that is made not at the time his work is being done but twenty-five or fifty years later" (Friedman and Friedman 1998, 442).

We have now entered that judgment period for the majority of Friedman's work. And given that many of his views on economics and public policy are being debated in the current economic and political climate, the timing of this book could not be better.

The objective of this book is to explain Milton Friedman's vast corpus of work so that the reader can judge for himself what to make of this interesting and controversial thinker. It also describes the personal and historical context of Friedman's thought while also showing how his work was received in his time as well as how it continues to be judged in the present. While economists and economic historians may find the original contributions offered here of interest, this book is intended for a general, educated audience rather than for specialists alone.

Friedman will never be ranked with the hallowed liberal thinkers of history such as John Locke and Immanuel Kant. However, he was a great economist whose scientific contributions place him on a footing with Irving Fisher, John Maynard Keynes, and Paul Samuelson—men who have vastly enlarged our understanding of the workings of the market. As economist and progressive columnist Paul Krugman argued recently, Friedman "was one of the most important economic thinkers of all time" (Krugman 2007).

Friedman, though, should not be viewed merely as a great economist. He was also a powerful purveyor of free-market and libertarian ideas, a Bastiat for the age of the welfare state, whose applications of both his economic knowledge and his liberal values made him an unrivaled public intellectual.[1] Indeed, Friedman's influence went well beyond his discipline.

Yet even this description of Friedman as an articulate, influential advocate of a certain vision of the good does not quite adequately capture his role in public life. Friedman was not a Krugman-like character—a powerful economist donning the cap of the partisan, general-purpose critic after earning his scientific bona fides. Instead, as he showed in his work on exchange rates, school choice, conscription, and the negative income tax, Friedman had great acumen in conducting and communicating policy analysis that was intellectually rigorous and rose above both the partisan and received wisdoms of his day. Yet he can be criticized for sometimes providing weakly grounded arguments that dodged or failed to capture the complexities of certain issues or the value trade-offs that bedevil less consistent or less ideological thinkers. Nonetheless, Friedman was certainly a world-historical figure who will be long remembered as both a first class economist and a beacon for individual freedom and free markets in an age with very mixed feelings about both.

* * *

Friedman achieved such a level of public stature that most learned people of a certain age have a fairly good picture of him in their heads: a physically diminutive, balding older man sporting large, thick-rimmed glasses and a conservative suit and tie. He seemed to look this way his whole life, though that says more about his longevity in the public eye than reality. Few think of him as the young vibrant man at Rutgers University or in wartime Washington. Indeed, the details of his early life and background are not common knowledge to most people.

Origins

Friedman was born in Brooklyn, New York, on July 31, 1912. He was the youngest of four children and only son of Jeno Saul Friedman and Sarah Ethel Landau Friedman. His parents were Jewish immigrants from Carpatho-Ruthenia, then in the Kingdom of Hungary within the Austro-Hungarian Empire but today on the western edge of Ukraine.[2]

Unlike John Maynard Keynes or even his contemporary, free-market economist Friedrich Hayek, Friedman came from a very humble background. Narrowly speaking, he grew up poor. In an interview later in his life, Friedman explained that "by today's standards, my parents in the whole of their life never had an income that came anywhere close to what we now regard as a poverty standard" (Academy of Achievement Interview 1991—hereafter AoA Interview). His father worked in New York City as a "jobber" and died at the early age of 49, while Milton was in high school.[3] His mother, once a seamstress in a "sweatshop," also had to work; she operated a dry goods store on the first floor of their house in Rahway, New Jersey, where the family had relocated when Friedman was 13 months old.[4] Despite the two incomes, Milton's parents still argued about money, often getting by through borrowing from relatives and check "kiting" (Friedman and Friedman 1998, 21; AoA Interview 1991). In contrast to many well-known thinkers such as John Stuart Mill,

Friedman's home environment was not all that intellectual given that his parents were neither very sophisticated nor even well educated (AoA Interview 1991; Capaldi 2004).[5]

Without veering overly into historicism, Friedman's background and upbringing most surely affected his basic outlook and assumptions about the world.[6] His great success must have likewise supported his view about the nearly limitless possibilities available for any hardworking person. Of course, Friedman's criticisms of policies such as the minimum wage certainly followed from his scientific understanding of markets and therefore stand on their own. However, his personal belief that these policies would have harmed his own poor family could not have helped but buttress his intellectual views. Indeed, Friedman often recalled that the minimum wage would have prevented his family from emigrating to the United States in the first place. Instead, in his opinion, they would have been "condemned indefinitely to remain in Hungary" (Rose Friedman 1976a, 28). Furthermore, the fact that he and his immigrant family were able to overcome financial poverty primarily through hard work, education, and thrift (rather than government aid) helps explain Friedman's later receptiveness to the virtues of the market. More importantly, his disadvantaged background probably accounts for his frequently voiced concern for poverty alleviation and the negative impact of government action on the lowest class of people. Yet there is some irony that this champion of laissez-faire had his college education financed by a state scholarship, and the local public library played a key role in his informal education (Friedman and Friedman 1998, 24).[7] Moreover, Friedman also fully understood the role that luck plays in life, noting on many occasions how chance worked to his advantage (Friedman [1986] 2004; AoA Interview 1991; Friedman and Friedman 1998).[8]

Rahway was a commuter city just 20 miles outside New York City. Friedman remained there until he went to college at Rutgers University in 1928. He had a fairly normal childhood for the times and has described his high school years as "mostly uneventful" (Friedman and Friedman 1998, 24). It was during high school, however, that he began to develop a love of mathematics and was inspired by his Latin teacher to go to college and become an educated person (Friedman and Friedman 1991, 24; AoA Interview 1991). Friedman also displayed signs of his later rhetorical prowess at this stage of his life, winning a bronze medal in the *New York Times*' National Oratorical Contest on the Constitution (Friedman and Friedman 1998, 24).

Friedman's parents were Orthodox Jews, and Milton attended Hebrew school until his bar mitzvah. However, Friedman "shifted to complete agnosticism" when he was roughly 12, later attributing the change to his realization "that there was no valid basis" for his religious beliefs or practices. From that point on, he never again authentically practiced a religious faith. Indeed, Friedman later noted that his wife, Rose, considered him "fanatically antireligious," displaying perhaps the hyperrationalism and empiricism that would guide his scholarly work (Friedman and Friedman 1998, 23). Yet Friedman firmly maintained until the end of his life that he was "not an atheist" either, since God's existence is "not capable of being proved either false or true" (Fox Interview 2004).

Fortunately for Friedman, the majority of his childhood coincided with the relatively peaceful and prosperous times of the "Roaring Twenties." Despite that era's own "irrational exuberance" at the end of the decade, 1920s America was characterized largely by real economic growth, low unemployment, a flourishing of art and architecture, and much progress (Shlaes 2007; Johnson 1997). It was a good time to be an American, though Friedman's own family remained poor, and the relative bounty of the decade was to disappear over the 15-year period starting in 1929.

The Education of an Economist

Graduating from high school at the age of 15, Friedman matriculated at Rutgers University in the fall of 1928. His tuition was covered by a competitive New Jersey state scholarship. Friedman paid his other expenses through a variety of jobs, including one as a waiter. This particular venture paid him what he described as a "free meal" at lunch (Friedman and Friedman 1998, 25). This anecdote is somewhat amusing – and perhaps surprising—given that Friedman is often erroneously credited with originating the saying, "There's no such thing as a free lunch" (Keyes 2006, 70).[9] Despite living on campus instead of at home, Friedman was "totally self-supporting" and engaged in a number of small-time entrepreneurial activities to supplement his conventional college jobs (Rose Friedman 1976a, 28; Friedman and Friedman 1998, 26–28).

When Friedman started at Rutgers, he majored in mathematics with the intention of becoming an actuary. However, after a couple of years of classes and a few failed actuarial exams, he switched to economics (Friedman and Friedman 1998, 29). Friedman also found time during college to work on the student newspaper and to fulfill his two years of compulsory ROTC training. Unsurprisingly for a future critic of conscription, Friedman had nothing good to say about the latter experience. He later explained: "I regarded ROTC as a burden to be borne with no significant benefits for me or for the country" (Friedman and Friedman 1998, 29).

As an economics major, Friedman was fortunate to study with two exceptional young economists visiting Rutgers: Arthur F. Burns (later a professor at Columbia University and then Chairman of the Board of Governors of the Federal Reserve System) and Homer Jones (a student of Frank Knight at the University of Chicago and later a key figure at the "maverick" Federal Reserve Bank of St. Louis) (*Business Week* 1967). These two professors were key early influences on Friedman's views and his fateful career choice.

Friedman took several classes from Arthur Burns, starting what became a lifelong friendship with the future Fed Chairman. These courses included a two-semester course on business cycles and a seminar with Burns and just one other student in which they carefully examined a draft of Burns's dissertation, *Production*

Trends in the United States. Friedman also may have audited a course Burns offered on Alfred Marshall's classic *Principles of Economics* (Hammond 2000). These latter two courses likely had a significant impact on the young student just starting to study economics seriously. Friedman directly noted the influence of the seminar on Burns's dissertation, stating that it "imparted standards of scholarship—attention to detail, concern with scrupulous accuracy, checking of sources, and above all, openness to criticism—that have affected the whole of my subsequent scientific work" (Friedman 1988c, 8). Readers of Friedman and Anna Schwartz's voluminous and exquisitely detailed *A Monetary History of the United States* would certainly agree that Friedman had internalized many of these scholarly standards!

However, Burns may have had his biggest impact on Friedman's thought by exposing the young man to Marshall and sharing his own views on the old master. This transmission was likely to have been especially important given that Friedman would come to be a standard bearer for the older, neoclassical tradition of economics that Marshall represented (Kirzner 1967, 102 cited in Cole 2007). Marshall's views also influenced Friedman's general scientific approach. Rose Friedman noted that Milton's "work has always been in the Marshallian tradition, directed at developing 'theoretical generalizations to fit as full and comprehensive a set of related facts about the real world as it is possible to get'" (Rose Friedman 1976b, 20).

The extent of Burns's (and Marshall's) intellectual influence on Friedman is difficult to judge, as how we come to hold certain views is an intricate process with many inputs. However, Friedman did later say that "Save for my parents and my wife, no one has influenced my life more than Arthur" (Friedman 1988c, 7). Indeed, he went so far as to call Burns his "mentor, guide, and surrogate father" as well as someone who "played a major role in shaping my scholarly activity" (Friedman and Friedman 1998, xi).

This influence was not isolated to Friedman's college days. The two economists interacted frequently over the decades, including long conversations that would go late into the night and morning. Friedman noted that these sessions "constituted a continuing course in scientific method, economic analysis, economic policy, and, more broadly, life that left a permanent imprint" (Friedman 1988c, 8–9). Burns's role in Friedman's life must have made it especially painful to Friedman when they had a bit of a falling out over the Fed chairman's policies in the 1970s (Ebenstein 2007, 186).[10]

Homer Jones, who taught the young economist in courses on insurance and statistics, was also a key influence on Friedman. Most importantly, as a Knight disciple, Jones introduced Friedman to "what was even then known as the Chicago view" (Friedman 1976b, 434).[11] Jones also emphasized individual freedom and deep skepticism about planning—key themes that Friedman would likewise stress during his career (Friedman 1976b). However, Jones's influence in this regard does not appear to have been immediate. Otherwise, it would be odd for Aaron Director, Friedman's future brother-in-law and professor at the University of Chicago, to write his sister in 1937 or 1938 complaining of Milton's "very strong New Deal leanings—authoritarian to use an abusive term" (Friedman and Friedman 1998, 81). Jones was keenly interested in practical matters and was a forceful questioner in the classroom, characteristics that came to be hallmarks of Friedman's teaching (Friedman, 1976b; Johnson 1976; Becker 1991). Lastly, Jones was vital in securing Friedman a graduate school scholarship in economics at the University of Chicago: the scholarship being critical for a self-supporting young man during the Depression (Rose Friedman 1976a; Friedman 1976b).

Friedman graduated from Rutgers in 1932. He won high honors for his bachelors, honors in economics, and the Bradley Mathematics Prize (Hammond 2000). His undergraduate course of study, though, was a bit narrow; he took 24 courses totaling 87.5 credits in math and economics alone (Hammond 2000). Given that Friedman's political thought often lacked philosophical depth, perhaps a more liberal education would have been of some later value.[12] However, his strong grounding in math paid great dividends for his economic career, and thus a less-focused course of study might have come at too steep of an opportunity cost.

With solid credentials in both economics and mathematics and the desire to pursue graduate study, Friedman won tuition scholarships at the University of Chicago for economics and at Brown University in applied mathematics. He ultimately decided to take the Chicago offer and embark on a career as an economist rather than as a mathematician. Friedman later explained his fateful choice was due to the "intellectual appeal of economics"; the influence of his two Rutgers professors; and perhaps, most importantly, the "times." The Great Depression had begun, and the young Friedman was eager to understand "the burning issues of the day" (Friedman [1986] 2004). Economic historian Daniel Hammond may be correct that Friedman's choice of courses at Chicago, not to mention his later study with mathematical economist Harold Hotelling at Columbia University, meant that he had not completely shut the door on the world of mathematics (Hammond 2000). However, Friedman may have considered such training necessary for even a purely economic career—or at least to conduct the kind of economics he wanted to do.

The Great Depression was the single most important historical event of Friedman's life. From 1929 to 1933, U.S. real gross domestic product (chained 2005 dollars) went from $977 billion to just $716 billion; unemployment went from an annual rate of 3.3 percent between 1923 and 1929 to a high of 25 percent in 1933 (and did not go below 14 percent until 1941) (Bureau of Economic Analysis; Van Giezen and Schwenk 2001; Lebergott 1964). The rest of the world was in much the same boat. A League of Nations report from 1933 noted that "Economic activity in the world as a whole had touched depths unprecedented during the present depression" (quoted in Garraty 1987, 162–63). This economic calamity not only influenced Friedman's career choice and his early adult life but also impacted much of his professional work as an economist. Moreover, Friedman, the public intellectual, ceaselessly attacked many of the policies enacted in the face of the Depression and contested the ideas that guided them. It was a tough time to be starting out in the world, but it was a propitious time to be studying and working in the field of economics.

Friedman's graduate career in economics at the University of Chicago was actually quite short. He was in residence for only two academic years, 1932–1933 and 1934–1935. Indeed, he did not even ultimately get his Ph.D. from Chicago, though he did earn a master's degree from the university in 1933. During his first year at Chicago, Friedman studied under such luminaries in economics as Jacob Viner and Frank Knight, as well as Henry Schultz, Lloyd Mints, and John Nef (Friedman and Friedman 1998; Hammond 2000). He also took a number of courses in mathematics.

Viner, Knight, and Schultz were the teachers who influenced Friedman most during his limited term at Chicago. Friedman took three classes from Viner, including the core economic theory course entitled "Price and Distribution Theory" that Friedman himself later taught at Chicago (Hammond 2000). This class had a dramatic impact on the young man. Friedman later noted it "opened up a new world" and described it as "unquestionably the greatest intellectual experience" of his life (Friedman [1986] 2004, 70).[13] Not only did the course contribute to his intellectual development and understanding of price theory, Friedman also met his future wife and collaborator, Rose Director, in it.[14] Viner's teaching style—perhaps inherited from his teacher F. W. Taussig—may also have rubbed off on Friedman, given that both were well known for intimidating—even terrorizing—students (Reder 1982, 9; Overtveldt 2007, 80). Though to be fair, Friedman probably never fully matched Viner's caustic classroom style (Reder 1982).

Knight, the arch classical liberal and fellow original Mont Pelerin Society member, was a second key figure from Friedman's student days at Chicago. Friedman noted in an interview that he was "much influenced by Knight" and, in his autobiography, referred to Knight as "our revered teacher" (Overtveldt 2007, 71; Friedman and Friedman 1998, 193). However, Knight played a less formal role than that of Friedman's other professors. Friedman only had one class with Knight and did not work under him for his thesis (Hammond 2000).

Nonetheless, Friedman was exposed to Knight's ideas through a number of indirect paths. First, as noted earlier, he was taught by Knight disciple Homer Jones at Rutgers and was thus brought into contact with Knight's views even before enrolling at Chicago. Second, Friedman was early on a part of what Chicago economist Melvin Reder calls the "Knight affinity group" that formed around the old economist (Reder 1982, 6). This coterie included Friedman's future wife Rose Director, her brother Aaron Director, and one of Friedman's best friends George Stigler—all of whom were Knight students and strong classical liberals themselves who brought Friedman into contact with Knight's views on a regular basis. Moreover, Knight, as the leader of this affinity group of gifted students, "contributed to the formation of their minds" even though he "did not influence the direction of their research" (Reder 1982, 6).[15] Knight was probably even more influential on Friedman when they were "particularly close" colleagues and neighbors following Friedman's return to Chicago in 1946 (see Friedman and Friedman 1998, 38 and 193). At that point, "the Knight affinity group" slowly morphed into the Chicago School (or second or even third Chicago School) that Friedman was soon thereafter to lead to prominence (see Reder 1982; Bronfenbrenner 1962; Rotwein 1983; Frazer 1988). Indeed, many would argue that Knight was the intellectual forefather or even founder of this school.

Some caveats about Knight's influence are worth noting. Recent scholarship argues that Knight may not have been as important a figure in the development of the Chicago School (especially compared to Friedrich Hayek and Aaron Director) as has often been suggested (see Van Horn and Mirowski 2009, 158). Moreover, later in life, Friedman provided qualifiers about

Knight's influence on him personally. For example, Friedman explained that he did not consider himself "a disciple" of the man as was the case with Director, Jones, and Stigler. One of the things that separated the two, according to Friedman, was their different levels of interest in science vs. philosophy (Overtveldt 2007, 71). An examination of their work would show even more differences.

Henry Schultz was the last of the three professors at Chicago who had a particularly strong impact on Friedman, though less intellectually than as a mentor. According to Hammond, "Friedman's fortunes at Chicago appear to have been tied to Schultz more so than to any other member of the faculty" (Hammond 2000). Friedman formally took two statistics courses from Schultz, sat in on other courses with him, and spent his second year at Chicago as Schultz's paid research assistant (Friedman and Friedman 1998). Schultz was also the supervisor for Friedman's master's thesis (Hammond 2000). Although he ultimately did not regard Schultz as a profound scholar, Friedman later admitted that he learned a lot about conducting research from Schultz and "even more about the pure theory of demand and supply, and the statistical analysis of time series" (Friedman and Friedman 1998, 52; Hammond 1992). Friedman's first published paper was an outgrowth of his work with Schultz (Friedman 1935; Friedman and Friedman 1998). Most importantly, Schultz was critical in getting Friedman a well-paying fellowship at Columbia University for 1933–1934 in order to study with Harold Hotelling (Friedman and Friedman 1998; AoA Interview 1991).

It would be an oversight not to mention Henry Simons as well. He was an important presence in the department who likely influenced Friedman to some degree given Simons's work on monetary policy. Hammond (2000) argues that Friedman "along with other Chicago students was 'Simonized'" despite not taking any classes directly from Simons. Friedman himself notes, in his controversial discussion of a Chicago quantity theory of money tradition, that Simons (along with Mints) was a key progenitor of the approach that he was restating (Friedman [1956] 1987). Indeed, it would be hard to imagine Simons not influencing the future monetarist par excellence to some degree, given Simons has been described as "undoubtedly the dominant figure in discussions of monetary and fiscal policy" at Chicago when Friedman was a student (Patinkin 1969, 51). Friedman suggests just this in an article he wrote on Simons's monetary views: "there is no doubt that mine [beliefs and values] would be different than they are if I had not had the good fortune to be exposed to Henry Simons" (Friedman ([1967c] 1969b, 81). However, it is worth noting that there was a heated debate between Friedman and fellow Chicagoan Don Patinkin over whether Friedman accurately represented the "oral tradition" on money at Chicago—and thus whether Friedman was building off the approach of Simons and others at Chicago or breaking with it under the influence of other sources, including Keynes (see Patinkin 1969; Leeson 2000; Leeson 2003). Moreover, Friedman suggests that Simons was not all that influential on his thought. As Overtveldt (2007) carefully points out, it is Mints, not Simons, whom the Friedmans later credit in their autobiography as exciting them about monetary theory. Moreover, Friedman's early career shows little sign that this education on money matters stuck, given that he ignored the monetary side in his work on inflation while at Wisconsin and at the Treasury Department (see below).

Friedman spent a year at Columbia University from 1933–1934 sandwiched between his two years in residence at Chicago. He also ultimately received his Ph.D. from Columbia. During that year, Friedman continued his graduate education, largely under the direction of Harold Hotelling and Wesley Mitchell (the eminent business cycle theorist). Hotelling had a lasting influence on Friedman (Friedman 1986 [2004]; Friedman and Friedman 1998). In particular, Hotelling cultivated Friedman's interest and skills in mathematical statistics. Friedman took to this area so well that, as Julio Cole notes, he at first "showed more signs of becoming an eminent statistician than a great economist"

(Cole 2007, 117). His training under Hotelling paid dividends in his career as an economist but also during World War II when he did research for the military. This time, Hotelling was a colleague rather than a mentor.

Wesley Mitchell's impact on Friedman was more limited but nonetheless quite critical. At Columbia, Friedman took two classes from Mitchell, including one on business cycles. More importantly, when Friedman was at the National Bureau of Economic Research in the late 1930's, Mitchell (as director of research) helped defend Friedman's work on professional incomes from an attempt to suppress a key part of it. In this work, Friedman discusses barriers to entry in the medical profession—something that drew a hostile response from certain interested parties (Friedman and Friedman 1998).

When his fellowship at Columbia concluded, Friedman returned to Chicago for the 1934–1935 school year. He spent much of his time working as Schultz's research assistant as well as sitting in on classes and successfully taking his Ph.D. exams (Friedman and Friedman 1998). This only lasted one year, though, as Friedman left Chicago and academia in the fall of 1935 for Washington, D.C. and a government job. This move seemed to be more about needing gainful employment in a tough academic marketplace rather than any particular desire to give up the ivory tower. Friedman thought that anti-Semitism also may have had something to do with his lack of academic options at this time (Friedman and Friedman 1998). Going to Washington meant that Friedman had to interrupt his studies, since he had not yet completed his Ph.D. In fact, he would not formally finish for another decade.

Mr. Friedman Goes to Washington

Friedman arrived in Washington in late 1935. The changing city was filled with great energy and was focused on waging the revolution in American politics represented by the New Deal. Indeed, President Franklin Roosevelt's state-building was in full swing despite its centerpiece, the National Recovery Administration, having been ruled unconstitutional by the Supreme Court in the *Schechter* case. The Wagner Act, the Social Security Act, and the Revenue Act were all enacted just as Friedman was joining the growing federal bureaucracy.

Aside from growing in terms of its power, Washington was also growing physically. According to the U.S. Census Bureau, the population of the city ballooned by 36 percent between 1930 and 1940, going from 486,869 inhabitants to 663,091. In addition, new construction changed the face of the capital, as many of the monumental neoclassical buildings we associate with the federal district were erected between 1933 and 1939 (Schivelbusch 2006, 7–8).

Friedman, like many talented young men and women who joined the effort, knew he was participating in a special period in American history. He later remarked that "There was a sense of excitement and achievement in the air. We had the feeling—or illusion—that we were in at the birth of a new order that would lead to major changes in society" (Friedman and Friedman 1998, 60–61).

It might seem surprising to some that Friedman was originally a supporter of the New Deal. At that time, he and his wife thought the dire economic circumstances required a vigorous government response—a fiscal one and not just a monetary change by the Federal Reserve. He later explained: "Like our teachers and fellow students at Chicago, and indeed most of the nation, we regarded many early New Deal measures as appropriate responses to the critical situation" (These included job-creation programs such as the WPA, PWA, and CCC, though not the price and wage-fixing aspects of the NRA and AAA) (Friedman and Friedman 1998, 59).[16] Some contemporaneous evidence of Friedman's early support for the New Deal can be found in the aforementioned letter that Aaron Director sent to Rose before her 1938 marriage to Friedman. In this letter, Aaron remarked on Milton's "very strong New Deal leanings—authoritarian to use an abusive term" (Friedman and Friedman 1998, 81). Although Director's words ceased to be fully accurate as time went on, it is still nonetheless the case that Friedman maintained his support for some of Roosevelt's New Deal programs given the desperate circumstances of that time (see Friedman and Friedman [1980] 1990, 94; Commanding Heights Interview 2000).

Even if there was some measure of hyperbole on Director's part, Friedman probably fit right into FDR's New Deal Washington. He was just one more energetic young person who became part of the "explosion of government" that allowed men such as himself to "achieve positions of far greater responsibility than was possible under more static conditions" (Friedman and Friedman 1998, 60). Friedman expert Daniel Hammond's research supports this view, as he argues:

> Friedman's quasi-libertarian ideology, so familiar to us now, is not evident in the biographical record from 1928 until 1946. His teachers and friends were not of any one ideological stripe, and there is little if anything in his educational record with definite ideological slant. The evidence suggests that his views of the role of government through the 1930s and 1940s were in the New Deal mainstream. (Hammond 2000, 29)

Hammond's conclusion, however, probably goes a bit too far. There are things in Friedman's past suggestive of his future libertarianism—things that would rise to the fore once the New Dealer was whittled out of him over time by other influences, study, and experience. Nonetheless, Friedman's work at the Treasury in the early 1940's—especially his testimony before Congress in 1942, discussed below—shows that he was far from the libertarian and monetarist he would become after the war. Indeed, he spoke like a standard Keynesian with his emphasis on countercyclical fiscal policies to control inflation![17] Friedman himself later noted that "During World War II when I was at the Treasury, I was essentially a Keynesian" (Booknotes Interview 1994).

Friedman's first job in Washington was at the newly created National Resources Committee (NRC). He was hired to assist with a detailed study of consumer purchases. Specifically, Friedman was a "technician" who worked on planning the study, including designing the sample—"the most difficult statistical problem" associated with the study according to Friedman (Friedman and Friedman 1998, 106 and 62). Although he left the position after less than two years, the expertise Friedman gained on consumption behavior and practical statistics was important to his later work. Indeed, Friedman believed that his work on the consumer study enabled him to write what he considered his "scientifically best piece of work": the *Theory of the Consumption Function* authored in 1957 (Friedman 1957; Friedman and Friedman 1998). While at the NRC, he also developed a new method of nonparametric analysis known as "Friedman's Test," which is still broadly used today and a standard inclusion in statistical software packages (Friedman 1937; SPSS 17.0; Elliott and Woodward 2006; Friedman and Friedman 1998). Clearly, Hotelling had left his mark on the young scholar.

Friedman left the NRC in 1937 for a job in New York under Simon Kuznets at the National Bureau of Economic Research (NBER). There he worked on studies of professional incomes, including one on independent professional practitioners that he turned into a book with Kuznets (Friedman and Kuznets 1945). This book also served as his dissertation at Columbia University (where he had been teaching on the side while at the bureau). Though the book was completed in 1941, both publication and the awarding of his degree had to wait several years because of a controversy that the manuscript generated at the NBER.[18] In short, Friedman's work fingered the American Medical Association for engaging in monopolistic practices that artificially raised the income of physicians. This suggestion raised the ire of a board member from the pharmaceutical industry who then blocked release of the study. With the aforementioned help of Wesley Mitchell, the book was ultimately published with the inclusion of some diplomatic caveats. Importantly, in the process of completing this study, Friedman developed some helpful theoretical innovations regarding consumption that proved essential to his seminal work on the consumption function.

Included among these innovations is his famous distinction between transitory and permanent income.

It was also while at the NBER that Friedman, on June 25, 1938, married his fellow Chicago graduate student Rose Director. This marriage lasted over 68 years until Milton's death in 2006. Rose and Milton were not only a romantic couple but an intellectual team as well. They collaborated on many projects, including the well-known *Free to Choose* television series and its accompanying book.

The Friedmans' marriage also yielded two living children, Janet (b. 1943) and David (b. 1945), four grandchildren, and four great-grandchildren.[19] Janet attended the University of California at Berkeley for her undergraduate degree and for law school. She has had a successful career as a lawyer and had one son with her first husband.

David, following somewhat in his father's footsteps, is professor of law at Santa Clara University. Although he writes and teaches broadly in the areas of politics, economics, and law, he actually holds a Ph.D. in physics from the University of Chicago. Like Milton, David has also been involved in the movement for individual liberty. However, he is far more radical than his "statist" father and is one of the most widely known advocates of anarcho-capitalism. His book *The Machinery of Freedom* is a powerful exposition of this position and a must-read for libertarians and anarchists alike (David Friedman 1973). He has three children, one from his first marriage and two with his current spouse.

David's son, Patri Forwalter-Friedman, is also following the family calling of promoting a free society. Patri is a self-described libertarian, but it is probably more accurate to describe his views as anarcho-capitalist. He is especially critical of both libertarian political "folk activism" and democracy (Patri Friedman 2009; www.patrifriedman.com). Instead, Patri hopes that liberty can be furthered by building city-states at sea that will compete with traditional governments. To that end, he founded and is the executive director of the Seasteading Institute.

The "Friedman Affair" at the University of Wisconsin

Friedman left the NBER in 1940 to assume a one-year visiting position at the University of Wisconsin. This turned out to be a brief but ugly phase in his academic career. Friedman had ostensibly been brought to Wisconsin by economist Harold Groves in order to work on the NBER income project, with which Groves had also been involved. However, Rose later concluded that this was a "Trojan horse" to get Friedman into the department on a permanent basis (Friedman and Friedman 1998, 92).

Unfortunately, Friedman stepped into an internal battle at the university that frequently places new, untenured professors in the crosshairs. Upon arriving in Madison, the Friedmans quickly found the department divided into two camps (something of which they had been warned in advance) and further discerned that they had already been assigned to one of them (Rose Friedman 1976c). This division was largely the result of a fight going on between a faction in the economics department and the school of commerce over a number of issues, including whether the two departments would merge. Despite the simmering departmental politics and coldness displayed by some of the faculty, Friedman stayed busy with his course preparation and research on professional incomes (Friedman and Friedman 1998). However, fuel was added to the fire when, at the request of Groves, Friedman penned a memo critical of the university's flawed statistical training (Friedman and Friedman 1998; Lampman 1993). Yet Friedman's life was still relatively quiet until the spring semester.

In March, Friedman's future at the university came under review (as was typical), and he moved to the center of the battle over the future of economics at Wisconsin. At that point, the department's executive committee, in a 4–5 vote, defeated a motion to appoint Friedman as an assistant professor. When the dean of letters and sciences intervened and proposed that Friedman be brought in as an associate without tenure for three years, the motion was defeated 2–7. The dean then secured the university president's permission to buck the department and offer Friedman a tenured position, which morphed into a three-year position without tenure. Friedman accepted the term position despite some misgivings. Undaunted, his opponents used the local press to continue the battle. Finally, Friedman decided to withdraw his acceptance and move on (Lampman 1993; Friedman and Friedman 1998; R. Friedman 1976c).

The so-called Friedman Affair likely resulted from a number of causes, though its origin remains unclear. The internal division at the university about the future of economics was certainly key. There was also some personal enmity among the principle players in that battle that likely spilled over into Friedman's case. As James Earley, a Wisconsin professor at the time, put it: "I tend to view the Friedman affair as part of the running battle, that became really acute after WWII, between Walter Morton and others over the control of the Department and its development" (Lampman 1993, 121). Moreover, Friedman's controversial memo on statistical training, not to mention his expertise in that area, may also have played roles since they no doubt threatened some in the department (Friedman and Friedman 1998).

However, it is unlikely that political philosophy or ideology had any role in the episode. As Leonard Silk argues:

> The image which Friedman's arrival at Wisconsin suggests is that of a libertarian Daniel walking into an institutionalist lions' den—a historic confrontation between the 'Chicago' and 'Madison' doctrines. In fact there was no such confrontation. Although Friedman's ideological sympathies lay with the free market, he had not yet actively taken up the cudgels in its behalf. His association with Wesley Mitchell—the student and admirer of Thorstein Veblen, and himself the most 'scientific' of American institutionalists—gave Friedman impeccable credentials. The young Friedman, moreover, worked primarily as a mathematical statistician. From a professional standpoint, he believed in a 'value-free' economics, he was politically inert. (Silk 1976, 58)

Further evidence for this argument lies in the fact that the liberals in the department supported Friedman, while the conservatives fought his appointment (Silk 1976; Lampman 1993).

Finally, several participants, including Friedman himself, thought that anti-Semitism played a role in the affair. However, Friedman admitted it was a "minor subtheme" rather than the primary issue (Lampman 1993; Friedman and Friedman 1998). Another minor cause may have been Friedman's status as "interloper" from Chicago and the east, suggesting a fusion of regional and institutional prejudice (Silk 1976, 59).

Back to Washington

After the debacle at Wisconsin, Friedman and his then-pregnant wife Rose spent the summer of 1941 in Norwich, Vermont. There, Friedman worked with Carl Shoup and Ruth Mack on the very Keynesian question of how taxes could be used to prevent inflation (Friedman and Friedman 1998). Their work resulted in a 1941 report to the Treasury Department and culminated in the 1943 book titled *Taxing to Prevent Inflation* (Shoup, Friedman, and Mack 1943). It also led to Friedman being offered a position in the Division of Tax Research at the Treasury Department, a job he quickly accepted. Before he assumed the position in Washington, the Friedmans suffered a personal loss as Rose's pregnancy ended in a stillbirth (Friedman and Friedman 1998).

Friedman was at the Treasury from 1941 to 1943 working on tax issues. In contrast to his earlier stint in government, this time he was a policy maker tasked with helping revise the tax structure in anticipation of war (Friedman and Friedman 1998, 106). Friedman's work at this time displayed no signs of his monetarist and libertarian future. Indeed, he himself noted that he was "thoroughly Keynesian" at the time, and despite his certain familiarity with the monetary teachings at Chicago—unique "oral tradition" or not—he did not emphasize money or monetary policy in his work (Friedman and Friedman 1998, 112–13; Leeson 2000; Leeson 2003). Friedman's May 7, 1942, testimony before Congress on fighting inflation supports the claim. There, he argued that: "If inflation is to be prevented, this [inflationary] pressure must be neutralized by measures that restrict consumer spending. Taxation is the most important of these measures; unless it is used quickly and severely, the other measures alone will be unable to prevent inflation." In addition, he thought that "price controls and rationing, control of consumers' credit, reduction in governmental spending, and war bond campaigns" could also be used (Friedman 1942; Friedman and Friedman 1998, 112–13). To their credit, though, Friedman and others in the Division of Tax Research favored a "spendings tax" (different than a sales tax) over forced savings measures (Friedman and Friedman 1998; Friedman 1943).

Friedman's most important contribution at the Treasury was his work on developing the U.S.'s present tax withholding system for collecting income taxes. In particular, the system changed from one in which taxes were collected from individuals at the end of each year to one in which taxes are collected on current wages at the source (i.e., from the employer). This made it possible for the government to inconspicuously increase revenues and collect the huge amount of taxes required for the war effort in the short term and to expand the federal government in the longer term. The latter result was something that Friedman only afterwards understood: "We gave no consideration to any longer-run consequences. It never occurred to me at the time that I was helping to develop machinery that would make possible a government that I would come to criticize severely as too large, too intrusive, too destructive of freedom. Yet, that was precisely what I was doing" (Friedman and Friedman 1998, 123). Although he later hoped that withholding could be abolished, Friedman had no apologies given wartime exigencies and because he thought it would have been introduced whether or not he had been involved (Reason Interview 1995; Friedman and Friedman 1998).

In 1943, with the United States now involved in World War II, Friedman accepted an offer from his friend Allen Wallis to become the associate director of the new Statistical Research

Group (SRG) (Friedman and Friedman 1998). He stayed in this position until his permanent return to the academy in 1945. The SRG, located in New York City and based at Columbia, was supported by the Office of Scientific Research and Development (OSRD) and served the military services (particularly the Navy) and some of their suppliers (Wallis 1980).

Friedman's research at the SRG centered on the optimal size of anti-aircraft shells, aircraft vulnerability, proximity "fuzes" [*sic*], procedures for sampling inspections, and high-temperature alloys (Wallis 1980; Friedman and Friedman 1998). While engaged in that applied work, Friedman also helped invent sequential analysis, an important tool for statistical research. He and Wallis first struck on the idea, after which they brought in statistician Abraham Wald to further develop what Friedman sensed early on might be a "bigger" idea than either he or Wallis would "hit on in a lifetime" (Wallis 1980).

Although economists were not a majority of the group, Friedman fit right in at the SRG given his background in mathematics. Indeed, he was one of the two members (along with Wald) most cited by their colleagues as having the greatest influence on them (Wallis 1980). Even after a very long and successful career, Friedman looked back on his time at the SRG as "among the most varied, interesting, and indeed exciting, professional experiences" he ever had (Friedman and Friedman 1998, 125). Moreover, Friedman's work there spilled over into his later economic research. The failure of some of his work on alloys—using projections from multiple regressions—led him to be skeptical of using complex methods, and his research on proximity fuses inspired some of his work on income distribution (Friedman and Friedman 1998).

Back to the Ivory Tower for Good

With victory on both fronts ending the war in 1945, Friedman's period of federal employment also ended—this time for good (though he was later asked to join the Eisenhower administration on the Council of Economic Advisors, an invitation he declined) (Bender 1971).[20] He now embarked on the academic career he was determined to have. George Stigler, his friend and fellow student at the University of Chicago (as well as a former SRG employee), helped arrange a one-year visiting position at the University of Minnesota which Friedman began in the fall. This quickly turned into a tenured position at the associate professor level (Friedman and Friedman 1998).

While at Minnesota, Friedman taught statistics and economics. He also finally received his Ph.D., which was granted by Columbia University rather than Chicago where he had started graduate school. He also wrote, with Stigler, a controversial but enduring critique of rent control titled, "Roofs or Ceilings?" (Friedman and Stigler 1946). Showing his penchant to weigh in early on ripe political debates, 500,000 copies of a short version were later distributed as part of a campaign by realtors to end rent control (Friedman and Friedman 1998).

The short piece was met by the kind of controversy Friedman became famous for creating. Some economists were irked by this piece, while it caused a mini-tempest among some of the few classical liberals left in America at the time. As writer Brian Doherty explains, this uproar among the latter was due to Friedman and Stigler's focus on the inefficiency rather than the immorality of rent control as well as hints of an egalitarian impulse (Doherty 2007). Ayn Rand—in her typical black and white outlook—responded to the piece by calling Friedman and Stigler "two reds" and the pamphlet "the most dreadful thing ever put out by a conservative organization" (Rand quoted in Doherty 2007, 191). Even the publisher, the Foundation for Economic Education, had a problem with the piece. It asked the two economists to cut a passage suggesting support for greater equality—which the authors refused to do—and then without permission added a special editor's note that Friedman and Stigler felt accused them of "putting equality above justice and liberty" (Friedman and Friedman 1998, 151).

Despite plans to remain at Minnesota, Friedman left in 1946 for a post at the University of Chicago, where he taught until his official retirement in 1977. Unfortunately, it was due to George Stigler's misfortune that Friedman received the offer from Chicago to replace his old professor Jacob Viner. The economics department had offered the position to Friedman's friend first. However, Stigler's appointment was vetoed by the president of the university when, as Gary Becker notes, "in an interview, Stigler alienated the central administration" (Becker 1991, 138). Chicago then turned to Friedman, who quickly accepted a tenured position at the associate level.

Chicago proved an excellent home for Friedman, and he quickly began establishing his reputation for superior scholarship. Indeed, not long after arriving at Chicago, he started to concentrate heavily on the study of money and banking—or more specifically, monetary theory and policy. This focus marks the beginning of the monetarist counterrevolution that would make Friedman famous (or infamous) as Keynesianism's chief antagonist. Friedman's unrelenting assault on Keynes and defense of neoclassical economics, joined by others at Chicago (in the economics department, business school, and law school), made the "Chicago School of Economics" that he headed a notorious but unrivaled center of a certain type of economic research.[21] Economist Mark Skousen even goes so far as to claim that "Friedmanite economics has become practically synonymous with the Chicago or monetarist school" (Skousen 2005, 2)

But why did Friedman concentrate so heavily on monetary policy in the first place? Economist and *New York Times* economics correspondent Leonard Silk, in an early biographical sketch, makes it sound as if Friedman's journey into the study of money was basically a happenstance of chance and ideology. He argues that the proximate cause of Friedman's monetarist work was Arthur Burns's decision at the NBER to parcel out Wesley Mitchell's business cycle research when it became clear that Mitchell was not going to be able to finish his huge study.

Friedman, Silk notes, simply "drew American monetary history" from Burns and then as his study in the area intensified, grew to believe that monetary policy was absolutely critical. Silk adds that Friedman's underlying motivation was a dislike of Keynesianism and what it implied for individualism and free markets (Silk 1976, 76). Silk's interpretation, though true in part, is problematic for at least one major reason. Although Friedman was invited by Burns to handle the NBER's study of monetary matters, he had already shown an active interest in money well before 1950 when he was asked to assume those duties (Friedman 1936; Friedman [1948] 1953; Friedman and Friedman 1998, 228).

In his first decade teaching at Chicago, Friedman produced an impressive body of work. Most of it was relatively straightforward scientific research (though these pieces had important policy implications), including seminal essays on methodology, price theory, and monetary theory and policy. Many of these pieces were ultimately collected in a book titled *Essays in Positive Economics* (1953) although the two most famous chapters—"The Methodology of Positive Economics" and "The Case for Flexible Exchange Rates"—had never been published before.[22] During this early period, Friedman also penned his initial case for school choice, an intriguing argument for why the American economy is depression-proof (to which he returned in a talk in Stockholm during the 1976 Nobel Prize ceremonies) and two important co-authored pieces on utility with Leonard James "Jimmie" Savage (Friedman and Savage 1948, 1952; Friedman [1954] 1968b; Friedman 1955b).

Then, in 1956, Friedman published an introduction to a collection of papers from his Chicago Money and Banking seminar that was a critical early shot in the monetary counterrevolution that he led against Keynesianism (Friedman and Friedman 1998, 228). In this introduction, titled "The Quantity Theory of Money—A Restatement," Friedman articulated his basic "monetarist" argument that money matters. In particular, he argued that the demand for money is "highly stable" (and due to relatively few factors that lead one to choose money rather than other assets) and that the supply of money is a key variable that affects important economic phenomena such as prices (Friedman [1956] 1987).

Friedman was promoted to full professor in 1948. In 1951, he was honored with the prestigious John Bates Clark medal, which is awarded by the American Economic Association to the "American economist under the age of forty who is judged to have made the most significant contribution to economic thought and knowledge" (AEA). As Rose later noted, "The move to Chicago was really the take-off point for my husband's teaching and scientific career" (Rose Friedman 1976c, 23).

Although the primary reasons for Friedman's scholarly success were his own hard work and genius, the young academic was certainly aided by the hothouse intellectual environment at Chicago. Friedman returned to the university surrounded by a plethora of keen minds and excellent scholars. The most important of these for him included Frank Knight, Ted Schultz, Gale Johnson, John Nef, Lloyd Mints, brother-in-law Aaron Director at the law school, Allen Wallis in the School of Business, and Jimmie Savage in the mathematics and then statistics departments. Stigler finally made it back to Chicago in 1958 and was also joined by Harry Johnson and Arnold Harberger. Friedman was especially close with Wallis and Stigler, both of whom he had gone to graduate school with and worked with before joining the faculty at Chicago (Friedman 1992b). Later as a more senior scholar, Friedman was blessed by yet more brilliant colleagues, including his former student Gary Becker, Ronald Coase, and Robert Fogel.

Friedman also benefited from the location of the Cowles Commission for Research in Economics at Chicago from 1939 to 1955. Although Friedman was very critical of the "Cowles approach"—namely, an emphasis on mathematical economics and econometrics, he found its seminars "exciting events" (Friedman and Friedman 1998, 197). It is also hard to imagine that the Commission's high-powered members, including eventual

Nobel-winning economists such as Tjalling Koopmans, Lawrence Klein, Kenneth Arrow, and Trygve Haavelmo did not help create at Chicago what must have been an unparalleled intellectual atmosphere in which to do economics in the postwar era. Nonetheless, there was enough antagonism between members of the economics department and the Cowles economists that Cowles's departure to Yale in 1955 was probably not mourned too greatly. However, Friedman later noted that "the move was a significant loss to Chicago" (Reder 1982; Christ 1994; Friedman and Friedman 1998, 198).

Finally, Friedrich von Hayek was among the Chicago colleagues who exercised the greatest philosophical influence on Friedman. Hayek came to Chicago in 1950—though not to the economics department—and soon engaged Friedman in discussions that "reinforced" his interest in public policy and political philosophy (Friedman and Friedman 1998, 333). Friedman also attended one of Hayek's seminars and was engaged with the "exceptionally able group" of libertarian students that came to study with Hayek (Friedman and Friedman 1998, 188 and 333). Even before coming to Chicago, Hayek had already impacted Friedman indirectly through *The Road to Serfdom* (which Friedman claimed was a "powerful book" that also reinforced his philosophical interests) and the founding Mont Pelerin Society meeting (Friedman and Friedman 1998, 333 and 158). Moreover, Hayek had enlisted Friedman's support in 1945 for the Free Market Study that Hayek (and the libertarian Volker Fund) had been hatching with Henry Simons before the latter's death. This eventually came to fruition at Chicago under Aaron Director, and some claim it was a key spark for the Chicago School that emerged (see Van Horn and Mirowski 2009; Overtveldt 2007).

Friedman in the Classroom

In the midst of Friedman's impressive scholarly productivity, it should not be forgotten that he was also an active teacher with classes to teach and students to supervise. When he started at Chicago, Friedman taught the graduate price theory class he inherited from Viner. This class became a staple of his early offerings and was his "most famous course" (Hammond 1999: xiii). Eventually, his lectures in that class were even organized into a price theory textbook (Rose Friedman 1976d; Friedman 1962b; Friedman 1992b). Nobel laureate Gary Becker was a student in one section and thought "Friedman was at his best in this course" (Becker 1991, 141). Friedman's deep respect for Marshall shone through in this class, with Marshall's *Principles* forming the backbone of the early syllabus (Hammond 1999).

Friedman taught a number of other courses during his career. Given the direction of his research and the retirement of Lloyd Mints, Friedman began teaching graduate monetary theory starting in 1963 (Friedman and Friedman 1998). He also taught graduate-level courses on income, employment, and the price level; monetary dynamics; and other seminars (Hammond 1999; Friedman and Friedman 1998). However, Friedman rarely taught undergraduates and did not seem especially interested in them. He offered an undergraduate course on money and banking at Chicago from 1946–1951 and an introduction to economics class while visiting at the University of Hawaii in 1972 (Hammond 1999). In addition, Friedman was a Fulbright fellow at Cambridge University in 1953–1954 and spent a term at UCLA in 1967.

One of Friedman's most important teaching outlets was not a formal class but the Workshop in Money and Banking that he first organized in 1951. Operating on a "no representation without taxation" basis—namely, one had to be willing to present research or one could not attend, Friedman used this workshop to further the study of monetary matters and develop a group of students interested in the subject (Friedman and Friedman 1998, 208). In the workshop, students and visitors would present papers that would subsequently be dissected by Friedman and the other participants. These sessions could be meat grinders but helped push the study of money forward. George Neumann, an economics professor at Chicago for a decade, called the department's workshops "a bloodbath" (Overtveldt 2007, 41). Friedman was not as negative in his assessment, noting that "The workshop was successful in teaching students methods of research, in fostering the rapid completion of doctoral dissertations, and in deepening the quality of work done in the field of money, both at Chicago and elsewhere" (Friedman and Friedman 1998, 209). His summary of its effects is borne out by the fact that a supermajority of the 75 or so completed theses he supervised were in money and banking and led to many published works, including a collection of them titled *Studies in the Quantity Theory of Money* (which includes Friedman's seminal essay "The Quantity Theory of Money—A Restatement") (Friedman [1956] 1987; Friedman and Friedman 1998; Hammond 1999).

Friedman's pedagogical style was intense and not for the meek. Becker noted that "Friedman encouraged give-and-take with students. He welcomed questions, restated them much more clearly than the struggling students were able to, and then usually showed why they revealed confused thinking" (Becker 1991, 141). Other former students have described Friedman's classroom personae with more dramatic terms. They have called him "demanding and unforgiving of sloppiness and error," as well as "intimidating." Moreover, he was "feared" and "an unforgiving taskmaster in terms of getting things right" (Dwyer 1999; Fand 1999). His last Ph.D. student, Gerald Dwyer, admitted that such a "harsh" portrayal is "deserved" in a sense (Dwyer 1999, 7). Nobel laureate James Buchanan went so far as to say that Friedman "relegated the student to the role of fourth-best imitation" and that, like Viner, he did not encourage "students to believe that they too might eventually have ideas worthy of merit" (Breit and Hirsch 2004, 144).

Friedman's approach was not intended to be cruel—at least according to one student. Instead, as Dwyer explained, it was meant to convey the message that "we could work out the argument ourselves." Furthermore, he was paying a compliment to his students by treating them as operating on the same playing field (Dwyer 1999, 7).

Despite the fear he frequently provoked—and perhaps in part because of it—Friedman's classes were at the same time regarded as great learning experiences. For example, Nobel laureate Robert Lucas explained that Friedman's class "was far more exciting than anything I had imagined" and further noted that "the quality of discussions . . . was unique in my experience" (Frängsmyr 1996; Breit and Hirsch 2004, 199). This was echoed by another former student who thanked Friedman for "making economics exciting" (Hammond 1999, xxviii). David Fand noted that Friedman's price theory had "extraordinary impact" since "Friedman was a brilliant lecturer," and "the course was intellectually stimulating and exciting" (Fand 1999, 20). Richard Timberlake likewise thought Friedman was a "scintillating teacher" (Timberlake 1999, 22). Finally, Becker noted that "no course had anywhere near the influence that Friedman's did. I looked forward with excitement to every lecture . . . it was a marvelous intellectual experience, and I was quite sad when the last lecture finished" (Becker 1991, 143).

With his emphasis on showing how theory could help untangle and shed light on real-world problems, his acumen at explaining difficult subjects, not to mention his debating skills, Friedman's lectures must have been powerfully seductive. Fand claims that "many students found Friedman's presentation both stimulating and convincing" (Fand 1999, 19). Nobel winner James Heckman found him "fascinating" (Frängsmyr 2001).

However, not everyone shared this view. Fand acknowledged that some students were indeed quite "skeptical." He continued: "Some students were turned off because they could not square their respect for 'enlightened opinion' with Friedman's conclusions; and other students thought that while Friedman was developing interesting economic theory, it was not the real world" (Fand 1999, 19). Friedman's style alone deterred some students from studying under him. Becker noted that many of the top students did not work with Friedman "because they could not take the heat: they could not handle psychologically his sharp and blunt criticisms, and his quick insights. In essence, they feared being overwhelmed intellectually" (Becker 1991, 144).

Yet Friedman was likely an excellent teacher and mentor. If one could handle his intensity and criticism in search of the truth, it is hard to imagine that Friedman's tutelage would not improve one's thought and work. Even though Friedman was a very busy man, as Becker related, "it was evident from the many written questions, criticisms, and suggestions, that he read [his students' work] very carefully" (Becker 1991, 143). In fact, he cared so passionately about good writing, something he inherited from Wesley Mitchell, that he pushed his students not only to get the economics right but to communicate them properly as well (Friedman and Friedman 1998, 75; Hammond 1999). In addition, Friedman was willing to go to bat for his students when necessary. For example, he sent a strong letter to the University of Chicago Press after it initially rejected Becker's manuscript on the economics of discrimination (Hammond 1999; Becker 1957). Lastly, as a testimony to his abilities as a teacher, it is worth noting that Friedman helped educate many fine economists who passed through his classes or workshop, including Buchanan and other Nobel winners such as Gary Becker, Robert Lucas, Harry Markowitz, and James Heckman (Ebenstein 2007).[23]

Despite his reputation for toughness, Friedman was reputed to care deeply for his students and to exhibit great patience in dealing with those who encountered problems in the course of their studies (Hammond 1999). He was also quite cheerful, gentle, and generous with people, especially those without his specialized knowledge (Dwyer 1999, 7). As his son David noted, Friedman had a "willingness to take other people, including one's own children, seriously in intellectual matters. What was important was not who was older or younger, father or child, but who had the better arguments" (Goldring Interview 2009). Indeed, it is likely these very qualities that made Friedman so popular and effective as a public intellectual.

Friedman Gets Religion

Although primarily focused on scholarship following his move to Chicago, Friedman also started to operate in more ideological circles. In 1947, he participated in a meeting put together by Friedrich Hayek in Switzerland, the goal of which was to discuss (classical) liberalism, its decline, and whether a society should be formed to help revive it (Hartwell 1995). He owed his invitation to Aaron Director, who knew Hayek, and who secured spots at the meeting for Friedman, George Stigler, and himself (Frank Knight also attended). The result of this meeting was the Mont Pelerin Society.

The Mont Pelerin Society (MPS) is a classical liberal organization whose members share a common concern for individual liberty and free markets. They also believe that the growth of the modern state represents a dangerous threat to a free society. The Society was founded to provide a forum for the discussion of liberal ideas among a small international group of people committed to individual liberty (Hartwell 1995). It meets regularly with both general and regional conferences.

Friedman was actively involved in MPS from its inception until 1992, when he attended his last regular meeting, though his participation was relatively limited before 1960 (Friedman and Friedman 1998; Cherrier n.d.). Friedman ultimately served as president of the society from 1970–1972. In the mid-1960s, he helped Don Lipsett start an American version of MPS that was called the Philadelphia Society. Friedman belonged to this organization for over 30 years, frequently attending its annual meeting and serving on its board for three terms (Friedman and Friedman 1998).

Friedman believed that participation in that founding MPS meeting was an important point in his intellectual development. He notes in his autobiography, "The trip provided my first opportunity to go abroad, introduced me to distinguished scholars in economics, as well as other fields, some of whom became close friends, and it strengthened my incipient interest in political philosophy and public policy." He also claims that it "marked the beginning of my active involvement in the political process" (Friedman and Friedman 1998, 158–59).[24] The opportunity for someone with his focus on mathematics, statistics, and mathematical economics to talk about philosophical ideas with a learned group of liberal thinkers must have certainly deepened, and even advanced, his budding interest and identification with liberalism.

Economic historian Daniel Hammond also sees this 1947 meeting as a key turning point in Friedman's outlook. Indeed, he goes so far as to argue that it "is probably the key single event in the formation of Friedman's ideology" (Hammond 2000). John Davenport, a journalist who attended the first MPS gathering, likewise emphasized its influence on Friedman. He later noted that Friedman, at the time of the meeting, "then had some distance to travel on his road to *Free to Choose*" (Davenport 1981 cited in Friedman and Friedman 1998, 160). This assessment of Friedman's ideology at the time seems credible, considering Friedman himself claimed it was not until after the war that he was "apparently cured, or some would say corrupted" of his Keynesianism (Friedman and Friedman 1998, 113). Indeed, just five years before in 1942, Friedman had offered very Keynesian and illiberal policy prescriptions during his aforementioned testimony before Congress on fighting inflation (*Power of Choice*; Friedman and Friedman 1998).

However, Friedman must already have been well down the road to classical liberalism before leaving for Europe. Otherwise, why would Stigler have written to him before the meeting that he assumed Friedman would be going with Aaron Director to a meeting meant "to save liberalism"? In addition, Stigler must have thought Friedman a liberal already, given that he told Friedman they, in addition to Director, needed to find a "fourth liberal" for bridge (Friedman and Friedman 1998, 158).

Stigler certainly had good grounds for this view since Friedman—even before he came back to Chicago—showed signs of supporting an active liberal agenda. For example, Friedman may have had ties to the group involved in setting up the Free Market Study at Chicago as early as 1945 and was certainly a hiring target as early as 1944 for those, such as Henry Simons, who were Hayek's key collaborators in trying to get the project off the ground (Van Horn and Mirowski 2009).[25] Furthermore, although Friedman's piece with Stigler on rent control troubled many classical liberals (due to its emphasis on efficiency and equality over justice and liberty), its publication by the libertarian Foundation for Economic Education suggests he was at least a fellow traveler by 1946 despite his egalitarian sympathies and support for the New Deal. Rose Friedman may provide a hint that her husband was sympathetic to classical liberalism even earlier. She related in 1976 that the modern liberalism and Keynesianism of the faculty and students at Wisconsin "furnished the grist for many arguments and discussions" while they were there in 1940–1941. She added, "Needless to say also, there was strong disagreement" (Rose Friedman 1976c, 19). Unless she was arguing with her husband as well, Rose's comment suggests that Milton was at least in part sympathetic to classical liberal views in 1940. Silk (1976, 58) certainly thinks this was the case, claiming that at Wisconsin, "Friedman's ideological sympathies lay with the free market." Thus is it possible, as economist Beatrice Cherrier (n.d.) argues contra Hammond, that MPS was merely "a catalyzer rather than a source of influence in Friedman's intellectual development." However, she admits it is hard to document whether "MPS *influenced* Friedman's political thinking rather than *reflected* it" and acknowledges that the meeting played a key role in Friedman's overall career since it "initiated his activism."

The debate about the importance of MPS to Friedman's intellectual and ideological development raises the question of when he did become a full-fledged libertarian. Unfortunately, this question is not easily answered since there was no single moment when Friedman saw the classical liberal light. Indeed, later in his life, Friedman told economist David Henderson that "there was no Saul of Tarsus moment" (D Henderson 2010, pers. comm., June 22).[26] Furthermore, economic historians provide few insights on the matter since, as Rob Van Horn and Philip Mirowski (2009, 162) admit, a detailed history of the "individual conversion experiences" of classical liberals like Friedman has not yet been written.

What can be said is that Friedman's classical liberalism emerged slowly over time due to a variety of factors and reached its full bloom in his 1962 classic, *Capitalism and Freedom*. We can say with some certainty that as a young man in college and graduate school, Friedman was not all that interested in politics. If he had any political sympathies as an undergraduate, they might even have been toward the Left, given that Friedman admitted in 2000: "it may well be that I harbored socialist thoughts at the time" (Commanding Heights Interview 2000). What he was most interested in was mathematics, statistics, and economics as a scientific endeavor (Frazer 1988; Ebenstein 2007; Silk 1976). This scientific focus continued in graduate school. Indeed, even up to his days at Wisconsin, he was, as Silk (1976, 58) notes, "politically inert." Fellow economists Martin Bronfenbrenner and Abba Lerner supported this contention in interviews with Frazer, the latter of whom "recalled Friedman as being non-political in 1937" (Frazer 1998, 151).[27]

Between that point and MPS ten years later, Friedman started to develop more interest in politics, not to mention more experience with it due to his work in the government. As noted above, Silk (1976, 58) thought Friedman's free-market sympathies were already evident by 1940. However, it was by no means a straight line from there to MPS and his emergence as a libertarian icon. He did not exactly sound like Adam Smith or Hayek while working at the Treasury. Moreover, he admitted he was a Keynesian before he was "cured" after the war.

This suggests that until he fully "got religion" at Mont Pelerin and beyond, Friedman was simply a sharp young economist prone to believe in pragmatic, even utilitarian-rooted, solutions to the ills he saw around him without dwelling too much on philosophy or philosophical consistency. Of course, this meant that he would have some faith in markets, even if he was still a Keynesian. He had clearly absorbed enough from the pen of Marshall; his experiences with Jones, Burns, Knight, Aaron Director, and Simons; and his friendships with Stigler and Wallis; to recognize the value of markets. Moreover, we should not underestimate the influence that his wife, Rose, had on Milton over the years. As Silk (1976, 57) concludes, "Professor Friedman appears to owe a measure of his libertarian zeal to his wife" (Cherrier n.d., in her analysis, stresses this as well, arguing that it "immunized" him from "the many progressive influences he encountered in his formative years"). Therefore, Friedman's views were sometimes consistent with the older liberalism. However, at other times, they were shaped more by the emerging Keynesian and New Deal consensus he was breathing in the air of New Deal America.[28] But eventually Friedman shed those tensions and transitioned into a thoroughgoing classical liberal.

In the final analysis, as Cherrier (n.d.) rightly argues, the ultimate transition is likely explained by the "interwoven" combination of personal and intellectual influences noted above, his own scientific investigation into economic science, and his experiences after leaving Chicago.[29] In terms of the first factor, Knight and his "affinity group" (comprised of the two Directors, Stigler, and Wallis) were probably most important, not to mention the indirect influence of Hayek and Marshall. Hayek's great impact on him can hardly be doubted, especially since Friedman specifically references *The Road to Serfdom*, discussions with the Austrian economist, and the "exceptionally able" libertarian students that Hayek attracted as influencing him (Friedman and Friedman 1998). His attendance, starting in 1956, at a series of summer programs on classical liberalism financed by the Volker Fund also undoubtedly contributed to his philosophical development (Friedman and Friedman 1998). However, Friedman was already at that point a firmly committed libertarian as seen by earlier, little-known pieces on liberalism (Friedman 1951d; Friedman 1955a) not to mention that his lectures at these programs were turned into *Capitalism and Freedom* (Friedman 1962a; Friedman and Friedman 1998). Cherrier, on the other hand, emphasizes Simons's *A Positive Programme for Laissez-Faire* as a key inspiration (which may go too far given the important differences between the two economists). As for the other factors, Friedman's study of professional incomes (and the controversy it sparked), monetary matters, and rent control—as well as his work in government and his increased contact with other classical liberals through the Volker Fund and MPS—likewise solidified his ideological vision.[30]

* * *

Although Friedman's days as a government employee ended with World War II, he consulted for the U.S. government for two extended periods in the 1950s. In 1950, Friedman spent three months in Paris for the U.S. government agency tasked with overseeing the Marshall Plan. Specifically, he analyzed the Schuman Plan for a common European market in coal and steel (Friedman and Friedman 1998). This plan resulted in the European Coal and Steel Community and was an early step toward the European Union. Friedman ultimately had deep reservations about the plan, thinking that it might result in "the substitution of a single super-monopoly for the present collection of monopolies" as well as "centrally directed and controlled industries" (Friedman and Friedman 1998, 181).

During this consultancy, Friedman also examined West Germany's balance of payments problem. After analyzing a variety of possible solutions, he concluded that the West German government could best deal with this issue by adopting a floating exchange rate. In other words, rather than being convertible into other currencies at a fixed rate set by the relevant authorities, the German mark would be traded on the market, and its value reflected by these private transactions. Given reigning ideas about the virtues of the Bretton Woods System of fixed exchange rates and hostility by German officials, Friedman's proposal fell on deaf ears. However, his research on the issue led to his influential article "The Case for Flexible Exchange Rates" (Friedman 1953; Friedman and Friedman 1998).

Friedman also consulted for the U.S. government agency that handled foreign aid, the International Cooperation Administration, in the fall of 1955. Specifically, he visited India at a time the Eisenhower administration was trying to influence that state to move in a more free-market direction. According to one Indian source, Friedman's recommendations to the Indian government were "wholly neglected" (Friedman and Friedman 1998, 268). This is unsurprising given this was not only the age of Keynes, but central planning was still very much in vogue, especially in the developing world.

It is worth lingering at this point on the historical context of Friedman's career since it underlines how much of an intellectual maverick he was at the time. Friedman's most important scientific and popular writings were completed from the end of World War II until 1980. This was a time that Friedman characterized as "a period of galloping socialism" (Wall Street Journal Interview 2006). At the least, it was one in which Keynes, the "mixed economy," and the welfare state dominated.[31]

When Friedman returned to the professoriate after World War II, the alleged free-market revolution that arose with Reagan and reached its peak following the demise of the Soviet Union was far, far away. Instead, planning—not capitalism—was the order of the day. Of course, capitalism was already suspect before the war, as the Great Depression had eroded people's faith in the market and spurred on a variety of government responses to deal with the crisis. These efforts included centrally planned and state-controlled entities in the United States like the Tennessee Valley Authority and even more far-reaching changes in the political economy of states such as Germany. By the end of World War II, as Daniel Yergin and Joseph Stanislaw (2002, 4) explain in their history of the postwar global economy, "In Europe and throughout much of the world, capitalism was discredited in a way that is not easily imagined today. It seemed infirm, inept, and incapable. It could not be counted upon to deliver economic growth and a decent life."

States around the globe responded in different ways despite this common view. Some looked to the Soviet example for an alternative to capitalism. Most others opted for someplace in-between, what British Prime Minister Clement Attlee called "the mixed economy." In this system, the government played a large role in regulating economic activity, even taking over and running industries in some cases, while providing a thoroughgoing welfare state to protect people from any manner of harm or insecurity. It stopped short of outright socialism, though classical liberals like Friedman thought it went pretty far, arguing that "Everywhere in the world, all of the emphasis was on central planning, on collectivism" (Mont Pelerin Society Interview 2002). This response took a slightly different form in the United States. As Yergin and Stanislaw (2002, 30) point out, Americans chose regulation more often than state ownership to control the market, and "This idea would maintain its grip for decades."

As might be guessed, intellectuals—including most economists—were quite friendly toward this shift in the political economy. Indeed, many of Friedman's own professors at Chicago, including Knight, Viner, and Simons, had been pushing for greater government involvement during the 1930s (Skousen 2001, 385). But in the postwar era, it was John Maynard Keynes who was the intellectual force behind the mixed economy and the use of fiscal policy to regulate the economy. As Yergin and Stanislaw note: "Keynes provided both a specific rationale for government's taking a bigger role in the economy and a more general confidence in the ability of government to intervene and manage effectively" (Yergin and Stanislaw 2002, 23). The dominance of Keynesianism and his followers such as Alvin Hansen and Paul Samuelson meant that old liberals such as Friedman were suspect in and out of academia. As Friedman recalled, "Those few of us who believed in freedom, in free markets, in minimum government were regarded as nuts over on the extreme fringe of the intellectual scene" (Mont Pelerin Society Interview 2002).

This hostile world—which the diminutive Chicago economist tried to turn on its head—remained this way throughout most of Friedman's career. Indeed, it was not until the 1970s when "stagflation" hit hard that this orthodoxy started to fall apart. The 1960s, on the other hand, were a particularly high point for advocates of the mixed economy and Keynesianism. Yergin and Slanislaw accurately note that "The good economic performance and long expansion of the Kennedy-Johnson years (until disrupted by the Vietnam War) marked the high point of Keynesianism, offering proof that the economy could be fine-tuned through macroeconomic management and the fiscal tools of taxation and spending" (2002, 41). The '60s were also notable for the broad expansion of the welfare state under Lyndon Johnson's "Great Society." This was followed in the early 1970s by Richard Nixon's own Keynesian declaration—both literally when he exclaimed, "I am now a Keynesian in economics"—and in terms of policy with deficit spending. Even worse, from Friedman's free-market perspective, Nixon went on to impose wage and price controls—something supported by another of Friedman's famous nemeses of the day, John Kenneth Galbraith.

Despite Keynes's dominance in the world around him and the large increase in the size and scope of government, the late 1950s and 1960s were an incredibly fruitful period for Friedman's scholarship. During this time, Friedman continued his assault on Keynes and led a band of other researchers to fully explore the role of money. One of the most important of these efforts was his massive, detailed study of the history of U.S. monetary policy, *A Monetary History of the United States, 1987–1960.* (Friedman and Schwartz 1963). This was the first of three books focused on monetary matters that he wrote with Anna Schwartz, and it was an instant classic. Another critical contribution from this period was his work on the consumption function and the permanent income hypothesis (which he had introduced earlier in his dissertation research). It was published in *A Theory of the Consumption Function,* a book that Friedman thought represented his "best purely scientific contribution (Friedman 1957; Friedman and Friedman 1998, 222). Other key publications from this time include his piece on velocity with David Meiselman (1963); his work on monetary and banking reforms, including the case for a monetary rule (Friedman 1960; Friedman 1962a); his pieces on the quantity of and demand for money (Friedman [1959] 1969b; Friedman [1961] 1969b; Friedman 1969b); and his influential 1967 presidential address to the American Economics Association, which critiqued the Phillips curve and introduced the idea of a natural rate of unemployment (Friedman 1968d).

Friedman the Public Intellectual

Although he became well known as a public intellectual and standard-bearer for a particular type of libertarianism, Friedman did not fully enter the political advocacy business until well into his career. Of course, his published works had contained hints of his promise analyzing public policies and offering his normative perspective, such as in his 1946 Foundation for Economic Education piece on rent control (Friedman and Stigler 1946) and in a few other infrequent pieces in the early 1950s, including his seminal article on education (Friedman 1951d, 1955a,b). He had also become more involved with several organizations on the "Right," including the American Enterprise Institute in 1956 (where he was a member of the Academic Advisory Board) and the Volker Fund (Friedman and Friedman 1998, 339 and 344). Of course, Friedman had entered the field of economics during the Depression because of its practical import. Therefore, much of his economic work had significant public policy implications. However, it was not really until the late 1950s and early 1960s and the publication of *Capitalism and Freedom*—when Friedman was already 25 years into his career—that he joined the fray as an active public intellectual. At that point, Friedman's public policy work became a consistent and increasingly prominent "part-time activity" to go along with his academic research (Friedman and Friedman 1998, 213).[32]

Friedman's late start as a public intellectual was due to a number of factors. A substantial one was that, as a young scholar, he was more interested in economics as a science than in public policy and political philosophy. His interest in these latter domains was, as he noted in his autobiography, "rather casual before he joined the faculty of the University of Chicago" (Friedman and Friedman 1998, 333). Furthermore, it took time for his budding interest to grow and for his philosophical commitments to harden. Another factor was that Friedman spent much of his early professional life involved in rather technical government service, especially while at the NRC and SRG. A fourth factor was his conviction that it was important to do solid scientific work lest one lose one's "sense of objectivity" and become a "pure ideologue" (AoA Interview 1991). Given such a view, Friedman would naturally have been reluctant to get too involved in normative work without first acquiring an extremely firm understanding of his own discipline. Finally, such reluctance may have also grown out of sheer prudence, especially after the experience at Wisconsin, where his opinions on World War II might have contributed to his problems there. In other words, he was a bit more careful about what he said until after he had made a solid mark as a scientist. This is consistent with the view he later expressed that you do not truly have free speech until you have a "solid," "independent" base so that you can then "stick to your principles" without having to modify them (AoA Interview 1991).

While Friedman was firming up his scientific bona fides in the 1940s and 1950s, he was also developing into a full-blown libertarian. As mentioned earlier, he was already moving in that direction by the time he went to his first Mont Pelerin Society meeting. However, that meeting and a number of other factors helped push him to the point where he could offer his finest statement of his libertarian principles in 1962 with the publication of *Capitalism and Freedom.*

Capitalism and Freedom, published in 1962, is arguably Friedman's richest political work and certainly his most philosophical. The introduction and first two chapters are especially important, as they explicate his general political theory. In particular, Friedman provides a libertarian argument about the proper role of government and defends the thesis that economic freedom is an indispensable condition for political freedom in general. The remainder of the book fleshes out his views on these matters in relation to particular areas such as economic policy, education, and social policy.

Capitalism and Freedom launched Friedman's career as a public intellectual and political advisor. In less than a decade, he would rise so far in these capacities as to be featured on the covers of both *Time* and the *New York Times Magazine* (Ebenstein 2007)—hardly where one would expect to find an academic without any official portfolio, especially a libertarian scholar!

Friedman's ability to communicate regularly to a broad audience was significantly aided when he became a columnist for *Newsweek* in 1966. According to his wife, he was initially "reluctant" to sign on after being approached by the weekly news magazine to pen a triweekly column in rotation with Paul Samuelson and Henry Wallich (Rose Friedman 1976g). However, Rose, Stigler, Henry Hazlitt, and even Samuelson convinced him to give it a shot. The decision proved wise, as Friedman ended up reaching millions of readers with each column for the next 18 years. He wrote on a wide array of topics in the over 300 columns he produced during that period (Friedman and Friedman 1998). Of course, the majority of these were on economic matters such as monetary policy, fiscal policy, and international trade. However, he also wrote on more purely political issues such as the draft, drug policy, education policy, welfare policy, and other areas far afield from strict economics.[33] Given the platform, Friedman used it to aggressively promote his philosophical commitment to free markets, monetarism, limited government, and individual liberty. He wrote the column for *Newsweek* until the magazine decided to go another direction in 1984.

In terms of party politics, Friedman was an advisor for a number of Republican officials from the 1960s up through the Reagan administration. However, he never took a formal full-time position in Washington with any of them. One of his first ventures came in the early 1960s when he advised a group of Republican congressmen who, according to Friedman, "were trying to develop a philosophy and legislative program for the Republican party" (Friedman and Friedman 1998, 344). His work with these congressmen resulted in a book titled *The Conservative Papers* in which he had an article on whether a controlled economy could work (Laird 1964). A few years later in 1967, Friedman wrote a piece further outlining his idea of a negative income tax for a similar book titled *Republican Papers* (Laird 1968).

Friedman's first significant role in partisan politics came during the Johnson-Goldwater presidential contest. After helping Bill Baroody put together a platform for Barry Goldwater in 1963, Friedman joined the campaign as an economic advisor. He claimed not to have done any "active campaigning" in this role. Instead, he later argued, he worked primarily in the background writing memos and advising on policy issues as they arose (Friedman and Friedman 1998). However, this is not entirely accurate, based on his own description of his activities. Friedman spent a great deal of time in the six weeks leading up to the election promoting his candidate at meetings, talks, and interviews (for example, see Rossant 1964; Friedman and Friedman 1998, 370). In fact, his activities sound a lot like active campaigning! Friedman also wrote a detailed piece just before the election for the *New York Times* explaining Goldwater's views on economics (Friedman 1964).

Four years later, Friedman again entered the political ring as an advisor to Republican presidential candidate Richard Nixon. He did not know the future President well at that point, though the two had met for one "long meeting" when Nixon was still Vice President. That rendezvous had left Friedman "favorably impressed" (Friedman and Friedman 1998, 375). It was about a decade later that Friedman joined Nixon's cause.

Specifically, Friedman was recruited by his longtime friend Arthur Burns to become a member of Nixon's economic advisory committee, which Burns was chairing. Instead of working on campaign matters, this group did advance planning for a potential Nixon presidency (Friedman and Friedman 1998). After Nixon's victory, Friedman and the rest of Burns's committee briefed the President-elect on economic issues for an entire day.

Friedman also met personally with Nixon after the election to discuss a memorandum he had written on the United States' balance of payments problem. In that memo, Friedman pressed for the United States to abandon the Bretton Woods system by stopping direct convertibility of dollars into gold and adopting a flexible exchange rate system—something he had advocated in a seminal article on the subject in 1953. Unfortunately, Nixon did not take Friedman's advice—largely because of Burns's vehement opposition (Friedman 1953; Freidman and Friedman 1998). However, Nixon eventually had to abandon Bretton Woods in 1971, and Friedman was vindicated.

After Nixon assumed office, Friedman became an outside resource for the new administration. He directly advised Nixon on several occasions, including at least one phone call initiated by the President (December 18, 1969) and at four lengthy meetings with Nixon in the Oval Office. George Shultz, Friedman's former colleague at Chicago and Nixon insider, was an especially important avenue of influence for Friedman and his ideas. Shultz was present at all but one of Friedman's Oval Office meetings, and it is probably no coincidence that Shultz was there for many of the administration's internal discussions in which Friedman's name and ideas were mentioned. According to the logs from Nixon's White House Tapes, Friedman was mentioned in as many as 60 discussions during the period from February 16, 1971, to July 12, 1973 (White House Tapes Subject Logs at www.nixonlibrary.gov; White House Tapes Subject Log Namelist).[34]

Friedman also served the administration as a member of two commissions: the Gates Commission on an All-Volunteer Armed Force and the Commission on White House Fellows. While a member of the latter from 1971–1973, he helped select three classes of fellows who would serve in the administration for a year (Friedman and Friedman 1998). The Gates Commission appointment only lasted a year, given its discrete purpose but was far more substantial and rewarding for Friedman.

Friedman had a long history of advocacy on the issue of military manpower policy. Specifically, he was vehemently opposed to conscription *in the United States* and favored an all-volunteer force (AVF).[35] He first wrote on the subject in 1962 in *Capitalism and Freedom*. There, he listed peacetime conscription as one of the many government activities that could not be justified on liberal grounds and proposed a shift to a voluntary system (Friedman 1962a).

He wrote a longer defense of a volunteer military in 1966 for a major conference on the draft in which he participated at the University of Chicago. This meeting, sponsored by the Ford Foundation, occurred on December 4–7, 1966. There were 73 participants from diverse backgrounds who held a variety of positions on conscription.[36] Friedman was active at the conference, though by no means the dominant force, and his paper appeared in a special volume on the conference (Tax 1967). His attendance at the conference was followed by multiple *Newsweek* columns on the issue (Friedman [1966b, 1968c, 1970b, 1974b] 1975) and a lengthy piece in *The New York Times Magazine* making the case for an all-volunteer force (Friedman 1967a [1987]).

While a candidate, Nixon had supported an end to the draft and its replacement with a voluntary force. Consistent with that pledge, Nixon created the Gates Commission shortly after becoming President and appointed Friedman as one of its 15 members. The group was specifically tasked with developing a plan to eliminate conscription (see Nixon statement of March 27, 1969, quoted in Henderson 2005). Despite its mandate, the commission was evenly staffed with five in favor of the draft, five opposed, and five uncommitted (Friedman and Friedman 1998, 379). Surprisingly given the group's initial make-up, the commission's final report was delivered without dissent in recommending an end to conscription and its replacement with a voluntary system (*Report* 1970).

Friedman was so intensely motivated by this issue that he even directly lobbied members of Congress (Friedman 1975, 188). His work paid off, as conscription was eliminated on January 27, 1973. Clearly, Friedman played an active role in the fight to end the draft, and one that many think was important to its success (see Henderson 2005, 2006). He later claimed it was the most satisfying public policy effort he had ever participated in since he thought the draft was "a major stain on our free society" (Friedman and Friedman 1998, 381). However, it is debatable how much influence Friedman personally had on the policy change (a topic that will be explored in more detail in Chapter 3).

When the manpower debate reemerged toward the end of the Carter presidency over whether to reintroduce the draft or at least draft registration, Friedman again defended the volunteer force and argued against registration (Friedman 1979a; Friedman 1979b; Friedman 1980b; Friedman 1980c). Although the draft was not reinstated, President Carter reestablished Selective Service registration for males in 1980 after it had been stopped by President Ford only a few years before.

Despite Friedman's access to the halls of power during the Nixon presidency, it would be inaccurate to cast him as a partisan for the administration and its policies. Friedman certainly defended Nixon when he thought the President was moving in the right direction, especially in the first two years of the administration. For example, he wrote an ill-timed piece on July 26, 1971, praising the "vision and courage" of Nixon's "steady as you go" economic policy (see Friedman [1971c] 1975). Indeed, Friedman later noted that he had, in the period before August 15, 1971, been largely on Nixon's side in public debate: "[my columns] mostly supported the general direction of policy and defended it against what I considered to be unjust criticism" (Friedman 1975, 40).

However, Friedman called it as he saw it and frequently criticized Nixon when the President strayed too far from the economist's free-market ideals. This was particularly the case after the President announced his New Economic Policy—which included wage and price controls—on August 15, 1971. At that point, Friedman hammered the administration's economic policies on both economic and moral grounds (although he agreed with the closing of the gold window, something he had urged Nixon to do two years earlier). He repeated these attacks over the course of the fall and into the next two years. For example, he excoriated Nixon for adopting wage and price controls in over a half-dozen *Newsweek* columns and in two *New York Times* op-eds (for some of these, see Friedman 1975). The *Times* op-eds were especially notable for making the moral rather than economic case against controls. Lastly, Friedman even took his argument with Nixon to the White House where he told the President—who agreed that the wage and price controls were a monstrosity and asked Friedman not to blame Shultz: "I don't blame George. I blame you, Mr. President" (Friedman and Friedman 1998, 387).[37]

Friedman was also a notable critic of the administration's "Family Assistance Program," given that it was a version of his negative income tax plan. He consulted on the project before it went to Congress and at first favored the plan. However, he soon grew "disenchanted" with what started to come out of the sausage-making process that is lawmaking (Friedman and Friedman 1998, 382). Friedman disliked the program's failure to properly incentivize welfare recipients to become self-supporting and the fact that Nixon "tried to implement a bold idea without seriously disturbing any existing programs" (Friedman 1970 cited in Friedman and Friedman 1998, 382; Friedman [1970d] 1975, 202). Despite the criticism, Nixon still felt warmly enough toward the economist that he phoned Friedman's doctor after Friedman's heart surgery on December 13, 1972 (or perhaps, cynically, Nixon was merely currying favor with an important public intellectual who represented many among his base) (see Friedman and Friedman 1998 and Nixon Library records).

Despite the access, Friedman's advice on economic matters seemed to have little influence on Nixon. For example, on June 8, 1971, Friedman directly counseled the President against more rapid monetary growth, but Nixon rejected this advice for personal political reasons (Friedman and Friedman 1998). More generally, the self-declared Keynesian President was more than willing to overlook Friedman's monetarism and concern for free markets as he increased the size and scope of government (Yergin and Stanislaw 1998, 42). Nixon's actions led Friedman to ultimately conclude that "Nixon was the most socialist of the presidents of the United States in the 20th century" (Commanding Heights Interview 2000). If Friedman was really an influential counselor to the prince (as some have claimed), it would be hard to square the libertarian advice he proffered with the frequently liberal (in the modern sense) policies and vast expansion of the state that occurred under Nixon.

On the heels of his role as sometime advisor to President Nixon, Friedman became quite active in a largely unsuccessful campaign to pass tax and spending limitation amendments to state and federal constitutions. Specifically, Friedman was one of the founders of the National Tax Limitation Committee, which in 1975 took up the cause of constitutional change as a mechanism to control spending and taxation. In 1973, Friedman had worked with then-Governor Ronald Reagan in California to promote a spending limitation amendment known as Proposition 1. This campaign, which lost narrowly, led to the broader movement that still exists today and in which Friedman had been extensively involved. This movement almost enjoyed success at the federal level in 1982, when a "balanced-budget tax-limitation" amendment passed the Senate with a two-thirds vote but failed to gain the requisite support in the House. During the 1982 amendment push, Friedman worked hard for it, speaking and writing in favor of the amendment, testifying on the Hill, and even advising key politicians in the fight. Indeed, he later noted that this was the only issue other than the AVF for which he had "done extensive lobbying in Congress" (Friedman and Friedman 1998, 354).[38] Clearly, Friedman believed this was an important cause.

The Nobel Prize and Chile

With his successful academic career drawing to a close in the 1970s, about the only thing missing from Friedman's curriculum vitae was a Nobel Prize in economics. This was remedied on October 14, 1976, when the Royal Swedish Academy of Sciences announced that he had been selected to receive the award (technically called The Sveriges Riksbank Prize in Economic Sciences in Memory of Alfred Nobel). The official press release noted that the prize had been awarded to Friedman "for his achievements in the fields of consumption analysis, monetary history and theory, and for his demonstration of the complexity of stabilization policy."[39]

Friedman's selection by the Academy was apparently not without some friction. This is unsurprising given how controversial a figure Friedman was in his time. Indeed, the Academy had already passed Friedman over on many occasions when lesser economists were chosen. According to one news report:

> Sources at the Royal Academy said the award to Dr. Friedman followed an extraordinary and sometimes heated debate, centered primarily over his political activity as adviser to conservative politicians and his journalism. Some academy members also reportedly felt his economic judgments were insufficiently scientific. (quoted in Frazer 1988, 354)

Despite this criticism, it would have been very difficult for the Swedes to forever ignore Friedman's original and influential contributions to the study of economics. Indeed, Rose was not hyperbolizing when she noted that "The overwhelming sentiment is that the prize is not only well deserved but long overdue" (Friedman and Friedman 1998, 444). Even the *New York Times* (October 15, 1976) noted that "Professor Friedman richly deserves the Nobel Prize." This was echoed in an otherwise critical piece in the *New Republic* that noted that no economist the author knew "was even mildly surprised at Friedman's selection" (Ulmer 1976). However, this positive response was not universal.

The announcement was also met with scorn and protest by a loud minority. Four Nobel laureates, though none from economics, led the charge. In two pieces in the *New York Times*—one by laureates George Wald and Linus Pauling and another by David Baltimore and S. E. Luria—these distinguished scientists criticized the Nobel committee for selecting Friedman because of his involvement with the Chilean government led by General Augusto Pinochet. Baltimore and Luria (October 24, 1976) went so far as to call Friedman "a supporter of the enemies of democracy."

These criticisms echoed earlier concerns that had been voiced about Friedman's Chilean connections. Minor rumbling about this relationship had begun in mid-1975, following a six-day trip to Chile during which Friedman met with General Pinochet once. Such criticism picked up steam in the fall when the *New York Times*, on September 21, reported that Friedman was "the guiding light of the junta's economic policy" (Kandell 1975; Friedman and Friedman 1998, 401). Anthony Lewis followed up on October 2 with a column, also in the *Times*, discussing the relationship between Chile's repressive policies and Friedman and the Chicago School. In this column, Lewis claimed that "The Chilean junta's economic policy is based on the ideas of Milton Friedman." He went on to ask, even though any theory can be perverted, "if the pure Chicago economic theory can be carried out in Chile only at the price of repression, should its authors feel some responsibility?" Lewis concluded that "There are troubling questions here about the social role of academics" (Lewis 1975). Soon, Friedman was the subject of frequent published attacks, including a notable article written by former president Salvador Allende's foreign minister Orlando Letelier, shortly before he was assassinated in Washington (Letelier 1976). Protests also began at the University of Chicago and other places where Friedman appeared. According to Friedman, these small but "annoying" protests continued over the next decade (Friedman and Friedman 1998).

The vocal opposition did not prevent Friedman from receiving his Nobel in Stockholm on December 10, 1976. The controversy over Chile, however, followed him over the Atlantic and must have marred what should have been a purely joyful trip. It certainly made his life more difficult while in Sweden. He and Rose were provided bodyguards, and their room was under 24-hour police surveillance for their protection. There were also large protests outside his appearances, including one of up to 5,000 people on the night of the award ceremony. Most egregiously, one protestor even interrupted the official ceremony. Just as Friedman was about to receive his award from the King of Sweden, this individual yelled from the balcony: "Down with capitalism, freedom for Chile" (Friedman and Friedman 1998).

Friedman gave two lectures in Sweden as part of the award visit. The first, for the Stockholm Club of Economics, was an update of an earlier lecture he had given in Sweden in 1954 on why the American economy was depression proof (Friedman and Friedman 1998). At the official lecture, Friedman defended economics as a science. Specifically, he argued that economics was a value-free science and illuminated this view with reference to how positive research on the relationship between inflation and unemployment had worked to produce a "drastic change" in the minds of economists—following "precisely the classical process for the revision of a scientific hypothesis" (Friedman [1977a] 1987, 349).

Given how much attention the Chile controversy attracted, it is worth exploring Friedman's precise relationship with the Chilean junta. In general, economist William Frazer (Frazer 1988, 327) is correct in stating that "There is little doubt that Friedman's involvement in Chile was greatly exaggerated by events." Indeed, if there was a Chicago professor behind the curtain in Chile, it was not Friedman but his colleague and chairman of the economics department Arnold C. Harberger. Nonetheless, Friedman *was* linked to those in and out of the Chilean government, known as the "Chicago Boys," who were pushing free-market reforms. Moreover, he did on two occasions unofficially advise General Pinochet on economic matters.

Friedman's primary connection to Chile and the Chicago Boys was through his capacity as a teacher at Chicago. From 1955 to 1964, the university had an arrangement supported by USAID with the Catholic University of Chile that helped bring graduate students from Chile to study in the economics department. Harberger was most closely tied to the program. These students would naturally have taken Friedman's core course in theory, and some would have studied money and banking with him as well. He was not involved in any other way with these students (Frazer 1988; Harberger 1976; Friedman and Friedman 1998).

Friedman's other link with Chile was his aforementioned six-day visit there in March 1975, arranged by Harberger as a side trip on the way to Australia and Japan. While in Chile, Friedman gave seminars and lectures to a variety of audiences in Santiago (Frazer 1988). He was also part of a group of about a dozen people who met once with General Pinochet for "three-quarters of an hour or so" (Frazer 1988; Friedman and Friedman 1998, 399). During this brief meeting, the group discussed economic matters, including the possibility of using "shock treatment" to deal with inflation and to get a handle on the country's dire economic situation (Friedman and Friedman 1998, 399). The general also asked Friedman to provide a written assessment of the situation following his visit, which Friedman did in a letter dated April 21, 1975.

In his letter to Pinochet, Friedman unsurprisingly told the president to adopt a package of free-market and monetarist reforms.[40] In particular, Friedman argued that Chile's inflation problem was so severe that "shock treatment" was necessary, despite his typical preference for gradualism. Such treatment would include drastically reducing the rate of increase in the money supply, cutting the fiscal deficit by substantially reducing government spending, and publicly committing to abjure printing money to finance future government spending. He also advocated that the government promote a "social market economy" by removing barriers (such as wage and price controls) to the effective working of market forces and freeing international trade. In short, Friedman counseled that "No obstacles, no subsidies should be the rule." Showing he was not unsympathetic to the hardships this would cause, nor unappreciative of the politics of reform, Friedman also argued that the government should "provide for the relief of any cases of real hardship and severe distress among the poorest classes" (Friedman and Friedman 1998, 591–94).

Despite the different circumstances facing the two countries, Friedman essentially offered advice similar to that which he had advocated publically to American audiences since at least the publication of *Capitalism and Freedom.* Specifically, government should keep inflation and spending low through monetary and fiscal discipline while promoting efficient markets by reducing barriers to individual success *and* failure.

Given the charges of his critics, it is worth noting that Friedman was not a supporter of the Pinochet regime. During the controversy that erupted in 1975 soon after his trip, Friedman explained that he did not approve of the junta or any other authoritarian regime that he had studied or advised on economic matters over the years (including the Soviet Union and Yugoslavia). A year later, when the issue returned to prominence after he was selected for the Nobel, Friedman added that he "deplore[d]" the political situation in Chile (see Friedman and Friedman 1998, 600). More telling, according to a letter from Harberger to the Nobel Foundation that was reprinted in the *Wall Street Journal,* Friedman turned down honorary degrees from two different Chilean universities because "he felt that acceptance of such honors from universities receiving government funds could be interpreted as implying political approval" (Harberger 1976). Lastly, during his university talks in Chile, Friedman had emphasized the importance and fragility of freedom—hardly an endorsement of an oppressive regime.

Friedman's letter to Pinochet was the last interaction he had with the Chilean junta. It is unlikely that his recommendations had much impact anyway given, as Pinochet would admit in a note thanking Friedman for his advice, that Chile's National Recovery Plan already contained much of what the economist had counseled (Friedman and Friedman 1998). Indeed, the government's plan was largely based on a 1970 document known as "The Brick," which outlined free-market reforms (Yergin and Stanislaw 1998). There can be little doubt that Friedman's scientific work on monetary policy influenced the Chicago Boys and the Chilean government's response to hyperinflation, especially since "The Brick" was authored by Chicago-educated economists at Catholic University. However, Friedman's influence was indirect and occurred largely through his writing rather than via his extremely brief trip to Chile or even his personal mentorship (especially compared to that of Harberger). Furthermore, the "Chicago Boys" and their reform proposals were not central to the coup or the regime's odious behavior. As Megan McArdle (2008) of the *Atlantic* has noted, "The policies that led to the economic miracle did not cause the dictatorship, which would have been just as horrible without the Chicago Boys."

Although it is difficult to believe that Friedman's limited attention to Chile's problems amounted to much, his decision to travel there and help such a repressive regime is still questionable. Friedman would argue in response—as he later did—that no one seemed to be all that upset when he traveled to communist China and gave similar advice to its leaders (Friedman 1988a; Friedman and Friedman 1998).[41] Furthermore, he argued in *Newsweek* in 1976 (in reply to a letter to the editor) that he did "not regard it as evil for an economist to render technical economic advice to the Chilean government to help end the plague of inflation, any more than [he] would regard it as evil for a physician to give technical medical advice to the Chilean government to help end a medical plague" (quoted in Friedman and Friedman 1998, 596). Friedman thought this was acceptable, as he noted in another letter in response to his critics, if conditions "were such that economic improvement would contribute both to the well-being of the ordinary people and to the chance of movement towards a politically free society" (quoted in Friedman and Friedman 1998, 595). But what if the positive relationship between wealth and political freedom—commonly believed by political scientists—is not as robust as Friedman seemed to think? What if one, by counseling morally problematic leaders in ways that improve their economic situation, only serves to sustain and advance their power and makes it that much easier for the state to continue its illiberal rule by giving it more resources for control or by forestalling domestic unrest? These seem to be the million dollar questions today with regard to how the West should interface with China.

Sweden, Chile, and China were just three of the many places that Friedman traveled during his life. Indeed, Friedman was a bit of a travel junkie, traveling extensively to all parts of the world even into his eighties. Of course, many of his trips were for academic research, lectures, and consulting work, formal or otherwise. These included a year-long mixed work/vacation in 1962–1963 during which he and Rose traveled around the world (visiting 21 countries in total), a series of trips to Japan, China, and Israel, and globetrotting for the *Free to Choose* documentary and its ill-fated update (Friedman and Friedman 1998). Friedman and his family also spent nearly every summer from 1948 to 1980 in New England.

Friedman did more than just win a Nobel Prize and become embroiled in the Chile scandal during the period between his famous presidential address to the AEA and the initiation of the *Free to Choose* project soon after his retirement. He also wrote several important scholarly pieces, most notably two articles on monetary theory that were later combined to form an extended essay that is part intellectual history and part original theoretical contribution (Gordon 1974, x; Friedman 1974a). Additionally, he participated in numerous talks, debates, and interviews, including a celebrated debate on monetary and fiscal policy with Walter Heller in late 1968 and a famous 1973 interview for *Playboy* magazine (Heinemann 1968; Kraus 1968; Friedman and Heller 1969; Playboy Interview [1973] 1975). Finally, after his retirement from the University of Chicago in 1977, Friedman and his wife moved to the Bay Area where he worked first as a visiting scholar at the Federal Reserve Bank in San Francisco and then at the Hoover Institution.

Free to Choose

Following their move west, Friedman and his wife began work on what became the popular *Free to Choose* PBS documentary and accompanying best-selling book by the same title. The brainchild of the project was Robert Chitester, head of PBS station WQLN in Erie, Pennsylvania. He contacted the Friedmans soon after they had moved to California in 1977 and quickly sold them on the idea. The project took almost three years to complete (Friedman and Friedman 1998).

As a first step, Friedman was filmed delivering 15 public lectures around the country on a variety of subjects that were intended for discussion in the documentary. During this lecture tour, the structure of the documentary started to take shape with the decision to focus on ten topics, one for each of ten episodes. Filming of the on-location footage began in March 1978 in San Francisco, followed by shoots at various locations around the country and then abroad in Hong Kong, Japan, India, Greece, Germany, and Britain. The next step involved filming nine multiparticipant discussion sessions and one concluding interview session with Friedman alone. These discussions ultimately included 33 different people who had a variety of backgrounds and widely divergent views on the issues. The Friedmans also quickly wrote a book based on the ten episodes to accompany the documentary but also to stand as an independent, more detailed discussion of the issues raised in the television series (Friedman and Friedman 1998; Friedman and Friedman [1980] 1990).

The documentary ultimately began airing in January 1980 on 196 PBS stations in the United States with an average of three million viewers. It also aired in a number of other countries, with the British version containing five new discussions. Each episode was an hour long, divided evenly between a slickly produced overview of the topic at hand (featuring Friedman's commentary) in the first half, followed by a group discussion on the same subject in the second half. The first half has the feel of a standard pre-Ken Burns educational documentary and features well-chosen on-location shots that highlight each episode's core issue. The second half is like watching a Sunday morning television roundtable, complete with a moderator and a group of experts. The two halves are a bit disjointed. However, the format allowed viewers to hear different arguments and counterarguments and gave Friedman's supporters and critics space to voice their arguments at some length.

The book is a more comprehensive and detailed discussion of the topics explored in the documentary. It ended up selling over a million copies in the United States alone as well as another 200,000 in a Japanese edition. It has also been translated into at least 16 other languages (Friedman and Friedman 1998).

In terms of its content, *Free to Choose* is a defense of liberty and capitalism via an application of free-market principles to particular policy issues. It is clearly aimed for a general audience but is not excessively dumbed down, especially in the book version. In particular, *Free to Choose* begins by explaining how markets work and the proper role of government in a free society. It then moves to the dangers of political interference in the market, followed by detailed "concrete" rather than "abstract" examinations of topics such as the Depression and monetary policy, the welfare state, egalitarianism, education, consumer protection, occupational issues, and inflation (Friedman and Friedman [1980] 1990: xiii). The series concludes with a look toward the future with a discussion of the problem of special interests and specific recommendations for Constitutional changes to advance freedom. In terms of Friedman's own intellectual development, the series and book are notable for reflecting the impact that public choice theory had on him since his earlier, more "abstract" and philosophical book *Capitalism and Freedom*—something Friedman acknowledges explicitly in the preface to the *Free to Choose* book and which also can be seen in his other later writings (Friedman and Friedman [1980] 1990: xiii).

Free to Choose aired in a period of shifting attitudes around the globe toward markets and government planning. This changing outlook helped usher in a new era in the international political economy. Free-market ideas had remained alive throughout the age of Keynes—partly through the work of mavericks like Friedman and Hayek in the academic world, Rand in the literary realm, and Goldwater in the political arena—but were largely dormant from the 1930s to the 1970s. The enthusiasm for the mixed economy and big government that defined that era, though, waned in the late '70s. Economic problems in the United States and Europe—especially stagflation—undermined the Keynesian consensus and revived interest in free markets. In the social policy realm, people started to realize that the Great Society and its promise of government-led poverty eradication had largely failed. As these attitudinal changes were occurring, conservative and libertarian think tanks in the United States and United Kingdom began laying the intellectual ground work for political change. As might be expected, they marshaled many of the ideas that Friedman had preached for decades and readied for a chance to implement a new approach.

The elections of Margaret Thatcher and Ronald Reagan, as well as the demise of the Soviet Union a decade later, were key events marking a significant shift in global perspectives on political economy. Indeed, liberalization was the dominant discourse for the rest of Friedman's life, especially if one looks outside of the North Atlantic community to places such as India and China. Yet big government never really disappeared despite the rhetoric of the 1980s and 1990s. Nonetheless, it is undoubtedly the case that important changes occurred in this period. In the West, these consisted of increased privatization, deregulation (especially the end of wage and price controls as serious policy options), the liberalization of trade, and a growing concern with economic incentives and disincentives in policy making. In the developing world, the change was even more stark as capitalism replaced socialism and communism as the reigning ideology of the "commanding heights" (see Yergin and Stanislaw 2002). Of course, Friedman's scholarship and popular works played some role in those shifting attitudes toward markets, though it is extremely difficult to judge how much any one individual matters in such large-scale events. But he also benefited from these changes since *Free to Choose* was certainly received quite differently than *Capitalism and Freedom* had been less than two decades before.[42]

Friedman also returned to politics in his retirement, again acting as a campaign and presidential advisor—this time for the far more sympathetic ears of politician Ronald Reagan. Friedman had known the President when he was governor of California from 1967 to 1975. During that period, Friedman had discussed education financing with Reagan and even traveled around the state with him at one point in support of Proposition 1 (an amendment to limit government spending). As the presidential campaign got under way in 1980, Friedman was named to Reagan's Economic Policy Coordinating Committee. This group, like the one he served on in 1968 for Nixon, was tasked with formulating economic policy in the event that Reagan was successful in his bid for the White House. Its primary product was a policy blueprint titled "Economic Strategy for the Reagan Administration" that Friedman claims was followed very closely after the election (Friedman and Friedman 1998).

After Reagan's victory, Friedman was appointed to the President's Economic Policy Advisory Board and served on it for a full eight years. This group, consisting of 12 economists, including Alan Greenspan, Arthur Burns, and Arthur Laffer, played a key role in advising the President on economic policy during a time of great economic change. For example, it met formally with the President six times during the first year of the new administration and provided firm support for Reagan's controversial attempts to rein in inflation (even at the cost of a severe recession), avoid tax increases, and continue with deregulation.

However, the Board was not always in accord with Reagan's moves, especially the decision to impose a "voluntary" export quota on Japanese automobiles. Moreover, it had less access to the President during Reagan's second term (Friedman and Friedman 1998). Indeed, Friedman's personal influence on Reagan is hard to gauge, especially relative to larger economic and political factors.

During and after his work with the Reagan administration, Friedman remained active as a distinguished public voice on political and economic matters. In particular, he wrote periodic op-eds for the *Wall Street Journal* and other outlets. Indeed, he published nearly 100 op-eds and small pieces during that time. Friedman also continued to write serious, extended pieces on monetary matters. For example, in the 1980s, he produced several pieces expanding his thoughts on monetary policy and the role of government in the area of money (see Friedman and Schwartz 1982; Friedman [1984b] 1987; Friedman and Schwartz [1986] 1987). Of course, even Milton Friedman ultimately slowed down, as the quantity and length of his writings declined in the last 15 years of his life. But given his age, Friedman's output in the 1990s and early 2000s is actually quite impressive and shows a mind still alive to ideas and the world around him. However, Friedman spent more and more time on personal matters as time went on, whether it was finally finishing his autobiography in 1997, traveling, or dealing with the natural problems of age.

Friedman died at his home in San Francisco on November 16, 2006. He was 94 years old. The cause of death was heart failure. Given his family history (his father suffered from angina and died at age 49 of heart trouble), Milton's own angina and resultant heart attack in 1984, and two heart operations (1972 and 1984), it is a testimony to an active life and modern medicine that Friedman lived so well for so long (Friedman and Friedman 1998). His wife, Rose, lived another three years after his death, passing away on August 18, 2009. The couple is survived by two children, four grandchildren, and four great-grandchildren.

Notes

[1] Frederic Bastiat was a nineteenth-century French classical liberal who, according to Joseph Schumpeter, "was the most brilliant economic journalist who ever lived" (Henderson 2008). Bastiat is the author of such clever works as "A Petition" (1845) and "What is Seen and What is Not Seen" (1850). Sheldon Richman (2000) correctly notes that Bastiat "has few peers when it comes to presenting the case for liberty with clarity and wit"—but I would add that Milton Friedman would certainly be among them.

[2] The biographical details in this chapter come largely from the basic sources on his life. These include his autobiography co-authored with his wife Rose (Friedman and Friedman 1998); a series of articles from 1976 and 1977 that Rose wrote for the *Oriental Economist* (Rose Friedman 1976, 1977); two short autobiographical pieces, one in a book on Nobel laureates (Friedman [1986] 2004) and another for the Nobel Foundation (Friedman 1992b in Lindbeck 1992); a variety of interviews (especially the Academy of Achievement Interview 1991); and a short piece by his student Gary Becker (1991). The only book-length biography of Friedman that I know of is Lanny Ebenstein's *Milton Friedman* [and leaving aside William Frazer's (1988) interesting, detailed, but unfocused two-volume work on Friedman and his ideas]. Although a fine summary of Friedman's life with an informative bibliographical essay attached, Ebenstein's book does not break much new ground to those familiar with the subject (which is not surprising given how exhaustive Friedman's autobiography is and how often he was profiled or interviewed throughout his long life). I purposely waited to peruse Ebenstein's book until I had a draft of this chapter nearly completed and thus only used it to ensure that I had not omitted anything significant. Any similarities in our treatments are thus due to common sources and common subject. Details gleaned from that work are properly referenced.

[3] Friedman was not consistent about the details of his father's death. In one interview, he said he was 13 when his father passed away (Academy of Achievement Interview 1991). In his autobiography, he notes that he was 15 at the time (Friedman and Friedman 1998, 23).

[4] Friedman's parents briefly had a "small textile factory" after they moved to Rahway, but this failed so they opened the store (Booknotes Interview 1994).

[5] Mill's father was James Mill, an important thinker in his own right. However, his mother was not known to be a very sophisticated or intelligent person according to Capaldi (2004).

[6] Long after writing this section, I came across Cherrier (n.d.), who also notes that Friedman's personal history played a role in shaping his views.

[7] Not to mention that he once argued: "This idea that's present now, that somehow or other it is necessary to have great government subsidies to enable people to go to college is not true" (Academy of Achievement Interview 1991).

[8] And note the title of his autobiography—*Two Lucky People*.

[9] He even gave this title to one of his article collections (Friedman 1975).

[10] Indeed, Friedman publicly criticized Burns's Fed policies, including in several *Newsweek* columns. See Friedman 1975. It is also noteworthy that Friedman essentially ignores this period of Burns's life in his *in memoriam* tribute, saying only "Those who will follow me at this podium are far better qualified than I to comment on that phase of Arthur's life" (Friedman 1988c, 10).

[11] That a "Chicago view" existed at that time could certainly be disputed (though one could say a Knight or Viner or Simons view existed then that later transformed into a Chicago view once a critical mass of scholars committed to a certain outlook was reached). According to Melvin Reder (1982), "Chicago economics was a mixed bag" well into the late 1930s. This was certainly the case in the early '30s when Friedman first met Jones (who himself was at least one year removed from Chicago). See Friedman 1976b. Likewise, Gordon Tullock has noted that "Until the 1930's, one could not refer to a Chicago School of Economics" (Tullock 1983, iv cited in Overtveldt 2007). Horn and Mirowski (2009) go even further, arguing that a Chicago view does not emerge until well into the 1940s [something certainly suggested by Viner's recollection, as reported by Patinkin (1981), that he had not heard about a Chicago School until after he left in 1946 and had not confirmed the existence of such a thing until 1951]. Friedman and others might argue that there was a Chicago School at this time—or at least a first Chicago School as some have argued (see Bronfenbrenner 1962; Rotwein 1983). Frazer (1988) even argues there were three Chicago Schools! For a discussion of the Chicago School idea and its history, see Overtveldt 2007.

[12] In the context of discussing his methodology, Friedman admitted that he had not read much philosophy in an interview with Hammond (1992, 99). Asked if he had read much philosophy as a graduate student, he answered "None that I recall. Not only that, I don't recall ever having read much philosophy."

[13] Despite Viner's influence, the two scholars frequently disagreed over the course of their careers. On their differences, see Rotwein 1983.

[14] Viner may also have influenced Friedman's view of monetary theory, given the important similarities between Viner's understanding during the early Depression and Friedman's work in that area more than two decades later—something Friedman himself realized in the early 1970s (see Gordon 1974, 167).

[15] Cherrier provides an argument about what Knight taught that helped shape Friedman's mind. She claims that "Knight's depiction of a society as a set of rational individuals endowed with diverging preferences and pursing their welfare and his claim that market oriented systems should be favored because planning presupposed unattainable perfect information struck a chord with the young student" (Cherrier, n.d.).

[16] In an interview in 2000, Friedman explained why he supported the New Deal: "Because it was a very exceptional circumstance. We'd gotten into an extraordinarily difficult situation, unprecedented in the nation's history. You had millions of people out of work. Something had to be done; it was intolerable. And it was a case in which, unlike most cases, the short run deserved to dominate" (Commanding Heights Interview 2000).

[17] See Cherrier (n.d.) for some sign that he was not completely enamored of standard Keynesianism either. Of course, Friedman's New Deal leanings beg the question of when and why he turns toward classical liberalism, something I attempt to explain below.

[18] Leonard Silk adds that the war also caused a delay in the publication. See Silk 1976, 60.

[19] In the summer of 1941, the Friedmans suffered a stillbirth with their first pregnancy (Friedman and Friedman 1998, 104).

[20] When later asked why he turned down the invitation to such an important post, Friedman answered: "I prefer being independent and more useful. I think society needs a few kooks, a few extremists. If you're in the Administration, it's right and natural to compromise" (Bender 1971).

[21] Friedman never met Keynes in person. Moreover, the only personal correspondence between the two giants of economics consisted of two rejection letters Keynes sent acting in his stead as an editor in response to articles submitted by a young Friedman (Friedman and Friedman 1998). Moreover, it is worth pointing out that some economists think the clash between Friedman and Keynsianism is overstated, given that in many areas, Friedman's work should be "seen properly as an outgrowth, or sophistication of Keynes's own

basic theoretical framework, and not as some radical, fundamentally antithetical departure" (Burton 1981, 61).

22 The chapter on flexible exchange rates had its origins in a memo Friedman wrote in 1950 while a consultant for the Economic Cooperation Administration, Special Representative in Europe, Trade and Finance Division which administered the Marshall Plan (Friedman and Friedman 1998, 622). The chapter on methodology was first drafted in 1947, with an origin in a book review Friedman wrote in 1946 (Friedman and Friedman 1998, 215).

23 Though it is no doubt the case that these were already quite talented individuals before they even arrived at Chicago and only one of them (Becker) had Friedman as his supervisor.

24 Friedman here seems to have forgotten his very political piece on rent control he wrote with Stigler (not to mention his very policy-oriented work at the Treasury). Nonetheless, it is true that this marked the beginning of a more active life as a public intellectual.

25 Though, to be fair, Simons had hoped to hire Friedman well before the Free Market Study had even been imagined. He wrote to Hutchins of this desire in November 1944 and repeated it in August 1945. See Van Horn and Mirowski 171, fn. 34.

26 According to David Henderson, "The context was that we were talking, at a dinner at Hoover, about my review of *Two Lucky People* in *Reason.* I had expressed in the review my disappointment that he had not made clear how he got from being somewhat of a statist, and definitely a Keynesian, to being much more of a free-market guy. He said that others had expressed the same disappointment but, unfortunately, 'there was no Saul of Tarsis moment.' (Those were his words.")

27 This contrasts with Rose Friedman's (1976e) claim that his "basic libertarian philosophy goes back to his student days and probably earlier . . ." However, Rose's statement conflicts with Milton's own recollection about his views as a student and the lack of strong evidence of any early libertarian views.

28 For example, in one piece Friedman wrote at the time but updated later, he noted his failure to include monetary effects in his earlier work as perhaps arising from "the prevailing Keynesian temper of the times" (Friedman 1953, 253).

29 Although she goes so far as to argue that these factors influenced, at the same time, his economic, methodological, and political views in such a fashion as to make them "inextricably interwoven."

30 According to Friedman (Commanding Heights Interview 2000), his big break with Keynesianism was after World War II when he started working on money and economic cycles: "Very shortly after the war, when I came to the University of Chicago and started working on

money and its relation to the economic cycle. I cannot tell you exactly when, but very shortly thereafter, as I studied the facts, they seemed to me to contradict what Keynesian theory would call for." On the role of the professional incomes study controversy, see Silk (1976, 61) and Cherrier (n.d.).

[31] This section relies heavily on Yergin and Stanislaw's wonderful synthesis focusing on changes in the postwar world economy and the ideas that drove them, *The Commanding Heights* (2002).

[32] Lanny Ebenstein suggests that Friedman's career after *Capitalism and Freedom* was increasingly more about public policy work than scientific research. He argues: "After the book's publication, he [Friedman] increasingly moved in the direction of attempting to influence public opinion directly and through government leaders rather than at a remove through academia. He transitioned over his career from a focus mostly on academic economics and teaching to involvement in public policy and advocacy." (Ebenstein 2007, 135). Although this transition did occur, Friedman was still very much involved in scientific research after *Capitalism and Freedom* and up until and even after his official retirement from the University of Chicago at the end of 1976. Yet it is true that his scientific production decreased, especially as his other work increased. Therefore, Friedman's own characterization of his public policy work as merely "a part-time activity" may be too cute by half. However, Ebenstein's suggestion may give the false impression that Friedman's shift in emphasis was more dramatic than it actually was.

[33] Three collections of these columns were printed as books: *An Economist's Protest* (1972); *There's No Such Thing as a Free Lunch* (1975); and *Bright Promises, Dismal Performances* (1983).

[34] Sixty comes from the tape subject log namelist in which Friedman is listed in 62 conversations minus the two times during this period that he visited the White House.

[35] Friedman did not oppose all conscription everywhere. For example, he thought small states like Israel and Switzerland might be justified in imposing universal military service (Friedman 1979, *Newsweek* May 14).

[36] Friedman notes that there were 74 invited participants at the conference (Friedman and Friedman 1998: 377). However, there were only 73 at the conference given that Erik Erikson could not attend but did write a paper (Tax 1967: ix).

[37] Unfortunately, I could not find this exchange on the White House Tapes as it may have occurred after the recorded part of their conversation on September 24, 1971, ended. The tapes are also difficult to hear.

[38] Friedman testified in front of Congress on many occasions, starting during his stint at the Department of the Treasury in the 1940s and continuing throughout his career. In particular, he testified several times for the Congressional Joint Economic Committee while his former Chicago colleague Paul Douglas was the chairman (Friedman and Friedman 1998, 196).

[39] Royal Swedish Academy of Sciences, Press Release, October 14, 1976.

[40] The text of this letter and Pinochet's terse reply are reprinted in full in an appendix in Friedman's autobiography. See Friedman and Friedman 1998.

[41] In 1988, Friedman met with China's General Secretary Zhao Ziyang and counseled him on political and economic reform. Specifically, Friedman argued that China should decentralize power (and loosen licensing), deal with inflation by controlling the money supply while ending price controls, free the currency exchange rate, and let interest rates be determined by the market. He also warned of the danger of " 'getting stuck' in the middle" with reform efforts. See the transcript of his meeting with Zhao and a memo he wrote to the General Secretary, both provided in Appendix C of Friedman and Friedman 1998. In a cheeky letter to the editor at Stanford, Friedman asked whether, given the protests of his similar engagement with Chile, he should prepare "for an avalanche of protests for having been willing to give advice to so evil a government? If not, why not?" Friedman 1988b. Friedman returned to China in 1993, meeting this time with Jiang Zeming. Interestingly, Friedman thought that Jiang was far less friendly to decentralized markets than Zhao had been. According to Friedman, Jiang "viewed the market strictly as a mechanism to be controlled closely from the center" (Friedman and Friedman 1998, 556).

[42] This section benefited from correspondence with Professor Marc Eisner of Wesleyan University.

Chapter 2

Economic and Political Thought

Attempting to portray the work of Milton Friedman in 5000 words is an impossible assignment. It is like trying to catch the Niagara Falls in a pint pot.

—*John Burton (1981, 53)*

In the quotation heading this chapter, economist John Burton notes the difficulty of capturing Friedman's enormous corpus of work in such a small space. Although this chapter exceeds Burton's attempt in length and detail, it is still a challenge to fully portray the thought of a prolific scholar who wrote his first piece in 1935 and his last nearly 70 years later. Nonetheless, this chapter attempts to do just that. First, it explains his scholarship and public policy work. Second, it provides an outline of the general political "theory" that both underpinned and was developed in Friedman's writings. From these summaries, a full picture of Friedman's worldview emerges.

Scholarship

As a young man, Friedman decided to study economics because of its real-world import at a time of crisis. His scholarship always shows that concern for relevance, consequently making it difficult to draw a strict dividing line between his scientific and public policy work. This distinction is also hard because economics has become more a way of examining social behavior than a discipline with strictly defined boundaries of what ought to be studied.

That being said, it is useful to differentiate between Friedman's work as an economic theorist and his work applying an economic mindset in conjunction with his personal philosophic commitments to public policy issues.

Given that Friedman considered himself a scholar first and a public intellectual second, it is appropriate to discuss his more academic work first. The bulk of this work was in the area of money and banking, with Friedman leading the Monetarist School of thought, which stressed the importance of money (supply *and* demand) and monetary policy to key economic outcomes such as inflation and income. However, he also wrote in a number of other areas of economics, making key contributions to the study of methodology, consumption, and exchange rate policy. What shines through his scholarship is a studied appreciation for the efficacy of markets reminiscent of Smith and other classical economists.

Methodology

Friedman's scholarship was rooted in a very specific understanding of the best way to do economics. Most generally, he thought economics should and could be—indeed is—a value-free science in which scholars aim to develop positive theory and analysis of economic phenomena broadly understood (Friedman [1967e] 1987, 1953). To Friedman, positive economics is "in principle independent of any particular ethical position or normative judgments" (Friedman 1953, 4). This is not to say that he opposed economists' speaking about normative issues in the realm of public policy—quite the contrary. Friedman was an eager participant in that arena. However, he maintained that economists qua economists are neutral scientific observers of their particular domain. Indeed, he went so far as to say that economists (and even "disinterested citizens") generally differ on policy because of differences in positive analysis of economic consequences rather than because of normative values, even if in practice those values sometimes affected their analysis (Friedman 1953, 1967e [1987], 1968d).[1]

More specifically, Friedman had a particular philosophy of science (in the loosest sense of that term) that he thought most appropriate to positive economics.[2] It is fleshed out in his seminal contribution to that realm, a 1953 piece titled "The Methodology of Positive Economics" (Friedman 1953). In that essay (hereafter referred to as F53, following convention), Friedman made a case for what many have called an "instrumentalist" approach to science (see Nagel 1963; Lawrence Boland 1979; Caldwell 1980).[3] Instrumentalism, as Boland (1979, 508–09) explains, is a view that "theories are convenient and useful ways of (logically) generating what have turned out to be true (or successful) predictions or conclusions." Others, however, have criticized those who interpret Friedman's approach as instrumentalist, arguing instead that he is a methodological "realist" (Uskali Mäki 1986, 1992, 2009; Hoover 2009) or a logical positivist (see Wood and Woods 1990, xviii; and Frazer and Boland 1983), among other possibilities. Indeed, there is a bit of a cottage industry in analyzing to which school Friedman belongs. These many different interpretations might exist because, as Mark Blaug has argued, F53 is so "wonderfully ambiguous and incoherent" (Blaug in Mäki 2009, 351). Whether this is true or not, Mäki (2009, xvii) is certainly correct in concluding that "The essay was to become the most cited, the most influential, the most controversial piece of methodological writing in twentieth-century economics" (Mäki 2009, xvii).

Regardless of where his approach fits within the philosophy of science, what exactly did Friedman argue in F53? His overarching concern in F53 is to determine how we decide when to accept a hypothesis or theory. In other words, he hopes to answer the question, "What is a good theory?" To Friedman, a theory "consists of an assertion that certain forces are, and by implication others are not, important for a particular class of phenomena and a specification of the manner of action of the forces it asserts to be important" (Friedman 1953, 24). But how do we recognize a good one?

After beginning with a discussion of the relationship between positive and normative economics, Friedman cuts to the heart of the matter. He controversially claims that the "ultimate goal of a positive science is the development of a 'theory' or 'hypothesis' that yields valid and meaningful (i.e., not truistic) predictions about phenomena not yet observed." Such theories will take the form of abstractions that "serve as a filing system for organizing empirical material and facilitating our understanding of it" (Friedman 1953, 7). Even more notoriously, Friedman—in what Samuelson (1963) referred to as the "F-twist"—also claimed that the assumptions upon which these theories are built do *not* have to be true as long as they produce theories yielding better predictions than alternative specifications. In short, predictive power—not "descriptive accuracy" or explanation—is the key to a good theory. Thus, we can test the power of a theory not by "comparing its 'assumptions' directly with 'reality' " but by seeing if its hypotheses yield predictions that conform with "observable phenomena" (i.e., data, including what has been used to develop the theory) (Friedman 1953, 40–41, 13).[4] Indeed, Friedman went beyond saying that theoretical assumptions are necessarily "unrealistic" to claim that "the more significant the theory, the more unrealistic the assumption" (14). The key to knowing whether you have the right assumptions—or "good approximations" of reality—is whether they yield "accurate predictions" (15). So the bottom line for Friedman is always the predictive usefulness of a theory, hence the reason scholars have pegged him as an instrumentalist.

There are a number of other key points in the essay. Following Popper, Friedman emphasized falsifiability as a key criterion for a sound theory and asserted that "factual evidence can never 'prove' a hypothesis: it can only fail to disprove it" (9, 13). He also stressed parsimony (something he repeated in his argument against complex attempts to save Keynes's consumption function in the face of contrary data) and the range of phenomena that could be explained as criteria of a good theory (see Friedman 1957, 231). He even went so far as to assert that "we cannot perceive 'facts' without a theory" (34). Finally, Friedman claimed that theory construction itself was closer to an art than a science: "a creative act of inspiration, intuition, invention" (43).

It may be useful to mention why Friedman wrote this essay, especially since he later sarcastically noted that he was more interested in doing economics than talking about how it should be done (consistent with that, he never replied to the critics of F53) (Friedman and Friedman 1998, 215; Friedman in Mäki 2009, 355). The consensus view is that the piece was a vehicle to counterattack a variety of critics. For example, a number of scholars (Breit and Ransom 1971; Mirowski and Hands 1998; Mirowski 2002; Backhouse 2009; and De Vroey 2009) suggest the essay was aimed at critics of Marshall and neoclassical economics, such as Veblen and Chamberlin (and perhaps critics of classical liberal political thought as well). Friedman himself later noted that while he had forgotten why he started writing the piece, it could have been a response to contemporaneous debates in economic theory such as "formalized theories of imperfect competition, and even more directly, the questioning of orthodox marginal analysis" based on interviews with businessmen (Friedman and Friedman 1998, 215). Similarly, Ebenstein (2007) and others speculate it was a way to criticize the Cowles Commission (then residing at the University of Chicago) and its econometric emphasis.[5] Finally, Friedman may also have been attacking the anti-empirical and "purely theoretical" perspective of Austrian economists such as Ludwig von Mises (Skousen 2005, 102; Backhouse 2009).

It is also worth noting how Friedman came to hold these controversial methodological views, given the essay itself does not evince a particular familiarity with the philosophy of science literature. Of course, some of his arguments were obviously organic, especially since Friedman started thinking about these issues long before talking to Karl Popper about them in 1947. However, in terms of influences, Friedman himself claims to have been affected by his background in statistics as well as discussions with Popper and Friedman's friend and co-author "Jimmie" Savage (Friedman and Friedman 1998, 215). Many scholars have stressed Popper's influence—just as Friedman did—and the similarities are obvious. Others have found within F53 hints of various sources, including Marshall and the pragmatism of

Charles Sanders Pierce and John Dewey. In terms of the last, Dewey may have had an indirect bearing on Friedman through Friedman's mentor Wesley Mitchell (Wible 1984; Hirsch and de Marchi 1984; Breit and Ransom 1971; Frazer 1988; Hirsch and DeMarchi 1990; Hoover 2009).

In conclusion, Friedman's methodological view was centered on the importance of prediction rather than descriptive accuracy and using data to falsify or lend confidence to a theory. This emphasis on empirics put him at odds with the Austrian tradition, and his "unrealism" put him at odds with many scholars, especially Samuelson. Whether Friedman always practiced what he preached is debatable. However, his work on the consumption function is frequently highlighted as his best exemplar of his method in action. It is to that work that we now turn.

Theory of the Consumption Function and the Permanent Income Hypothesis

One of Friedman's most highly regarded academic works is his book *A Theory of the Consumption Function.* He considered this to be his "best purely scientific contribution" (Friedman and Friedman 1998, 222). Here, Friedman proposed and tested the "permanent income hypothesis" that challenged Keynes's understanding of the consumption function. However, as John Burton notes, he challenged it from within by "*building upon* the Keynesian revolution" and accepting the aggregate consumption function concept (Burton 1981, 57). Despite this, his critique is no less important for hollowing out a key component of Keynesianism.

Keynes argued in his classic *The General Theory of Employment, Interest, and Money* that current consumption is essentially a function of current income. Specifically, he explained that "the propensity to consume is a fairly stable function so that, as a rule, the amount of aggregate consumption mainly depends on the amount of aggregate income (both measured in terms of wage-units)." Therefore, when peoples' income rises, consumption does as well—but crucially to Keynes, because of human psychology, "not by as much as the increase in their income." This leads to a situation where there is "a greater *proportion* of income being saved as real income increases" (Keynes 1936, 96 and 97). In short, the higher your income, the more you save as a percentage of your income. The result of this aggregate behavior can be what American Keynesian Alvin Hansen called "secular stagnation" (Hansen 1938, 1941). In this model, rising incomes cause rising savings (and proportionately lower levels of consumption), which, in addition to declining investment opportunities, lead to economic stagnation (including reduced production and less than full employment). This stagnation can be broken, though, by raising the propensity to consume (and thus aggregate demand) via income redistribution through government spending (see Friedman 1957, 236–37).

Friedman argued that this Keynesian "absolute income" theory was flawed. In particular, it could not account well for new data collected on the first half of the twentieth century, nor could it explain the post-World War experience in which rising income did not yield a savings ratio consistent with the Keynesian theory (Friedman 1957, 3–4). This failure led researchers to develop more complex theory-saving arguments, including the "relative income" and "wealth income" hypotheses. Friedman thought these were unsatisfactory compared to an original alternative specification: namely, his permanent income hypothesis.

Building on his prior work on professional incomes (Friedman and Kuznets 1945), Friedman argued that, regardless of income level, current consumption behavior is determined primarily by people's estimation of their long-run or "permanent" income rather than their current income. In other words, people do not focus on what he called their "transitory" income when making consumption decisions. Instead, they have their "permanent" income in mind, a longer time "horizon" of approximately three years, to which they adjust their spending (Friedman 1957). This means that short-term fluctuations in income—up or down—have no significant impact on consumption as long as individuals do not perceive these changes as affecting their expected long-run income. Friedman also argued, consistent with his theory, that the "savings ratio is independent of the level of income" (Friedman 1957, 234). Not content with merely postulating a theory of consumption, Friedman proceeded to test the permanent income hypothesis on a large body of data and found substantial empirical confirmation for it.

The permanent income hypothesis yields a number of important conclusions. One of these, as Friedman explains, is that income inequality is unnecessary for economic development since income equality will not mean a low savings rate. Likewise, it is not necessary to reduce inequality in order to avoid secular stagnation since savings levels are not related directly to income. When high savings do result, they are caused by "uncertainty about income prospects" rather than to a diminished marginal propensity to consume (Friedman 1957, 235). Along with the similar "life-cycle hypothesis" developed at roughly the same time by Franco Modigliani and Richard Brumberg (1954), this work radically infirmed the Keynesian "secular stagnation" thesis and undermined the economic rationale behind government tax and spending initiatives (Friedman and Friedman 1998, 223).[6] Moreover, it helps us understand why permanent tax cuts will have a greater impact on consumption than tax rebates.

Flexible Exchange Rates

While his book on consumption was one of his most important scholarly works, Friedman's case for a flexible or floating exchange rate system for international currencies was arguably among his most influential. However, at the time he first began making the argument in 1948, it was considered a fantasy—especially given that he did so at the height of the Bretton Woods system of fixed exchange rates in which national currencies were pegged to the dollar and traded within relatively narrow set bands (Friedman [1948] 1953; Friedman and Friedman 1998, 219). Yet, within two decades of the publication of his argument in "The Case for Flexible Exchange Rates" (Friedman 1953), the world shifted to a flexible exchange rate system.

In contrast to the Bretton Woods system, Friedman argued for a flexible system in which currency values are determined in an open-market inhabited by private traders. He thought this approach had many advantages while avoiding the problems inherent to other mechanisms for adapting to the inevitable "real" and "monetary" changes that affect international trade and the balance of payments. According to Friedman, the problem with a fixed system is that it tends to delay needed changes in currency values until large disequilibria cumulate, leading to a crisis and the need for "drastic action" (Friedman 1953, 163). It also increases the incentives for "a maximum of destabilizing speculation" while giving cause for undesirable controls on domestic prices or international trade that are often difficult to impose or enforce anyway (Friedman 1953, 164).

A flexible system, on the other hand, has many virtues. First, a flexible system would avoid major crises since it produces spontaneous "corrective movements before tensions can accumulate and a crisis develop" (Friedman 1953, 163). Thus, contrary to what one might think, a flexible system would actually be more stable despite exchange rates varying day to day. Second, a floating system gives states more freedom to pursue monetary and fiscal policy independent of exchange rate considerations and its demand for policy coordination. Third, a flexible system is more compatible with trade liberalization (and its many benefits) than a fixed system since liberalization puts "substantial and unpredictable pressures on balances of payments" that cannot be handled with rigid exchange rates short of ultimately restricting foreign trade (Friedman 1953, 198). Friedman also thought that fears of such a flexible system producing a "wage-price spiral," destabilizing speculation, and increased uncertainty were overstated or even wrong. He did not think a flexible system solved all problems related to changes in the international monetary system; however, ever the realist, he thought it was the best, most efficient way to adapt to these changes while doing a minimum of harm (see Friedman 1953, 202).

The Monetarist Counterrevolution

Although known best by noneconomists for his defense of free markets, Friedman is most well known within economics as the leader of a monetarist counterrevolution that reasserted the importance of money as a cause of key macroeconomic outcomes. Indeed, his name and the macro side of the Chicago School he captained became synonymous with an emphasis on money. Yet one would not have predicted this at the time that Friedman returned to the academy after the war. Before that point, by his own admission, he "was essentially a Keynesian" (Booknotes Interview 1994). He showed this in his work at the U.S. Treasury where he focused on fiscal policy to prevent inflation and basically ignored the role of money. However, he was quickly "cured" of or "corrupted" away from his Keynesianism after turning to the study of money and banking, especially following his assignment to examine that area at the NBER (Friedman and Friedman 1998, 113).

Soon thereafter, Friedman adopted a very different approach to macroeconomics that eventually coalesced into a broad assault on Keynes that became known as "monetarism."[7] The reason it was a counterrevolution is that money—once seen as a key explanatory variable—had fallen into disrepute in an economics profession dominated by Keynes and focused on fiscal policy variables during and after the Great Depression (see Friedman 1960, 1–2). Friedman led the charge to put the stock of money back onto center stage, showing that "money does matter and matters very much" (Friedman 1960, 2). Over the course of his long career, he developed the basic logic behind this argument, assembled evidence to confirm it, and fleshed it out with further refinement and analysis of related issues (in particular, see Friedman ([1948] 1953; [1951a,b,c] 1953; [1956] 1987; 1957; [1958b] 1969b, [1959] 1969b, 1960; [1961] 1969b;

[1962c] 1987; [1966a] 1969b; 1968b; [1968d] 1987; 1969b; 1974a; [1984b] 1987; [1987] 1987; Friedman and Meiselman 1963; Friedman and Schwartz 1963, 1970; 1982; [1986] 1987). Given the extent of this work on money, what follows can, of course, only skim the waves of his deep understanding.[8]

Quantity Theory of Money

Although it was not the first time he challenged Keynesian orthodoxy, Friedman launched the monetarist counterrevolution with his 1956 piece "The Quantity Theory of Money—A Restatement."[9] Here, in an introduction to a book containing other monetarist works by his Ph.D. students, he articulated the basic monetarist argument that "money matters" while fleshing out a theory of the demand for money. In contrast to Keynes, who thought that people's liquidity preferences and the velocity of money vary widely, Friedman argued that the demand for money is "highly stable" as there is "a fairly definite real quantity of money that people wish to hold under any given circumstances" (Friedman [1956] 1987, 297; Friedman 1974a).

As for what causes the demand for money, he originally thought it was determined by a relatively few major factors. These included total wealth (including "all sources of 'income' "), the price of and return on wealth (money, bonds, equities, physical nonhuman goods, human capital), and the tastes and preferences of the wealth owner (Friedman [1956] 1987, 286ff). In short, the demand for money is related to the opportunity cost of holding it versus other things. Burton (1981) argues that by 1959, Friedman boiled it down to basically being a function of permanent income (Friedman [1959] 1969b). However, Friedman thought these types of arguments about his views were misrepresentations, as evidenced by his 1966 assertion that "interest rates affect the real quantity of money demanded" (Friedman [1966a] 1969b, 142).

Given that the demand side of the equation is rather stable (even though velocity is not constant), Friedman thought that what is really important to understanding important economic phenomena such as prices is the stock of money. As he summarized in 1974 (a, 3):

> On an empirical level, it [the quantity theory of money] is the generalization that changes in desired balances (in the demand for money) tend to proceed slowly and gradually or to be the result of events set in train by prior changes in supply, whereas, in contrast, substantial changes in the supply of nominal balances can and frequently do occur independent of any changes in demand. The conclusion is that substantial changes in prices or nominal income are almost invariably the result of changes in the nominal supply of money.

This quantity theory of money has important implications for our understanding of the bogeymen of inflation and deflation. If, as Friedman repeated over and over during his career, "substantial inflation is always and everywhere a monetary phenomenon," then we should look to the creators of money as those responsible for these ills. Of course, given that Friedman correctly argued that "Government and the government alone is responsible for any rapid increase in the quantity of money," the state rather than trade unions, businesses, foreigners, OPEC, or low productivity is thus ultimately liable for the level of inflation ([1980] 1990, 253ff). Given this scholarly position, it is easy to understand why Friedman was so critical of the Federal Reserve and the Nixon administration during the 1970s when stagflation reigned despite the use of controls to ward it off.

Two last points about the quantity theory are in order. First, critics have responded by arguing that income causes money stock rather than other way around. However, Friedman and other economists have provided evidence that this is not the case in any significant way (see Burton 1981, 61). Second, although critics such as economist Robert Solow joked that "Everything reminds Milton Friedman of the money supply. Everything reminds me of sex, but I try to keep it out of my papers," Friedman did not actually assert that money is the only variable worth examining. Indeed, he explicitly rejected this view and called it "a straw man" of his argument. On the contrary, Friedman offered a plethora of variables that explain the causes of wealth, such as institutional structure, technology, and even individual values (Friedman and Heller 1969, 47), and hence the demand for money.

Friedman also empirically challenged Keynes's famous multiplier (the idea that exogenous—i.e., government—spending can increase output and real national income even beyond the initial expenditure as it circulates through the economy). In collaboration with his student David Meiselman, Friedman tested the comparative power of the quantity theory versus the Keynesians' "autonomous expenditure" ("income-expenditure") model in predicting consumption. They found that the quantity theory outperformed the Keynesian approach. Namely, changes in the money stock explained changes in consumption better than expenditures did (Friedman and Meiselman 1963).

Monetary History and the Causes of the Depression

Friedman's research on monetary matters was not merely theoretical. He wrote a number of important works on the history of money and monetary policy, including three lengthy volumes with Anna Schwartz on monetary history in the United States (Friedman and Schwartz 1963, 1970, 1982; Friedman [1992c] 1994).[10] The most famous of these, and perhaps Friedman's chef d'oeuvre, was *A Monetary History of the United States, 1867–1960* (Friedman and Schwartz 1963).

A Monetary History was crucial because it provided solid empirical confirmation for Friedman's quantity theory of money. The long historical record, the authors discovered, largely supports the notion that the stock of money was a key variable affecting "changes in economic activity, money income, and prices" and was not itself the result of those changes (Friedman and Schwartz 1963, 676, and see 686ff). Moreover, the book laid out a fairly novel interpretation of the causes of the Great Depression that had a deep impact on our understanding of that critical episode in American history.

Friedman and Schwartz's book catalogues—in daunting detail—changes in the stock of money in the United States from 1867 to 1960. In the process, it explains why these changes occurred and what effect they had on the economy and politics of the country. The book is important not merely for this critical data provision and exhaustive historical survey but also because it offers a number of striking challenges. One of these is its perhaps counterintuitive conclusion that the "blind" and "impersonal" pre-1914 gold standard performed better at ensuring monetary stability than the more managed system that followed (despite strong performance by the Federal Reserve System in the 1920s under Benjamin Strong) (10).

More controversially, Friedman and Schwartz argued that the Federal Reserve System itself—not the unstable market—was largely responsible for what they call "The Great Contraction." In short, the System turned a business cycle contraction into the Great Depression by ineptly managing the money supply. Specifically, the System not only failed to take the appropriate actions necessary to stem the bank crisis (i.e., providing liquidity), but it actually increased the problem by pursuing deflationary policies. For example, toward the beginning of the crisis, "the downward pressure on income produced by the effects of the stock market crash on expectations and willingness to spend . . . was strongly reinforced by the behavior of the stock of money," which declined due entirely to "a decline in Federal Reserve credit outstanding" (307, 308). Thus, the Fed exacerbated the problem. Likewise, later in the crisis, in early 1931, when a revival looked possible and an expanded money stock could have helped, the Fed reduced credit and offset positive signs elsewhere (313). A similar thing happened in 1937 when the government increased the reserve requirements and sterilized gold, thus retarding the growth of the stock of money and the economy at large (544).

Importantly, Friedman and Schwartz do not attribute the System's failures to a lack of appropriate power to deal with the monetary problems that emerged from 1929 to 1933. On the contrary, the System had all the tools it needed to increase liquidity and stave off the worst of the crisis. Instead, the collapse "was a result of the policies followed during those years." Therefore, Friedman and Schwartz argue that the "monetary collapse from 1929 to 1933 was not an inevitable consequence of what had gone before" (300). They conclude that "The monetary system collapsed, but it clearly need not have done so . . . . Pursuit of the policies outlined by the System itself in the 1920s, or for that matter by Bagehot in 1873, would have prevented the catastrophe" (407). In particular, "prevention or moderation of the decline in the stock of money, let alone the substitution of monetary expansion, would have reduced the contraction's severity and almost as certainly its duration" (301). Unfortunately, this was not in the cards, especially since Benjamin Strong was no longer around to exert his powerful force on the tiller of the System (412–13).[11] Until Friedman revived monetarism, this interpretation of the Great Depression would not have been entertained even within the field of economics, and especially not by Keynesians, who thought the Great Depression proved that money does not matter very much. Thanks to Friedman, it is now a major part of the conversation, though (surprisingly) rarely heard outside economics.

It is important to note that Friedman and Schwartz's finding on the Great Depression is not unique to that period. Their emphasis on money stock changes helps explain other times and significant economic events in U.S. monetary history as well.

Against the Phillips Curve: The Natural Rate of Unemployment Hypothesis

Friedman's next salvo against Keynesianism came in his 1967 presidential address to the American Economics Association.

In that speech, Friedman criticized the Phillips Curve and offered an alternative hypothesis about the relationship between inflation and unemployment (Friedman [1968d] 1987; Phillips, 1958). Friedman's argument, along with Edmund Phelps's contemporaneous research on the subject (1967), theoretically damaged this aspect of traditional Keynesian thought. However, the real blow came when the "stagflation" of the 1970s provided evidence for the Friedman/Phelps position and severely infirmed the original Phillips Curve argument.

The Phillips Curve hypothesis essentially states, as Friedman noted in his Nobel speech, that there is "a stable negative relationship between the level of unemployment and the rate of change of wages" (Friedman [1977a] 1987, 350). If correct, this means that policy makers can utilize either monetary or fiscal levers to, in essence, choose the rates of inflation and unemployment. However, early Keynesians thought that monetary policy was not very useful (especially when the economy was mired in a liquidity trap); therefore, the key mechanism for economic fine-tuning (especially to achieve "full employment") would be fiscal policy—either tax cuts or government spending (Friedman [1968d] 1987, 388). Later Keynesians thought that monetary policy could be used to exploit a long-run trade-off between inflation and unemployment.[12]

Friedman (and Phelps) challenged the notion that fiscal or monetary policy could be used to select a level of unemployment and inflation, arguing that "there is no permanent trade-off" (Friedman [1968d] 1987, 396). In the long-run, inflation will have no real effect on employment since market participants will factor inflation into their thinking, and employment will settle at what he called its "natural rate" or less controversially, NAIRU (the "non-accelerating inflation rate of unemployment" (Friedman [1968d] 1987, 393ff). Friedman did agree that the short run was potentially different (assuming that individuals did not accurately anticipate any inflationary changes in the offing). Unanticipated changes in aggregate nominal demand spurred by fiscal or monetary policy will temporarily cause nominal wage growth to accelerate and unemployment to drop as well. People are temporarily under Irving Fisher's "money illusion." However, Friedman argued, this does not last long, as "perceptions will adjust to reality"—and unemployment will soon find the natural rate (Friedman [1977a] 1987, 353). Therefore, the "Expectations Adjusted Phillips Curve" is basically vertical. In other words, higher inflation—if expected—does not yield lower unemployment, so policy makers cannot choose between various mixes of inflation and unemployment. Indeed, it is possible that the Phillips curve is positively sloped, meaning both high inflation and high unemployment can coexist, at least in the short term (Friedman [1977a] 1987).

Stagflation in the 1970s provided empirical support for the Friedman/Phelps position. The combination of theory and the reality of economic problems in the 1970s was quite harmful to the Keynesian notion that government could fine-tune the economy. In fact, the economy proved difficult to manage in the manner Keynesians believed they could.

The Role of Government in Money and the "Monetarist Rule"

Although he was generally skeptical of arguments for government intervention in the market, Friedman believed that the state has a positive role to play in the area of money. In short, he thought that government should establish a stable monetary system. As he argued in *Capitalism and Freedom*: "It is desirable that we use government to provide a stable monetary framework for a free economy—this is part of the function of providing a stable legal framework" (Friedman 1962a, 38). Friedman originated a rule for establishing this stable system, which will be discussed shortly below.

But why did Friedman think such a government role was crucial? He thought the state had to intervene because "a moderately stable monetary framework seems an essential prerequisite for the effective operation of a private market economy"—and he doubted the market could provide this framework on its own (Friedman [1948] 1953, 134; Friedman 1960, 8; Friedman [1984b] 1987, 405). Without government intervention, market failure in this realm would occur, to Friedman, for four main reasons:

> [1] The resource cost of a pure commodity currency and hence its tendency to become partly fiduciary; [2] the peculiar difficulty of enforcing contracts involving promises to pay that serve as a medium of exchange and of preventing fraud in respect to them; [3] the technical monopoly character of a pure fiduciary currency which makes essential the setting of some external limit on its amount; and finally, [4] the pervasive character of money which means that the issuance of money has important effects on parties other than those directly involved. (Friedman 1960, 8)

Because of these issues, Friedman rejected "free banking" (in which private banks are free from regulation and are allowed to issue their own currencies) and thought the state had ample warrant to step in.[13]

However, Friedman advocated a dominant government role with some trepidation. He understood well that he was handing government a mighty power, "a potent tool for controlling and shaping the economy" or even destroying society, as he remembered Lenin saying (Friedman 1962a, 39; [1962c] 1987, 429). Moreover, Friedman recognized that there could be significant "government failure" in its maintenance of that monetary framework. Indeed, his works—especially his chef d'oeuvre (Friedman and Schwartz 1963)—document many historical instances of poor management. This led him to conclude that "Government intervention in monetary matters, far from providing the stable monetary framework for a free market that is its ultimate justification, has proved a potent source of instability" (Friedman 1960, 23). Yet he did not think there was a viable alternative and instead advocated reform of the governmental system, for example, the monetarist rule discussed below, rather than returning money to the marketplace.

Friedman's preferred monetary system is one in which the state is the monopoly provider of a purely fiat currency (money with no objective or intrinsic value and not backed by or convertible into any commodity such as gold). He preferred monopoly government provision for two main reasons. First, Friedman thought that fiat currency issuance is a "natural" or "technical" monopoly. Therefore, the advantages and presumption of leaving its supply to the competitive marketplace disappear (Friedman 1960, 7). Second, monopoly state provision solves the problem in alternative arrangements of the government inevitably having to intervene in the lending and investing markets (Friedman [1951b] 1953, 217–19; Friedman [1962c] 1987, 431).

Friedman also preferred a fiat currency despite knowing well the many real and potential problems with it. For example, he understood that fiat currencies are prone to inflation, given the allure for government to start the printing presses as a way to indirectly tax money holders without a vote (Friedman [1962c] 1987, 429–30; Friedman [1992c] 1994, 253). Yet Friedman still considered it the best option compared to other arrangements. He ruled out a commodity standard such as the gold standard or a commodity-reserve standard for a number of reasons (see Friedman [1951b] 1953, 249). These included the tendency in practice for commodity standards to become mixed systems anyway with significant government intervention (Friedman [1962c] 1987, 431; Friedman [1951b] 1953). Even more importantly, these commodity-based systems involve a significant cost in resources just to produce currency that is often stored away, as notes take the place of the commodity itself in day-to-day transactions (leading to the joke that "People must work hard to dig gold out of the ground in South Africa—in order to rebury it in Fort Knox or some similar place") (Friedman 1960, 4–6; Friedman 1962a, 40).[14] A fiat currency, on the other hand, has the huge advantage of being "essentially costless" to produce, as well as not requiring otherwise useful resources to be diverted to warehouses to sit unused (Friedman [1951b] 1953, 242).

Recognizing the danger of a fiat currency, Friedman thought the monetary framework had to be thickened with rules to limit the discretion of the government to tinker with the money supply. This distinction and his preference for rules followed directly from a 1936 article on monetary policy written by Chicago professor Henry Simons (Breit and Ransom 1971, 246). Friedman's preference for rules is in sharp contrast to many who favor the idea of central bank independence and discretion to engage in stabilization policy and to "fine-tune" the economy. Moreover, it bucks the tide of history in which authorities have been given leeway to meet general goals—with bad results according to Friedman (1960, 84–85). Instead, paraphrasing Clemenceau, Friedman argued that "Money is too serious a matter to be left to the Central Bankers" (Friedman 1962a, 51).

Friedman's case against discretion was part philosophical, part economic. In terms of philosophy, he thought it repugnant to the ideals of a liberal democracy to give so much power to a small coterie of men "free from any kind of direct, effective political control." Instead, he favored the rule of law while conceding that it was impossible to write rules without providing some administrative discretion. In terms of the "technical" or economic arguments, Friedman thought an independent central bank is flawed because it fosters "shirking" due to the dispersal of responsibility among different parts of the government, relies too greatly on particular personalities (thus inducing instability from regime to regime), and ties monetary policy too closely to the banking community (Friedman [1962c] 1987, 432–41; Friedman 1962a, 44–51).[15] He also thought there was a fundamental knowledge problem involved with fine-tuning, whether monetary or fiscal: we cannot possibly predict the future with enough accuracy to fine-tune effectively (Friedman and Heller 1969, 49–50). In practice, "we do not know when to do so and by how much," therefore it is better to stick with rules that are a safer bet for success (Friedman 1960, 98). Lastly, Friedman's research on lags shows that "monetary actions affect economic conditions only after a lag that is both long and variable" (Friedman [1961] 1969b, 238). The same could be said for fiscal policy. This means that stabilization policies are not likely to achieve their desired goals of alleviating short-term economic problems, but they can impact things further down the line when conditions might be quite different and the real impact quite unintended. For example, easy money in downturns, by the time it takes effect, may have the undesired effect of overheating an economy already in recovery. Moreover, Friedman understood that there is a political lag between changing economic conditions, recognition of the problem, and the ability to change policy (see Friedman [1947a] 1953, 313–16; Friedman [1948] 1953, 144–48). Together, these are further reasons not to give central bankers discretion; they are likely to tinker in the hopes of "fixing" things but only make things worse.[16]

Friedman pointed to the United States' troubling experience with government discretion as evidence of the problem of relying on individuals rather than rules. The result has been that we have not had stable, effective policy but "continual and unpredictable shifts" in the methods and content of policy making (Friedman 1960, 85).[17] Moreover, this independence allowed the mistakes of a few men to have far-reaching and terrible consequences during the Great Depression when central bankers failed to pursue proper policies in the face of a massive decline in the money stock (Friedman 1962a, 50; Friedman and Schwartz 1963).

Opposing both a commodity standard and an independent discretionary system, Friedman eventually argued in favor of what has come to be known as the "monetarist rule" to provide for a stable monetary order. This was not Simons's price-level rule, which Friedman rejected because monetary policy makers cannot easily or directly keep prices stable with the tools at their disposal (Friedman 1962a, 53). Nor was it his original proposal from 1948, in which the money supply would be linked to the federal budget (surpluses would shrink the stock of money and deficits would increase it) and there would be a 100 percent bank reserve requirement (Friedman [1948] 1953, 135–36). Although he continued to think this early proposal would contribute to monetary stability, Friedman later changed his policy prescription because he thought his original idea was unnecessarily complex.

Instead, starting in 1960, Friedman advocated his famous simple monetary rule—or Friedman's "k-percent rule"—that he preached with only negligible differences over the next two decades.[18] According to Friedman (1960, 90), this rule would mandate that the stock of money should "be increased at a fixed rate year-in and year-out without any variation in the rate of increase to meet cyclical needs" (90). Although he preferred one of a number of possible operationalizations of the stock of money, Friedman ultimately did not believe the particular choice is all that important as long as a clear choice is made, the definition includes currency and adjusted demand deposits, and the rate of increase reflects that choice (91).[19] Therefore, the stock of money should increase, using the central bank's open market powers, 3–5 percent per year in order to keep up with real growth in output and populations, achieve a stable monetary framework, and "correspond with a roughly stable long-run level of final product prices" (Friedman [1958b] 1969b, 184; Friedman 1960, 91, 100). Importantly, his prescription did not focus on interest rates (see Friedman 1969b, 74ff). Additionally, as part of his overall reform proposal, Friedman thought the central bank's powers also needed to be curtailed, including repeal of its ability to make loans, discount paper, or vary reserve requirements (100). He continued to support the 100 percent reserve requirement as well. Although he was originally content to let the Federal Reserve System adopt the rule on its own, Friedman soon added that it should be formally legislated and eventually argued that it ought to be formally written into the Constitution (Friedman 1962a, 54; Friedman and Friedman [1980] 1990, 308).

He also changed his view slightly on the size of monetary growth mandated under such a rule. In 1969, he shrunk the target rate to a 2-percent rule for growth of the money stock (Friedman 1969b, 48). By 1984, Friedman advocated (because of lower velocity growth) a 1–3 percent M1 growth per year (Freidman [1984b] 1987, 411, 427).

There is one important caveat to the foregoing discussion of Friedman's views on government's role in money. In the mid-1980s, his views shifted in important ways (not represented in the foregoing summary, which attempts to describe Friedman's longest-held position). First, starting in 1984, Friedman argued for a more radical change in the monetary framework. At that point, he believed the "best real cure" was to "abolish the money-creating powers of the Federal Reserve, freeze the quantity of high-powered money, and deregulate the financial system" (Friedman [1984b] 1987, 425). However, he was pessimistic about this or his earlier monetarist rule ever being enacted, given the powerful bureaucratic self-interest of the Federal Reserve System (425). Second, Friedman endorsed the idea, associated with Hayek and other libertarians, of rescinding the government's legal monopoly on currency provision, thus allowing competitive currencies. He even considered the idea of getting government out of the business of money supply altogether. He thought both were "intellectually exciting" ideas but doubted they would ever be accepted or that government would "long keep aloof" even if private currencies came into being (Friedman [1984b] 1987, 418–20; Friedman and Schwartz [1986] 1987, 511). However, he did admit that private arrangements would have been better than government involvement in the first place, even if the government's monopoly position is "largely a dead letter" (Friedman and Schwartz [1986] 1987, 513).[20] Friedman's shift in this area is reminiscent of his evolving thoughts on education. After his initial publications on the subject, longer personal experience and historical research done by others led him to change his mind in a more radical free-market direction.

Other Notable Scholarship

To round out this discussion of Friedman's scholarly work, it is worth touching briefly on a few of his other contributions. Early in his career, Friedman wrote several important pieces on demand (Friedman 1935, 1936, [1949] 1953) as well as on methods and statistics (Friedman 1940, 1947b; Friedman et al., 1948). Also noteworthy was Friedman's examination (with Simon Kuznets) of professional incomes. In it, he argued that we need to distinguish between transitory, quasi-permanent, and permanent income (Friedman and Kuznets 1945). Importantly (and controversially), he also found that the difference between the earnings of physicians and dentists could be related to a "deliberate policy of limiting the number of entrants" into the medical profession, thus indicting the American Medical Association (Friedman and Kuznets 1945, 395). This research, which served as his dissertation, paved the way for his later pathbreaking work on the consumption function. Friedman also published two articles on the concept of utility with statistician Jimmie Savage (Friedman and Savage 1948, 1952). One of Friedman's more interesting predictive pieces—to which he returned when he received his Nobel prize—concerned why the American economy is now "depression proof" (Friedman [1954] 1968b). He argued that institutional changes, ideas, and attitudes generated by the Great Depression made another depression "almost inconceivable." However, he worried that while we had learned the proper lessons to avoid deflation-inspired troubles, we had not yet learned that overcorrecting and spurring on inflation is also dangerous to our economic health (Friedman [1954] 1968b, 74 and 89). Lastly, Friedman delivered an address at the 1972 Mont Pelerin Society meeting on capitalism and Jews that continues to inspire debate almost four decades later (Friedman 1984a [1987]; and see Muller 2010). There he argued that Jews benefit immensely from free markets but generally have an anti-capitalist mentality, largely because they are trying to debunk anti-Semitic stereotypes of Jews as excessively concerned about money.

Friedman's Political Theory

Friedman's overarching political theory was a relatively unoriginal, amalgamated expression of the classical liberal tradition. He regarded individual liberty as an intrinsic good, largely trusted free markets to maximize economic well-being, and conceived of government as a necessary but dangerous mechanism for securing and advancing freedom and human welfare.[21] Friedman's thought was influenced by classical liberal thinkers—Adam Smith above all, as well as John Stuart Mill, Friedrich Hayek, and perhaps even Herbert Spencer.[22] His outlook also contained more than a hint of Henry Simons's particular variant of liberalism and, in his later work, of public choice theory. However, especially in Friedman's case, we should be careful not to overemphasize the role of classic works in influencing an intellectual's views versus other inputs. For Friedman, these other inputs would include his direct study and internalization of the general disciplinary knowledge and outlook of classical economics; the personal influences mentioned previously, such as Jones, Knight, and the two Directors (Rose and Aaron); and his own sensibilities and life experiences, including his stints in government and his increased contact with other classical liberals after World War II.[23]

In terms of the content of his political thought, Friedman believed that the primary ends of our "social arrangements" are individual liberty and well-being (Friedman 1962a, 12; also see Friedman [1948] 1953, 134; Friedman 1951d; Friedman 1955a; Friedman and Friedman [1980] 1990).[24] Indeed, his writings brim over with a deep concern for freedom, human welfare, material progress, and economic efficiency (Friedman's specific views on these ends will be discussed in more depth later). As might be expected of a libertarian and an economist, Friedman believed that markets, if left largely unrestricted, could satisfy most of these concerns without the encroachments on freedom inherent in the coercive means of the state. Moreover, free markets would accomplish these goals more efficiently while also preventing the dangerous accumulation of power and providing a counterweight to the state (Friedman [1978c] 1983, 89).

Nonetheless, Friedman doubted that the market alone could best achieve even these limited ends, especially given his view of humans as "imperfect beings" (Friedman 1962a, 12, 25, and 34). Despite his obvious contempt for the state, Friedman ascribed to government a positive role in securing and advancing these goods. Thus, he shied away from anarchism (unlike his son David). Indeed, Friedman did not regard anarchism as a "feasible social structure," particularly because social coordination often necessitates limits on our absolute freedom (Reason Interview 2005; Times Herald Interview 1978; AoA Interview 1991).

Therefore, Friedman was essentially a "statist," with these important caveats: he argued the state should be limited in size and scope and restricted to a largely night-watchman role.[25] Moreover, the state should be highly decentralized in order to prevent the concentration of power and all the negative things that flow from it (Friedman 1962a, 2, 3, 15; Playboy Interview [1973] 1983; Friedman [1948] 1953, 135; Friedman 1976a). Following Spencer, Friedman favored the smallest government "consistent with the maximum freedom for each individual to follow his own ways, his own values, as long as he doesn't interfere with anybody else who's doing the same" (Uncommon Knowledge Interview 1999). Put a little differently, this time following Mill, Friedman thought "The proper role of government is to prevent other people from harming an individual. Government, he [Mill] said, never has any right to interfere with an individual for that individual's own good" (Paige Interview 1991). However, at many points he went further, especially in the cases of market failure.

Specifically, Friedman thought government should perform a limited but important set of specific functions. Nearly all are encompassed by Adam Smith's three duties of a sovereign, something Friedman explicitly recognizes in *Free to Choose.* First, the state should be responsible for national defense against foreign enemies (Friedman and Samuelson 1980, 6; AoA Interview 1991).

Second, the government should be "a forum for determining the 'rules of the game,' including the definition of property rights (Friedman 1962a, 15 and 27; AoA Interview 1991). Third, the state ought to act as both "umpire" and "enforcer" of these rules. Thus the government would maintain law and order through a judicial system and a domestic police force. Some of its specific tasks would include the enforcement of contracts and the prevention of coercion of one individual by another (Friedman 1962a, 15 and 27; AoA Interview 1991). Fourth, government should do things that "technical" conditions such as monopoly or market failure make it difficult for markets to do without their being "exceedingly costly or practically impossible" (Friedman 1962a, 28; Friedman and Friedman [1980] 1990). This would include the provision of certain goods such as the financing of education for children up to a certain age. Fifth, it should be responsible for the maintenance of a competitive market order and a stable monetary framework (Friedman 1951d). Lastly, and most controversially among his fellow libertarians, Friedman also thought the government should "relieve acute misery and distress" and "provide for people who cannot take care of themselves—people who are in dire distress" (Friedman 1951d; Friedman and Samuelson 1980, 6). This would include some role in protecting and providing for those who "draw blanks in the lottery of life" and those not responsible for themselves such as children and the insane (Friedman 1951d; Friedman 1955a, 362; Friedman 1962a; Friedman and Friedman [1980] 1990).[26] How he fleshed out this broader political philosophy in particular public policy areas is discussed at length, below.

There are several other aspects of Friedman's philosophical outlook that are worth mentioning in brief. First, Friedman was a supreme individualist. Therefore, he despised paternalism and collectivism—and frequently used these very terms as pejorative labels to criticize policies that would restrict individual liberty. Friedman went so far in his individualism that he characterized the country as merely "a collection of individuals who compose it" (Friedman 1962a, 188, 2). Likewise, he asserted that only individuals, not businesses nor governments, can have responsibilities (see Friedman [1970c] 1987; Business and Society Review Interview 1972). However, Friedman leavened his individualism by claiming that the family is the basic social unit and expressed deep concern for families in his work (Friedman 1962a, 87; Friedman 1955a).[27] Moreover, Friedman recognized that even he was not as faithful to the spirit of individualism, in terms of his political theory, compared to his liberal intellectual ancestors, noting "By the standards of nineteenth century individualism, we are all collectivists in smaller or greater measure" (Friedman 1951d).

Second, somewhat uncommonly, Friedman grew more radical as he got older. In the 1940s and early 1950s, under the banner of "neoliberalism," Friedman's rhetoric was much less positive about laissez-faire and much friendlier toward state action aimed at remedying ills such as monopoly and poverty (Friedman 1951d). At that time, Friedman was also more vocal about the importance of equality of economic power and the role of the state in reducing inequality (see Friedman and Stigler 1946; Friedman [1948] 1953; Friedman 1951d).[28] As time went on–and almost certainly under the influence of public choice theory—Friedman saw greater and greater problems with government action. This was the case even in areas in which he thought the government could theoretically play a legitimate role, such as antitrust regulation (see Friedman and Friedman [1980] 1990, 189–227). Friedman also became more radical in education policy (more favorable to complete privatization), social welfare policy (questioning whether even a negative income tax was justified in principle), and monetary policy (more friendly to free banking/competitive currencies). By the 1990s, he was arguing that government had become "a self-generating monstrosity" (AoA Interview 1991).

Despite his radical political philosophy, Friedman was always pragmatic in his approach to politics. In particular, he was amenable—much to the chagrin of some of his fellow libertarians—to compromises and half steps that would produce a freer society even if only incrementally. As he noted in 1995, "The difference between me and people like Murray Rothbard [another leading libertarian] is that, though I want to know what my ideal is, I think I also have to be willing to discuss changes that are less than ideal so long as they point me in that direction. So while I'd like to abolish the Fed, I've written many pages on how the Fed, if it does exist, should be run" (Reason Interview 1995). This willingness to compromise was likely part of the reason for his unparalleled success (for a radical and a libertarian) in being taken seriously by political actors.

Third, Friedman typically privileged having institutions in place, rather than relying on virtue or a certain political culture, to protect a flourishing free society. To that end, he campaigned for tax limitation amendments and, in *Free to Choose*, advocated a broad set of constitutional amendments to overcome the advantages of special interests. However, at times, Friedman acknowledged that institutions alone were not sufficient for his libertarian political philosophy to work; certain virtues or principles held by the citizenry were required as well. For example, in 1975, Friedman noted that a free society cannot be maintained without "a self-denying ordinance of the most extreme kind. It requires a willingness to put up with temporary evils on the basis of the subtle and sophisticated understanding that if you step in to try to do them, you not only may make them—to do something about them—you not only may make them worse, but you will spread your tentacles and get bad results elsewhere." (Open Mind Interview 1975). Likewise, in *Free to Choose*, he admitted that "In order for a written—or for that matter, unwritten, constitution to be effective it must be supported by the general climate of opinion, among both the public at large and its leaders. It must incorporate principles that they have come to believe in deeply . . ." (Friedman and Friedman [1980] 1990, 300). Additionally, in the particular case of his negative income tax plan, Friedman recognized that it would only work if the public exercised "self-restraint and good will" (Friedman 1962a, 194). Skeptical that superior virtue would triumph, however, Friedman preferred to rely on institutions. Regarding the problem that only hypocrites seem to survive in elected office, he commented, "There is little point in looking to the moral regeneration of either politicians or ourselves for a solution to this basic weakness in our political system. We shall do far better to seek a change in our effective political constitution that will narrowly limit the power of those whom we elect and thereby alter the incentives of both politicians and voters" (Friedman [1980a] 1983, 121).

Fourth, Friedman was remarkably optimistic about the future, especially for someone whose basic view of human nature was not particularly rosy. In fact, Friedman thought mankind was "selfish and greedy" and corruptible by power as Lord Acton famously noted (Open Mind Interview 1975). Moreover, he was aware that people have seldom been free and that freedom has not been a stable equilibrium (Open Mind Interview 1975; Reason Interview 1995). Yet Friedman still maintained a dogged optimism and was well known for it. This sensibility was rooted in some faith in people to pull back from the worst, a long-run approach, and perhaps even his own psychological needs. As he told one interviewer: "I think in the end, you've got to remain an optimist" (Roberts Interview 2006).

* * *

Friedman political theory was not a tight philosophical system in which he resolved or even seemed to seriously grapple with the possible tensions among the values he cherished. In fact, he had little interest in wrangling with any of the fundamental philosophical issues within liberal thought, including the defense of individual freedom or material welfare as the highest ends. As Brian Doherty (2007, 302) notes in his history of libertarianism, "Friedman has never shown much interest in arguing basic questions of 'why liberty.' He simply assumes that men of good will favor the same things . . ." Given this view, Friedman generally posited the importance of both individual liberty and prosperity and moved on to push a freedom agenda that he thought would best secure them.

It is not entirely clear why Friedman never delved to go deeper into the philosophy of freedom as did Robert Nozick, Hayek, or other contemporaneous libertarians (including his son David). One likely reason is that Friedman was simply more interested in doing economics and pushing for a freer society through his engagement in public policy debates than he was in exploring the philosophical nuances of liberal thought. Moreover, he probably found resolution or debate of such nuances of little utility outside of what he liked to call "bull sessions," especially once he had settled into his basic libertarian outlook (see Friedman and Friedman 1998, 94, 49). After all, he had taken a similar approach to the area of methodology. Friedman was generally unwilling to spend time exploring methodological issues, including defense of his own foundational 1953 essay, once he had settled on a particular view (Friedman 1953). As Friedman noted later in life about his long silence, "I decided that I would rather do economics than spend more time writing about how economics should be done" (Friedman and Friedman 1998, 215).[29] Friedman may also have thought it was not in his comparative advantage to do so. In addition, Friedman may have had a rather panglossian perspective when it came to freedom and human welfare. For example, in 1978, Friedman commented in *Newsweek* that "The preservation of liberty, not the promotion of efficiency, is the primary justification for private property. Efficiency is a happy, though not accidental, by-product—and a most important by-product because liberty could not have survived if it had not also produced affluence" (Friedman [1978e] 1983, 100–01). In a very American way, Friedman wanted it all and thought freedom and the kinds of outcomes he preferred almost always came together harmoniously (and that coercive plans led to bad outcomes). It is perhaps unfair to criticize Friedman too much in this regard since he was an economist, not a political or moral philosopher, and never pretended to be otherwise. Instead, when it came to politics, he was an applied theorist and populizer of a certain type of political thought that had been explored in more detail by others.

However, Friedman's unwillingness to explore tensions in liberal thought may lead some of his readers to want for more. In particular, Friedman's normative works can be frustrating because he did not maintain a consistent rank-ordering of ends and was not averse to trading off one good to meet another end in certain circumstances. Moreover, he lacked a general principle or consistent approach to determine when certain ends should be "trumps" or even privileged and when they should be compromised or traded-off against other ends.[30] Instead, Friedman made what sometimes seemed to be ad hoc determinations. This reflected his unwillingness to concern himself with possible tensions in his thought and an interest in promoting pragmatic policies that would increase freedom or well-being. When Friedman did attempt to justify state action that was not rooted in the law of equal freedom, Friedman most frequently used monopoly, neighborhood effects, and paternalism for children and "irresponsible individuals" as rationales (Friedman 1955a, 362; Friedman 1955b; Friedman 1962a, 23). However, if freedom is really the ultimate goal, as he claims in *Capitalism and Freedom* (1962a, 12), why would government intervention be justified simply because "technical" conditions such as monopoly or market failure make it difficult for markets to do things without their being "exceedingly costly or practically impossible" (Friedman 1962a, 28; Friedman and Friedman [1980] 1990)?[31]

Two examples, out of many, highlight Friedman's frequent willingness to allow his concern for what he thought were good outcomes to trump freedom. In the case of conscription, Friedman argued that involuntary military service was a violation of a person's basic individual freedom and "inconsistent with a free society" (Friedman [1966b] 1975, 189). Yet even though he compared conscripts to "slaves," he thought such a system was justified in small states and in times of major war (Friedman 1979a, b; Tax 1967, 202; Friedman and Friedman 1998, 380–81). Friedman went so far as to argue that coerced universal military training could be justified on liberal grounds

(Friedman 1962a, 36; Tax 1967, 206). Likewise, he thought positive neighborhood effects were a sufficient ground for the public financing of education despite the coercion involved. In these and other cases, Friedman clearly suggested that some level of coercion was preferable to liberty if the latter would not yield the right results.

These points would not be a big deal for most thinkers except that Friedman was so emphatic about how evil coercion was and how individual liberty was an intrinsic good. Indeed, Friedman said that freedom of the individual was the "ultimate value" for liberals and frequently stressed the importance of freedom as a moral end that overshadowed even efficiency and economic well-being (Friedman 1955a). For example, he argued that the main justification for the free market was "its moral strength, not its superior efficiency" (Friedman and Friedman 1998, 469). Additionally, Friedman thought that free people should be free to make mistakes without government interfering for even their own benefit (Friedman 1962a, 188). Moreover, he often made arguments that were rooted in a deontological moral position he seemed to reject in other cases where he applied consequentialist standards. For example, in the case of business ethics, he thought (contra a strict utilitarian approach) that business and union leaders had a duty to their principals even if following that duty led to suboptimal results for society as a whole (see the discussion of corporate social responsibility below; and see Hasnas 1998). Thus, Friedman's position almost approached the notion that freedom is the ultimate value—except when it's not![32]

However, it is difficult to pigeonhole Friedman as a mere utilitarian or consequentialist who conceptualized freedom as simply an instrumental good. Examples abound that confound such an easy categorization. Yet Friedman was far from a deontological thinker. Indeed, it might be impossible to impose a system on Friedman's thought other than to say he was a classical liberal. Despite his lack of consistency, however, it is probably closer to the mark to characterize him, as David Boaz and others have, as a "consequentialist" who in some cases was willing to privilege good outcomes or "efficiency" even if getting there meant impinging on individual liberty and, in other cases, simply saw all good things going together (Boaz 1997, 82; Doherty 2007, 192 and 302). Indeed, Friedman himself referred to his position as "conseqentialist libertarianism," which certainly fits his attachment to writers such as Mill (Uncommon Knowledge Interview 1999; Friedman 2002).

One area in his political philosophy that Friedman does explore in more detail concerns the relationship between economic freedom and political freedom. In his famous opening chapter of *Capitalism and Freedom*, Friedman argues that the various aspects of freedom are inseparable. In his schema, economic freedom is an end in itself as well as the means to promote human welfare *and* political freedom (Friedman 1962a, 8).[33] Indeed, at one point, he claimed that "freedom is one whole, that anything that reduces freedom in one part of our lives is likely to affect freedom in the other parts" (Friedman [1980] 1990, 69). However, even in *Capitalism and Freedom* and at the end of his life, he admitted that economic freedom could exist without political freedom in the narrow sense of voting, especially if the state allows a large measure of civic freedoms (Friedman 1962a, 10; Liberty Fund Interview 2003). Hong Kong would be one example where economic freedom flourished without political freedom. But Friedman ultimately thought economic freedom would help cause political freedom—though political freedom could lead to a decline in economic freedom (Liberty Fund Interview 2003).

* * *

Given his political philosophy, it is unsurprising that Friedman unabashedly accepted the liberal moniker and tried to revive its use to describe himself and other advocates of individual liberty and free markets. Despite this, Friedman was often mischaracterized as a conservative, an appellation at which he bristled for many of the same reasons stressed by Friedrich Hayek (1960) in his famous epilogue to *The Constitution of Liberty* (for one of many examples, see Open Mind Interview 1975).[34] As time went on, Friedman accepted the unsatisfying designation as a libertarian and frequently described himself as "a small-l libertarian" (but importantly, "a large R-Republican" rather than a member of the Libertarian Party). However, he distanced himself from the anarchist strain of libertarianism as much as he ran away from the Libertarian Party (see Times Herald Interview 1978; Reason Interview 1995; AoA Interview 1991).

Public Policy

Education

Friedman was especially active in the realm of education policy. Specifically, he was a vocal advocate of school choice or "vouchers." Other than monetary policy, for which he had both a scientific and policy interest, no other subject occupied so much of his time and energy for so long (Friedman and Friedman 1998, 348). That Friedman and his wife established the Friedman Foundation for Educational Choice shows how devoted he was to this cause.

Friedman first took an active interest in education policy during his year at Cambridge University in 1953–1954 (Friedman and Friedman 1998). There, he wrote a piece titled "The Role of Government in Education" (Friedman 1955b), which emphasized the use of vouchers and the separation of school funding from school administration. According to Robert Enlow and Lenore Ealy (2006, 1) in their edited volume reexamining that piece on its fiftieth anniversary, these proposals "launched the modern school choice movement." It is interesting, given how important the issue became for Friedman, that he undertook this study not because of a pressing social problem at the time or any particular zeal for education policy but as an outgrowth of his overall interest in the philosophy of freedom (Friedman [2005] 2006a, b; Enlow and Ealy 2006, vii; Brandl 2006).[35]

Friedman begins his examination with a foundational statement about the proper role of government in a free society. He argues that the state's primary purpose is "to preserve the rules of the game by enforcing contracts, preventing coercion, and keeping markets free." He further specifies that the government can legitimately intervene under three special conditions: "natural monopoly" or similar market imperfections that prevent truly voluntary exchange, substantial "neighborhood effects" (what economists refer to as "externalities"), and a "paternalistic concern for children and other irresponsible individuals" (Friedman 1955b).

Unfortunately, Friedman does not explain in much detail why these grounds warrant impingements on individual liberty. This is especially regrettable in the case of positive externalities. The only real justification he gives for the first two conditions is that they "make voluntary exchange impossible," though his specific discussion of education suggests he is concerned about the general welfare (Friedman 1955b). Some liberty-minded observers might argue that the neighborhood effects justification for state intervention is exactly the "camel's nose in the tent" that leads down the path to socialism. Of course, the third condition is far less problematic from the standpoint of liberty, given liberalism's general difficulty handling children and those who cannot give proper consent.

Friedman then applies his general theory to education and argues that government does have a role to play in education because of its significant positive neighborhood effects. In particular, he explains that "a stable and democratic society is impossible without widespread acceptance of some common set of values and without a minimum degree of literacy and knowledge on the part of most citizens" (Friedman 1955b). Given that general education meets these common needs, and we cannot identify the specific beneficiaries or the "money value" of the externalities so as to charge for them, Friedman believes government involvement is justified.

According to Friedman, meeting this citizenship goal warrants compulsory schooling laws up to a certain minimum. This government imposition raises the question of who should pay for meeting such an expensive mandate. Friedman toys with the idea of forcing parents to pay, with the government handling special circumstances. However, he concludes that this option is "hardly feasible" and thus advocates full state financing of general education, with the form and quantity of schooling decided by the political community. Friedman also argues that public subsidies for education beyond these minima is justified because it will provide "better social and political leadership"—yet more positive neighborhood effects (Friedman 1955b). He does not endorse, however, public vocational or professional training on the grounds of externalities since these forms of education primarily benefit the student rather than the community. They are merely different types of capital investment (Friedman 1955b).

To this point, Friedman's position is not that remarkable. What differentiates his view on education from others' is that he proceeds to argue there are no grounds for generalized government administration of education even if the state pays for schooling. In other words, government should finance education but not run schools except in the limited cases where there is a natural monopoly in small, isolated rural communities. Instead, the government would provide vouchers tied to individual students, and their parents would then decide where to send them to school (including parochial schools). The only restriction for the vouchers would be that they could only be used for "'approved' educational services." The government's job would be to ensure "that the schools met certain minimum standards such as the inclusion of a minimum common content in their programs" (Friedman 1955b).

Friedman thought separating the administrative and financial functions of government education policy would have large benefits. Furthermore, he did not think the costs, including the transaction costs of moving from the current system to a voucher system, would be all that high. In terms of the benefits, Friedman thought such a system would empower parents to be able to "express their views about schools directly" by moving their children rather than by moving their residence (Friedman 1955b). It would also provide for greater competition among providers. This would have a number of positive consequences, including increasing the variety of schools and exposing teacher salaries to market forces. In short, school choice would increase efficiency. Contrary to what many have argued, Friedman also thought that a voucher system would reduce, rather than increase, class and religious stratification.

As noted above, Friedman also argues that the government should subsidize higher education on the grounds that it, too, contributes to the common good by training citizens and future leaders. Such financing would likewise be voucher-based and would work just as the G. I. Bill does except that states would provide the funding. Notably, Friedman does not think government universities and colleges are justified by the criteria he set out, but he did muse in a footnote that the subsidization of basic research might be one way to legitimize them (Friedman 1955b, fn. 4).

Finally, Friedman believes that government may be justified in playing a role in financing even vocational and professional training, although it mainly benefits individuals rather than the public at large. He bases this on the notion that there is a market imperfection in capital investment markets in human capital, such that "the full use of our human resources" would not be realized in a pure market. He notes that such imperfections would work to "perpetuate inequalities in wealth and status" (Friedman 1955b). Although he does not advocate full subsidization, Friedman thinks government should help solve the problem by engaging in "equity investment in human beings" and stimulating "private arrangements directed toward the same end" (Friedman 1955b). Such a program would be "self-financing" by requiring the loan recipient to pay back the state a percentage of future earnings.

Although Friedman's work on school choice seemed novel at the time, he was not the first liberal thinker to advocate such a plan. Classical liberal icons such as Adam Smith, Thomas Paine, and John Stuart Mill all favored educational plans in which the state provided at least some educational funding but did not necessarily operate schools (Smith [1776] 1976; Paine [1791] 1955, 630; Mill 1859, Ebenstein 2007). Moreover, Popper launched the postwar liberal attack on public schooling at the second Mont Pelerin Society meeting in 1949—something Friedman may have heard about even though he was not in attendance (Hartwell 1995, 88). Therefore, Friedman's proposals are not as original as they may have seemed in the context of widespread satisfaction with American schooling in the pre-Sputnik 1950s. Despite the older pedigree, it remains the case, as education professor Eric Hanushek argues, that "Perhaps no idea about schooling is as directly linked to a single individual as school choice is to Milton Friedman" (Enlow and Ealy 2006, 67).

Friedman repeated his call for a voucher system in *Capitalism and Freedom* (Friedman 1962a) and *Free to Choose* (Friedman and Friedman [1980] 1990). His views on education policy, though, changed over time, evolving subtly at first and then shifting quite dramatically in a radical direction.

In *Capitalism and Freedom*, Friedman discusses education policy in a chapter that is a slightly revised version of his original 1955 piece. Indeed, much of the chapter is copied verbatim. However, some slight changes presage his later more radical turn.

One of these changes is a shift in the style and tone of his discussion. Friedman's original work is predominantly theoretical, with very little discussion of the actual state of education in America. This is unsurprising given that, as noted above, he was not motivated to write the piece by any sense of crisis or even unhappiness with the American educational system. However, the few additions Friedman made from 1955 to 1962 are more empirical than theoretical and are largely negative in tone. This suggests he was starting to learn more about our educational system and its problems. For example, the largest new section concerns increased public school expenditures on things unrelated to real education and the difficulty that parents face controlling this problem in a nonmarket arena. This new section also raises the problem of teacher salaries that are "too uniform and rigid" and result in poor teachers being overpaid and good ones underpaid (Friedman 1962a, 95). Friedman blames these problems largely on school administration provided by the government—often further and further removed from parental control.

This more negative tone is also present as he introduces a distinction between schooling and education. He notes, in the first section of this chapter, that "it is important to distinguish between 'schooling' and 'education.' Not all schooling is education nor all education, schooling. The proper subject of concern is education. The activities of government are mostly limited to schooling" (Friedman 1962a, 86). He proceeds, in place after place where he previously used the term "education," to replace it with "schooling."

Unfortunately, Friedman is not especially careful with his usage—more often routinely changing the terms rather than applying the careful distinction he pointedly makes up front. For example, when noting that "neighborhood effects" justify state action, he uses the term "schooling" to refer to what is justified (Friedman 1962a, 89). However, it is hard to imagine that Friedman actually believed this rather than the original formulation that neighborhood effects justify a minimal level of public education and financing. After all, "schooling" alone, as he derisively uses the term, would not really produce positive neighborhood effects that would justify its cost to the public. Likewise, he argues that "public expenditures on higher schooling can be justified as a means of training youngsters for citizenship and for community leadership" (Friedman 1962a, 99). It is doubtful that mere "schooling," rather than a true college education, would accomplish this. Thus, schooling alone would not be justified under Friedman's conditions.

Another difference between the two pieces is an expanded section on the feasibility and desirability of requiring direct parental payment for education rather than general public financing. Although he ultimately rejects the former in both treatments, Friedman seems to be groping toward the more radical view in his 1962 update. For example, he notes there are "many areas in the United States" where parents could afford to pay for compulsory education while the state subsidizes "needy families." He argues this would have many benefits, even including a "better distribution" of family sizes! In his conclusion that, despite the benefits, the direct payment requirement is not feasible, he adds the words "in many parts of the United States" rather than repeating the blanket conclusion for the whole country found in the original piece (Friedman 1962a, 87). This may be an early indication of willingness to move beyond vouchers (with full public financing) to a radical system of near-complete privatization of education in both the administrative and financing areas—something he tersely embraces almost as an aside in *Free to Choose.*

Friedman also admits he is not sure his voucher program would have been as desirable in the American past as when he developed it. In particular, given that public schools might be necessary on the grounds of "technical monopoly" in some locales, the need to promote some conformity in a nation of immigrants might also require a government system. He was not sure this was true, but he thought there was a stronger case for public schools in our past than when he wrote.

The interesting question for us is whether that same argument applies today given recent high levels of immigration. Friedman thought that, in his time, we needed more diversity of education—not more conformity (Friedman 1962a). Do the recent changes in American society suggest, consistent with the minimal conformity Friedman thought necessary in the nineteenth century, that public schools are needed today in order to promote a certain level of integration? Or is the imposition of basic standards (such as the teaching of English) on private schools that receive vouchers enough? Or should liberals be ecumenical about what schools teach, even in the age of radical Islam and madrassas, as long as they teach basic skills?

By the time he wrote (with his wife Rose) *Free to Choose* in 1980, Friedman's views on education had changed significantly.

Of course, he still pushed vouchers as a means of financing general education. He thought such a system would improve education substantially even if vouchers would not eliminate every problem inherent in a publically financed scheme. They would provide consumers with greater educational alternatives, introduce greater competition (even among remaining government schools) and higher quality schools, waste fewer resources, and create movement toward "direct parental financing" with public financing for hardship cases (Friedman and Friedman [1980] 1990, 160–63 and 187). Importantly, he asserted that these arguments stood up without any assumption that private schools are better (*Power of Choice*). Friedman did not think that vouchers would increase inequality or racial segregation; indeed, he thought they would have the opposite effect (Friedman and Friedman [1980] 1990).

Friedman's support for vouchers, however, was in this work only as a "partial solution" and one that was simply a pragmatic, incremental step toward a complete and radical rethinking of education policy (Friedman and Friedman [1980] 1990, 161). In *Free to Choose*, Friedman seems to reject the arguments for both compulsory schooling and public financing, thus favoring a purer market in education. This is supported by later comments that the voucher system was only "a step in moving away from a government system to a private system" (Doherty 1995, 36).

Much of the reason for his shift was, as education scholar James Tooley argues, due to research stimulated by his original proposal (Tooley 2006). This research showed that education was not underprovided in the absence of public schools, and hence "compulsory attendance at schools is not necessary to achieve that minimum standard of literacy and knowledge" (Friedman and Friedman [1980] 1990, 162). E. G. West's work on the history of schooling in Great Britain and the United States—especially the extent of education in those countries and the role of self-interested teachers and government agents in pushing public schooling—was particularly important to Friedman's shift (see Friedman and Friedman [1980] 1990; West

1965; Tooley 2006). As he and Rose noted in 1998, "We have since been persuaded by the empirical evidence on the extensiveness of schooling in the absence of government involvement that neither [compulsory schooling or public financing] is justified" (Friedman and Friedman 1998, 628 fn. 18). West's problematizing of the basis for compulsory attendance struck at the heart of the argument for government involvement at all, since as Tooley notes, it was "a prime justification for public funding" (Tooley 2006, 140).

It is a testament to Friedman's pragmatism (and perhaps his acceptance of the positive side of his role as a "court libertarian") that his deepest views on education were for the most part left underdeveloped and undersold in his popular works (Rothbard in Doherty 2007, 406). For example, his rejection of a government role in financing education is in a footnote in his autobiography rather than in the main text, where he describes at length his support for vouchers. In *Free to Choose,* although Friedman straightforwardly stresses his disagreement with compulsory education requirements, he expresses his preference for direct parental financing less bluntly while suggesting some public role for hardship cases. He then quickly moves on, noting his views on the matter "will appear to most readers to be extreme" (Friedman and Friedman [1980] 1990, 163).[36]

Yet Friedman was not shy about lambasting opponents of his program whom he believed were effectively preventing adoption of voucher programs despite rising public support. In *Free to Choose,* he argued that the "key obstacle" was "the perceived self-interest of the educational bureaucracy" (Friedman and Friedman [1980] 1990, 171). Toward the end of his life, he fingered "centralization, bureaucratization, and unionization" as key enablers for public school administrators and union leaders who wanted to block such a powerful "threat to their monopolistic control" (Friedman 2005a, 157). Moreover, he thought these forces were preventing necessary changes as educational "output" declined, especially in poor inner city communities.

Friedman was more blunt about his shifting view on public higher education. In his earlier work, he provided a positive neighborhood effects rationale for a public role in higher educational funding. In *Free to Choose*, however, he argues, "There is no case for subsidizing persons who get higher education at the expense of those who do not. Insofar as governments operate institutions of higher education, they should charge student fees corresponding to the full cost of the educational and other services they provide to them" (Friedman and Friedman [1980] 1990, 183). In the interim, he stopped believing that higher education provided strong social benefits that the individual could not capture in terms of higher economic productivity (179). In addition, he rejects the argument that public schools are necessary for equal opportunity, especially since (in his view) state universities just ensured that the poor ended up subsidizing middle and upper-class college attendance (183). However, Friedman continued to believe government had a role in "equity investment" schemes to finance individual attendance. He thought that the "least bad way" to subsidize education, given political realities, would be a voucher system like the G. I. Bill (185).

Fiscal Policy

In general, Friedman advocated a stable fiscal policy that reflected the proper role of government. Ideally, the government would spend and tax to finance the limited tasks that a liberal regime must fulfill and nothing more. However, even if the citizenry wanted to do more, he thought government's agenda ought to be set "entirely in terms of what the community wants to do through government rather than privately, and without regard to problems of year-to-year economic stability" (Friedman 1962a, 79; and see Friedman [1948] 1953, 136–38). In other words, just as with monetary policy, Friedman opposed government fine-tuning and stabilization policies via fiscal means. He simply did not think fiscal stimulus works in terms of the multiplier, as Keynesians argue (Friedman 1962a, 79). Moreover, he thought even if fiscal policy could effectively stimulate the economy, inevitable lags meant that such mechanisms would not have the desired effects at the right time—thus leading to unintended negative consequences (Friedman [1948] 1953, 148; Friedman [1947a] 1953, 313–16; Friedman [1961] 1969b). Additionally, there is a basic knowledge problem inherent to trying to predict the future accurately enough to fine-tune (Friedman and Heller 1969, 49–50). Although he did approve of tax and spending cuts, Friedman did not see them as a "stabilization device" (Friedman and Heller 1969, 73; Rossant 1964; Hawkins Interview). Lastly, he also advised fiscal policy makers to avoid "erratic changes" in either spending or taxation (Friedman 1962a, 79).

Spending

As for the spending side of the ledger, Friedman was always in favor of cutting government expenditures. He advocated spending cuts for a number of reasons. First, Friedman wanted to eliminate a number of government programs because they could not be justified on liberal grounds. Indeed, he thought the government simply consumed too much of our resources (Friedman 1962a; Friedman [1967b] 1975, 88; Friedman [1981] 1983, 304). Second, Friedman did not think we were getting our money's worth for what we were spending. He frequently argued that "the U.S. federal budget is too large compared to what we're getting for it" (Friedman and Heller 1969, 74; and see Friedman [1978d] 1983, 324; Friedman [1972a] 1975, 101). A prime reason for this, he argued, was that much of the money designated for particular programs ended up paying for "well-paid" bureaucrats in the middle (Friedman [1981] 1983, 304). Third, Friedman believed that much government spending benefited the well off, and this could not justify taxes on lower income people (Friedman [1981] 1983, 304).

Taxation

Friedman did not favor the tax system in existence during his lifetime and which remains in effect today. He thought it provided perverse incentives and frequently benefited politicians at the expense of the general good, among other defects (Playboy Interview [1973] 1983). Moreover, bracket creep due to inflation results in the government invisibly capturing more and more of society's wealth (Friedman [1980d] 1983, 317). Given his disdain for such a tax system and how it empowered the government to spend on illiberal programs, it is not surprising that Friedman supported tax cuts. Indeed, he argued, "I am in favor of cutting taxes under any circumstances and for any excuse, for any reason, whenever it's possible. The reason I am is because I believe the big problem is not taxes, the big problem is spending" (Hawkins Interview).

Friedman had an ulterior motive in mind when it came to tax cuts. He considered them a means to "starve the beast" so that spending could be restrained (even if deficits resulted). Indeed, Friedman finally concluded this was the only way to rein in expenditures. He argued repeatedly that: "Government is going to spend whatever the tax system will raise plus a little more—lately a good deal more. The only effective way to keep down government spending is to keep down the amount of money available to government to spend. There is no other way you can do it" (Times Herald Interview 1978; and see Friedman [1976c] 1983, 327; American Prospect Interview 2005).

Friedman usually argued that the ideal or "least bad" tax system was a flat tax. In particular, it would be a tax with "a low flat rate—less than 20 percent—on all income above personal exemptions with no deductions except for strict occupational expenses" (Friedman and Friedman [1980] 1990, 306; and see Friedman 1962a, 174; Playboy Interview [1973] 1983; Times Herald Interview 1978).[37] He also wanted such a flat tax locked in by making it an amendment to the Constitution. Friedman would abolish corporate and inheritance taxes as part of this plan (Friedman and Friedman [1980] 1990, 306; Playboy Interview

[1973] 1983). On at least one occasion, Friedman argued in favor of the esoteric Georgist tax. He claimed in 1978 that Henry George's property tax on the unimproved value of land was the "the least bad tax" (Times Herald Interview 1978). Unsurprisingly, this exotic idea did not pass muster for *Free to Choose* less than two years later.

Regulation

Friedman believed that government should set and enforce basic rules for society, including the definition and protection of property rights but otherwise leave social coordination largely to the voluntary activities of individuals. Therefore, he opposed specific government regulation of commercial activity except in cases of monopoly and where significant neighborhood effects exist (Friedman 1962a). One of the reasons he thought regulation should be avoided is that it frequently makes us worse off in the end despite its good intentions. As he claimed in an interview with *Playboy*: "All of these interferences with the market are justified as protection of the public interest, but, in fact, they endanger the public interest" (Playboy Interview [1973] 1983, 26). What follows are brief descriptions of his views on a number of different areas of regulation.

Friedman's bête noires in the regulatory realm were wage and price controls. He had particular disdain for minimum wage laws. Although Friedman (perhaps naively) thought such controls were often well intended, he argued that the economic consequences of such polices were very bad. In particular, he thought minimum wage laws increased unemployment while favoring special interests that often benefit at the expense of low-skilled, low-income, and younger people. He also argued these laws were especially harmful to African-Americans (Friedman 1962a, 180–81; Friedman and Friedman [1980] 1990, 237–38). As for price controls, he thought they have "always failed" at controlling inflation (since inflation, to Friedman, is a monetary phenomenon) (Friedman 1975, 120). Moreover, he argued that such controls interfere with the transmission of information via the price system and are thus harmful to a well-functioning economy (Friedman and Friedman [1980] 1990).

Despite the dubious economic consequences of wage and price controls, Friedman opposed these restrictions mainly for political and ethical reasons. He had argued back in 1951 that controls "threaten the foundations of a free society" (Friedman [1951a] 1953, 264). Indeed, he thought they were the most likely route to collectivism (Friedman [1973] 1975, 141). Friedman was especially concerned that controls "undermined individual morality" by "encouraging men to spy and report on another, by making it in the private interest of large numbers of citizens to evade the controls, and by making actions illegal that are in the public interest." They would also induce contempt for the law and increase corruption, both of which are corrosive to a well-functioning free society (Friedman [1971a] 1975, 129). In view of these economic, political, and moral objections, it is not surprising that Friedman favored a constitutional amendment forbidding wage and price controls (Friedman and Friedman [1980] 1990, 305).

Friedman also opposed occupational licensing. Indeed, similar to wage and price controls, he advocated a constitutional amendment preventing states from adopting such restrictions (Friedman and Friedman [1980] 1990, 305). He had particular contempt for this type of regulation since, like medieval guilds, it abridges "the freedom of individuals to use their resources as they wish"—often to satisfy the narrow self-interest of groups with members in that profession. He even opposed licensing in the medical field, though he allowed that the strongest case for licensing could be made in that area. Yet Friedman was open to registration in some cases and preferred certification over licensing (Friedman 1962a, 137–38, 139ff).

As might be expected, Friedman was not enthusiastic about consumer and worker protection laws either. Of course, he thought the state should enforce violations of basic rules, thus entailing that the government uphold contracts and punish fraud.

However, Friedman thought most regulation enacted in the name of protecting consumers and workers often served to harm their interests. He frequently argued that regulations are expensive and inefficient, create powerful institutions that misuse their power in favor of special interests, regularly cause more harm than good, reduce innovation, and restrict our freedom to choose (Friedman and Friedman [1980] 1990, 189–227). He was particularly hostile to the regulatory actions of the Food and Drug Administration and the Federal Communications Commission, not to mention individual reformers such as Ralph Nader.

Friedman did see a role for specific government intervention in two special regulatory areas: environmental protection and anti-monopoly. With regard to the environment, he argued that market failure due to the existence of neighborhood effects justifies government action to protect the environment and prevent pollution in certain qualifying cases. However, he thought the downside of regulation is that we often get poor results for all of the effort and expense as the government fails to achieve the desired effect. Therefore, Friedman favored incentive-based programs like effluent taxes (Friedman and Friedman [1980] 1990, 213–17).

As for anti-monopoly regulation, Friedman considered monopolies a problem that in theory justified government interference in the market (because they prevent voluntary trade). However, he argued that monopolies were frequently the product of government actions such as tariffs, tax laws, or pro-union laws (that promote labor monopolies). Therefore, he advocated first removing these supports as well as freeing international trade so that global competition could undermine and prevent monopolies (Friedman and Friedman [1980] 1990, 53 and 225; Friedman 1962a, 121–25, 132–33). Friedman also worried that this justification for state action would in practice lead to either inefficient public monopolies or the creation of the regulatory means by which businesses could rent-seek through "cartelization" of an industry (Friedman and Friedman [1980] 1990, 198).

Thus, he ended up following fellow Chicago School economist George Stigler in concluding that "if tolerable, private monopoly may be the least of the evils." Nonetheless, he carefully recognized that the choice among regulation or private/public monopoly would be context specific (Friedman 1962a, 28).

Social Welfare Policy

Throughout his long career, Friedman frequently discussed social welfare policy. Indeed, one of his first public policy pieces was on rent control (Friedman and Stigler 1946). Although Friedman disagreed with many government-run welfare programs, it would be inaccurate to describe him as a "heartless conservative" or Social Darwinist given that he did support a government role in welfare provision. Indeed, early in his career, Friedman was especially concerned with the problem of inequality and supported "general fiscal measures" to alleviate it (Friedman [1948] 1953, 134). His opposition to most welfare programs stemmed largely from his belief that they were bad for the poor. Friedman's chief contribution to the welfare policy debate was the idea of replacing existing programs aimed at alleviating poverty with a negative income tax.

Friedman's early view of welfare mirrored that of many modern liberal and conservative commentators of his era. Namely, he supported the idea that government play a positive role in alleviating poverty and reducing basic inequality. In a 1948 article on monetary and fiscal policy, Friedman supported "substantial equality of economic power" as a basic long-run policy objective. He thought a "truly free market" would reduce inequality, but supplementary measures would be required in the interim. He added: "I should hope that the community would desire to reduce inequality even further." Presaging his negative income tax proposal, he described "general fiscal measures" as preferable to "specific interventions" for both ends (Friedman [1948] 1953, 124).

In *Capitalism and Freedom,* Friedman provided another basis for government social welfare. He argued that private charity alone would be insufficient to meet the needs of the impoverished in "large impersonal communities" because of the collective action problem (Friedman 1962a, 191). Therefore, government intervention was justified to overcome this market failure and meet our generally held wish to help those in need.[38] This support should take the form of a government-provided "floor under the standard of life of every person in the community" (Friedman 1962a, 191). Friedman also thought that paternalist grounds, combined with the inadequacy of private charity, justified government action to supplement private care of the insane and, in some cases, children as well (Friedman 1962a, 33–34).

Friedman's novel policy prescription, formally introduced first in 1962 and expanded upon in 1968, was that the best way to provide that "floor" (while minimizing disincentives for self-reliance) was a fractional negative income tax (NIT). This welfare plan via the federal tax system would basically provide a guaranteed net "income" for every individual in the country. It would do so by "supplementing the income of the poor by a *fraction* of their unused income tax exemptions and deductions" (Friedman [1968a] 1987, 58). While providing an income floor as in standard guaranteed income schemes, it would avoid those plans' disincentives to work and self-help by allowing workers to keep a fraction of earned income up to a certain level without suffering a commensurate subsidy loss. Friedman also supported states' supplementing such a federal program with their own state NITs where necessary (Friedman [1968a] 1987, 63).

Friedman argued his NIT plan had many advantages over existing welfare programs. First, it would focus aid directly on the poor and in the most fungible way (cash) rather than indirectly (and in potentially market-distorting ways) as do "broadside" programs such as minimum wage laws, farm aid, and Social Security (Friedman 1962a, 191; Friedman [1968a] 1987, 60; Friedman and Friedman [1980] 1990, 122). Second, as previously noted, it would mitigate the negative incentives of traditional guaranteed income plans while recognizing that all welfare programs create negative incentives to some extent (Friedman 1962a, 192). Third, assuming it replaced existing programs with the same end, the NIT would cost a lot less since administration could be handled through the existing tax system rather than through large, cumbersome, and intrusive bureaucracies (Friedman 1962a; Friedman [1968a] 1987). Fourth, it would prevent the welfare system from being used as a tool for political patronage, as has been the case in the past (Friedman [1968a] 1987). Fifth, the NIT would treat the "indigent as responsible individuals" rather than as wards of the government, thus promoting "the development of habits of independence and self-reliance" (though Friedman failed to specify exactly how it would achieve this) (Friedman [1968a] 1987, 60). Along these lines, it would neither undermine families and private charities nor limit the freedom of recipients, as he claimed traditional government welfare programs do (Friedman and Friedman [1980] 1990, 123, 127). Lastly, the NIT would help individuals "regardless of the reasons for their need"—thus obviating the necessity of bureaucrats to make decisions about who is eligible or determine how to "run other people's lives" (Friedman and Friedman [1980] 1990, 120, 123).

Friedman thought the negative income tax was only worth enacting if it were a substitute for rather than an addition to extant welfare programs. When he first proposed the NIT in 1962, Friedman was not explicit about this. In 1968, he expressed willingness to accept an NIT as a substitute for direct public assistance alone, despite his preference that it be a replacement for "*all*" welfare programs (Friedman [1968a] 1987, 64). In later writings, Friedman argued it would be a "satisfactory reform of our present welfare system only if it *replaces* the host of other specific programs that we now have. It would do more harm than good if it simply became another rag in the ragbag of welfare programs" (Friedman and Friedman [1980] 1990, 122).

Unfortunately for Friedman, this was never going to be in the cards. By the time he wrote *Free to Choose*, he saw the inability of politicians to implement such a radical change despite its appeal. Friedman ultimately testified in Congress *against* President

Nixon's Family Assistance Plan despite his initial approval and its roots in his NIT proposal (Friedman 1970d; Friedman and Friedman 1980, 124; Friedman and Friedman 1998, 381–82).

Although Friedman supported the NIT, he strongly disagreed with the existence of other welfare measures. He opposed them primarily because he thought they produced largely negative consequences for society as a whole and even for the recipients themselves. As he noted in a 1973 interview for *Playboy*, "The actual outcome of almost all programs that are sold in the name of helping the poor . . . is to make the poor worse off" (Playboy Interview [1973] 1983, 19). To Friedman, welfare corrupts recipients (and politicians for that matter) and erodes their capacity for self-governance, undermines and destroys their families, and reduces the incentive for good behavior such as working and saving (Friedman and Friedman [1980] 1990, 119, 127). Furthermore, he thought programs like the minimum wage actually work to increase poverty because they artificially produce unemployment at the bottom rungs of society (Friedman 1962a, 180). Society as a whole is worse off too, according to Friedman, because welfare tends to "rot the moral fabric that holds a decent society together" while "poison[ing] the springs of private charitable activity" (Friedman and Friedman [1980] 1990, 127, 123). It is also a big waste of money.

Instead of helping the poor, Friedman thought that "The major beneficiaries are intermediaries—the bureaucrats who administer it, the agencies or organizations that benefit from it—and that is also the major obstacle to reform" (Times Herald Interview 1978). He finally concluded in the 1980s that the system was such a "mess" that welfare—not the Soviet Union—was the greatest danger to the United States! (Times Herald Interview 1978; Spokane Chronicle, March 3, 1982).

Of course, Friedman also opposed most welfare programs because they could not be justified on liberal grounds and violated individual liberty. Thus, he lists, in *Capitalism and Freedom*, rent control, minimum wage laws, social security programs, public housing, and the like as among those government activities inconsistent with his overarching political theory (Friedman 1962a, 35–36).

Friedman's emphasis was clearly on the negative effects of welfare. Most likely, he well understood this would be the most effective way to sell his policy preferences to a public largely moved by consequentialist arguments rather than appeals to principle (especially since many in his audience would not share his fairly radical views in whole or in part). However, it may also have been because his philosophical position did not actually preclude the use of government to achieve collective ends when market failure exists, which he admits it does in the case of charitable giving to alleviate poverty. Thus, it is not clear whether even those programs listed above would be automatically ruled out in principle—as he thought they were—since they could easily be justified as poverty alleviation measures if they were the best means to meet that goal. Once market failure becomes a justification for governmental action, it is merely a question of prudence (or an empirical question) which policies we choose.

Friedman's rationale for government involvement in the provision of welfare may have changed over the course of his life. As in a few other areas such as education policy, he may have become more radical as he got older. In the case of welfare policy, he hints that he may have changed his mind about whether governmental action in this realm was justified in principle. [That being said, Friedman's initial justification for the minimal role he supported was fairly weak to begin with. After all, it was not based on positive rights or a political obligation animated by a vision of what human dignity required but mostly on the grounds of market failure in charitable giving (and the assumption rather than an argument that greater economic equality is desirable)]. Support for this radicalization hypothesis comes in 1973, when he even questioned his endorsement of a negative income tax—the lone pillar of his welfare program. Indeed, he went out of his way to state during his *Playboy* interview that

> If we were starting with a clean slate—if we had no government welfare programs, no Social Security, etc.—I'm not sure I would be in favor of a negative income tax. But, unfortunately, we don't have a *tabula rasa.* Instead we have this extraordinary mess of welfare arrangements, and the problem is: how do you get out of them? You can't simply abolish them, because when we enacted these programs, we assumed an obligation to those who are now being helped by them. In fact, we have *induced* people to come under the protection of these programs (Playboy Interview [1973] 1983, 43).

At this juncture, Friedman seems to support a government role simply because of obligations incurred by bad decisions in the past. In short, the government has a responsibility to the poor because its programs got them "into trouble," not because government has a principle-derived proper role to play in this area (due to market failure or paternalistic concerns for the irresponsible) (Playboy Interview [1973] 1983, 45; Friedman 1962a). Friedman was enough of a pragmatist to realize we could not abolish programs overnight but would have to "ease" out of them (Friedman and Friedman [1980] 1990, 119).

* * *

It is worth briefly touching on Friedman's views on a number of specific welfare programs, especially since he offered particular arguments against them and prescriptions about how to proceed given their existence.

One of the most important government welfare policies in the United States is Social Security. Unsurprisingly, Friedman was a consistent opponent of it. In *Capitalism and Freedom* (1962a), he argued that this public retirement system could not be justified in a free society based on a liberal political philosophy. He more than once described Social Security as "a combination of a bad tax and a bad expenditure program" (Times Herald Interview 1978; Friedman and Friedman [1980] 1990). Less charitably, he—toward the end of his life—called it a "vicious program" (Fox Interview 2004).

Friedman opposed Social Security because he thought it was inconsistent with basic liberal principles and also economically unsound. In terms of principle, he thought that income redistribution from the young to the old, regardless of means, was arbitrary and that the compulsory purchase of government annuities (a diversion of a "sizable fraction of our income") was paternalistic and a violation of individual freedom (Friedman 1962a, 182–89). Friedman also thought such a system involved "a large-scale invasion into the personal lives of a large fraction of the nation" (Friedman 1962a, 182). Additionally, he believed it was being presented in a misleading, even Orwellian, fashion (Friedman and Friedman [1980] 1990, 103).

Friedman also disliked the program because he thought it was a bad deal for many. Specifically, he thought that the young would not get a good return on the money that they and their employers were forced to pay into the system. Moreover, Friedman thought the system discouraged employment while reducing personal savings and the accumulation of capital (and all of the good results that flow from this). He disliked that Social Security favored the better-off at the expense of the less well-off (Friedman and Friedman [1980] 1990, 104, 106, 124, 127). Meanwhile, it weakened family ties and "drastically reduced the feeling of obligation that members of society traditionally felt towards others" (Playboy Interview [1973] 1983, 43). To Friedman, all of these costs could only be justified on liberal grounds by a desire to avoid some small percentage of the elderly being "public charges": a case he did not find compelling (Friedman 1962a, 189).

Instead of a government retirement system, Friedman believed that individuals should be allowed to decide whether and how much to save for retirement based on their own interests and appraisal of their future (Friedman 1962a, 187–88; Fox Interview 2004). Thus, in theory, he favored scrapping Social Security and not even mandating private retirement plans. Considering prior obligations, this would mean "winding down" Social Security by continuing payments to current beneficiaries, appropriately compensating present workers who had paid into the system, while ending payroll taxes and any additional accumulation of benefits (Friedman and Friedman [1980] 1990, 123–24).

Friedman understood that his plan was a pipe dream when he proposed it. However, he thought that it might be feasible in the future (Friedman and Friedman [1980] 1990, 126). By the end of his life, Friedman believed privatization was possible, given the problems faced by the system. He thought a good first step towards his dream would be to maintain mandatory payments but allow some portion of the money to go into a private account that individuals could control in terms of how it is invested (Fox Interview 2004). If this could not work, his fallback would likely have been to at least convert it to a system funded outright by general revenues rather than by a payroll tax (Times Herald Interview 1978).

Friedman's view on housing policy was similar to his views on other government programs, especially wage and price controls. In short, he thought the market should determine the quantity, quality, and price of housing. It is safe to assume, flowing from this, that Friedman opposed all public housing programs. At one point he even argued for the abolition of the Department of Housing and Urban Development and was willing to sell existing public housing to tenants for a dollar as part of a deal to close down the department (Uncommon Knowledge Interview 1999).

Friedman disagreed with public housing programs designed to aid the poor and the middle class because of the negative consequences of such efforts. Much to the chagrin of fellow free-marketeers such as Ayn Rand, he did not make any overarching, principled argument against government intervention in this area (Doherty 2007, 192).[39] Instead, it was all about the relative efficiency of two different methods of housing allocation: government vs. free markets.

Specifically, Friedman argued that housing programs benefit few people while harming a great many others, including a large share of those who are supposed to be helped by these programs. Beneficiaries include the few lucky enough to get subsidized housing. However, Friedman thought the people who gained the most were those who did not need help at all. To that point, he argues:

> The beneficiaries have, rather, been the owners of property purchased for public housing or located in urban renewal areas; middle and upper-income families who were able to find housing in the high-priced apartments or townhouses that frequently replaced the low-rental housing that was renewed out of existence; the developers and occupants of shopping centers constructed in urban areas; [and] institutions such as universities and churches that were able to use urban renewal projects to improve their neighborhoods. (Friedman and Friedman [1980] 1990, 111–12).

Experience has since largely confirmed his views.

Friedman also observed that many have actually suffered from government housing policies. In particular, public housing has frequently evolved into slums overcome by crime and delinquency (Friedman and Friedman [1980] 1990, 110). These units also physically deteriorate over time as residents fail to maintain properties in which they have no stake. Moreover, he argues that justifiable income limitations led to a high density of "broken families" in public housing areas, with sequelae that one would expect (Friedman 1962a, 180). Even more damning, Friedman noted that "Public housing and urban renewal programs have subtracted from rather than added to the housing available to the poor" (Friedman and Friedman [1980] 1990, 96). This is quite the opposite of the original intent.

Friedman was especially critical of rent control policies. Although he was not an urban economist, Friedman co-authored an important early piece on the subject titled "Roofs or Ceilings." He wrote it with fellow economist George Stigler while the two of them shared an office at the University of Minnesota.

Published in 1946 by the Foundation for Economic Education, it was, as Paul Krugman claims, "his debut as a populizer of free-market economics" (Krugman 2007). Indeed, a condensed pamphlet version was eventually sent out by the National Association of Real Estate Boards in its campaign against rent control (Friedman and Friedman 1998, 150).

The basic argument of the piece is that rental housing, like any other scarce resource, is best allocated or "rationed" by the price mechanism. In this case, the free market will ensure that there are always rentals available at different price levels, people will be noncoercively incentivized to economize until new construction occurs, and high rents will stimulate new construction. Furthermore, this method will not require an expensive bureaucracy to determine who gets what. Friedman and Stigler argue that the two competing options—rationing by rent control and rationing by public agency—have significant downsides. In terms of rent control, the authors claim that "Rent ceilings . . . cause haphazard and arbitrary allocation of space, inefficient use of space, retardation of new construction and indefinite continuance of rent ceilings, or subsidization of new construction and a future depression in residential building." Against the latter, they note that "Formal rationing by public authority would probably make matters still worse," including the empowerment of an agency to determine family space requirements, among other "stupendous administrative and ethical problems" (Friedman and Stigler 1946).

Friedman never swerved from this argument. For example, he restated his views in a 1971 article for *Newsweek* during a housing crunch in New York City (Friedman 1971b [1975]). He also likened housing to any other good—i.e., price controls will ultimately lead to shortages. Thus, he was not surprised that New York's experience with rent control was exactly what he had predicted a quarter of a century earlier.

Before ascribing to Friedman any heartless Social Darwinism in this area, it is worth remembering that, in *Free to Choose,* he called the objectives of programs such as these "noble." However, he thought the results were "disappointing" and even harmful (Friedman and Friedman [1980] 1990, 96; Uncommon Knowledge Interview 1999). Surprising perhaps for such a champion of liberty, Friedman—at least in 1946—thought that it would be better to address the problem of inequality directly through government intervention than through indirect methods such as rent control (Friedman and Stigler 1946).[40] Consistent with this concern for the poor, Friedman later proposed a negative income tax that would provide low-income individuals the means to purchase basic necessities such as housing (Friedman 1962a; Friedman [1968a] 1987). He simply thought the provision itself should be left to the market, as it would produce an adequate supply of housing at different price points and quality levels as long as the government just allowed the price system to work.

How would Friedman have accounted for the sheer number of human welfare problems for government or the private sector to have to solve in the first place? An important part of the answer, to Friedman, was almost surely basic human inequality. He attributed much income inequality to fundamental differences in initial endowments of "human capacities and property" as well as imperfections in the market (Friedman 1962a, 163). However, he also thought some measure of this inequality was created by the government itself. Perhaps naively, Friedman went so far as to argue that "most hardship and misery" in the United States was due to government interference with the right to cooperate voluntarily with others (Friedman [1972b] 1975, 206). Given this position, he thought creating freer markets, rather than welfare or taxes (progressive or inheritance), would be the best way to help the poor. Indeed, he thought freedom and a capitalist economic system had already decreased inequality around the globe, especially since most of the market's benefits have helped "ordinary" people even more than the rich (Friedman 1962a, 169 and 195; Friedman and Friedman [1980] 1990, 147). As he preached on the *Phil Donahue Show* in 1980, "The record of history is absolutely crystal clear that there is no alternative way so far discovered of improving the lot of ordinary people that can hold a candle to the productive activities that are unleashed by a free enterprise system."

Conscription and National Service

Although hardly an expert on defense policy, Friedman was actively involved in the military manpower debates that occurred from the 1960s through the early 1980s. As noted in Chapter 1, he even served on the presidential commission tasked with studying the draft that unanimously recommended its elimination. Unlike many of the policy proposals he floated over the course of his career, Friedman's prescription to end conscription actually won the day, as he saw the draft eliminated in 1973 after a decade in which he had promoted an all-volunteer force (AVF). This result no doubt contributed to his feeling, toward the end of his life, that "no public-policy activity that I have ever engaged in has given me as much satisfaction" (Friedman and Friedman 1998, 381). This victory was trimmed a bit when selective service registration was reinstated in 1980 (despite Friedman's vehement opposition).

Friedman's case against the draft was based on both instrumental and deontological grounds. In terms of the latter, he thought involuntary military service was a violation of a person's basic individual freedom and thus "inconsistent with a free society" (Friedman [1966b] 1975, 189). As he noted in 1962—well before the Vietnam War brought the draft debate to center stage—conscription "seriously interfere[s] with the freedom of young men to shape their lives" (Friedman 1962a, 36). Friedman also thought conscription has deleterious effects on freedom of speech and assembly since the threat of being drafted could have a chilling effect on young men (particularly if draft boards used it as a political weapon). In contrast, a volunteer system preserved "the freedom of individuals to serve or not to serve" (Tax 1967, 201).

Friedman also argued that the selective conscription necessary in peacetime or during limited wars was arbitrary and introduced major inequities. In particular, he argued that the draft as practiced tended to place most of the burden of involuntary service on the upper lower class and the lower middle class, as the poorest are rejected for a variety of reasons, and the better off find ways around it (Tax 1967). For this reason, he argued (during a major conference on the draft held in 1966) that we should eliminate educational deferments (Tax 1967, 314).

In terms of pure consequences, Friedman argued that an all-volunteer force would actually be better for the military itself than one generated by conscription. First, he thought morale would be better since the military would be a chosen career rather than a forced period of service that, by definition, was not that person's preference. In addition, military service itself would rise in public estimation once it was no longer considered a necessary chore that "men have to be dragooned into performing." Second, he argued that the AVF would produce greater military power by allowing more "intensive training, a higher average level of skill, [and] the use of more and better equipment" while necessitating fewer people in uniform (Friedman [1967a] 1987, 71).

Friedman also thought society at large would benefit greatly by doing away with conscription. He argued, contrary to what a lot of people might think, that the AFV would be cheaper for society than a conscript force, especially once one accounts for the "real cost" rather than the "money cost" of the draft system. To support his logic, Friedman wittily noted that "the construction of the Great Pyramid with slave labor was a cheap project" if you only look at the money cost to the government (Tax 1967, 204)! In addition, he thought there would be savings resulting from the AVF's reduced training burden, higher skill levels, decreased waste, and lower costs to the community (such as the elimination of college enrollments and "unwise marriages" made to avoid the draft, removal of uncertainty for potential draftees, and fewer distortions to the market for young labor).

A volunteer force would also be a possible constraint on the government's ability to use the military for unpopular activities since these would make recruitment and retention potentially more difficult (Tax 1967; Friedman [1967a] 1987). Lastly, Friedman thought conscription undermined popular support for the strong military that he argued the United States needed, thus potentially compromising the government's core security function (Tax 1967, 366).

Defending the move to a voluntary force, Friedman attempted to demolish or deflect counterarguments. For example, he argued that while a professional army detached from society is a potential danger to a free society, a volunteer military would not increase the threat since officers (who are volunteers even under the draft) are the problem in such cases, not enlistees. Moreover, recruiting policy could be designed to counter any tendency with an AVF toward separation and ensure proper civilian control. Friedman rejected the notion that a voluntary military would be racially unbalanced or too inflexible when policy needs dictated expanding the force (Tax 1967).

Despite his work to eliminate the draft before and during the Vietnam War, Friedman did not oppose conscription in all cases. This might seem at odds with his frequently stark, unalloyed claims about how bad such a system was, especially in terms of its detrimental effect on freedom. For example, in his autobiography, Friedman described the draft as "a major stain on our free society," and in a frequently-cited argument with General William Westmoreland during the Gates Commission hearings, he compared conscripts to "slaves" (Friedman and Friedman 1998, 380–81).

In particular, Friedman allowed for two major exceptions to his opposition to the draft. First, he thought that conscription, even during peacetime, was justified in small states. As Friedman noted in 1979, "Universal *military* service may be justified for countries like Israel or Switzerland with populations so small that the military can readily use the temporary service of every young adult in peacetime, and which need to muster into service a large fraction of the civilian population in time of war" (Friedman 1979b). Second, Friedman believed there is a "strong case" for compulsory service during times of major war because many of the advantages of the AVF evaporate (Tax 1967, 202). Thus he was amenable to "standby provisions for conscription" if necessary (Tax 1967, 206). It is also worth noting that Friedman thought coerced universal military training could be justified on liberal grounds (Friedman 1962a, 36; Tax 1967, 206).

These exceptions show that Friedman was not as universally committed to individual freedom as he sometimes claimed. Rather, they suggest that he was strongly motivated to favor means that would ensure good consequences (as he saw them) even if it meant restricting individual freedom to choose. Even more surprising, if Friedman assumed that the larger cause of freedom might demand it, he trusted government to best decide when individuals needed to fight for freedom, since individuals could not be counted on to volunteer when it was necessary. This would seem either to violate some of his core assumptions about the world or expose an unresolved tension between his utilitarian side and his deontological concern for freedom as an end in itself!

Two more points on the subject are worth noting. First, Friedman's position on the draft may have changed slightly during his life. In 1962, he listed "Conscription to man the military services in peacetime" among a number of existing government activities that could not be justified on the basis of his normative political theory (Friedman 1962a, 36). This suggests Friedman did not think conscription in wartime would be unjust. By 1966, he explicitly acknowledged a strong case for a draft for "major wars." (Tax 1967, 203). This addition of "major" may have been explicit, indicating Friedman had changed his mind about using the draft in more limited conflicts due to the country's experience with the draft during Vietnam. However, it is possible that Friedman consistently opposed using the draft except in major wars and simply failed to qualify his 1962 statement. Second, Friedman made an interesting case in 1966 and again in 1980 that the United States should utilize "horizontal recruitment" to help fill the ranks.[41] Namely, the military should be open to "lateral recruitment" that would bring those who already had related civilian skills directly into military positions (ostensibly at higher rank as well). This would reduce the need for expensive training, expand the pool of potential recruits, and overall "improve both demand and supply" (Tax 1967, 207; Friedman 1980b).

Not surprisingly, Friedman also opposed universal national service. Plans for compulsory community service popped up regularly once they started being seriously considered during the Vietnam era. Although Friedman thought national service plans were fairer—given the universality of service—compared to the selective service of a military draft, he argued that a system of involuntary service was "a monstrosity utterly inconsistent with a free society" (Friedman 1979b). He worried that the power to conscript the youth would be a dangerous tool that could "fall into the wrong hands" since it would empower the government to indoctrinate an army of young people and decide for what "good purposes" they should be used. Although he could be criticized for being rhetorically extreme, to Friedman, national service plans had an "uncanny resemblance" to the Hitler Jugend (Friedman 1979b; Schwartz 1989; Friedman 1967a). In response to George H. W. Bush's particular plan, Friedman added that he thought it represented "more wasteful government spending" (Maralee Schwartz 1989).

Foreign Policy and International Relations

Friedman may appear to have been relatively quiet on foreign policy matters compared to other subject areas important to a free society. However, this might be an overstatement given that his work on money matters had important implications for U.S. foreign policy and international relations in general. For example, his advocacy of a flexible exchange rate system was directly related to U.S. foreign relations given, at the time, the United

States' leading position in the Bretton Woods pegged exchange rate system. Moreover, his arguments and actions in opposition to the draft had wide-reaching effects on American foreign and defense policy. Nonetheless, outside trade and exchange rate policy, Friedman did not emphasize this area during his career.

Free Trade

Friedman was a vigorous advocate of free trade. Indeed, like the Manchester liberals who overturned the Corn Laws in Britain, Friedman favored unilaterally opening up the American market to outsiders. In *Capitalism and Freedom*, he argued it would be "far better for us to move to free trade unilaterally" than to engage in the slow process of reciprocal negotiation of tariff reductions (Friedman 1962a, 73). He also warned about the danger of nontariff barriers (NTBs) such as voluntary export restrictions and wanted to end these too (see Friedman [1981] 1983, 369). Despite his advocacy of free trade, the conservative and pragmatic side of Friedman led him to propose that both tariffs and NTBs be gradually reduced over time rather than ended immediately (Friedman 1962a, 74).

Friedman's main argument for unilateral free trade is that the United States would be better off economically and politically from adopting such a policy. He disagreed with the notion that tariff reduction only makes economic sense if others reciprocate. Instead, Friedman argued that "our tariffs hurt us as well as other countries. We would be benefited by dispensing with our tariffs even if other countries did not" (Friedman 1962a, 73). This position is grounded in the view that we in the United States actually benefit from imports and should not be overly concerned about an unfavorable balance of trade. As Friedman noted during the dark economic days of the 1970s, "Imports contribute to our standard of living. Exports are a cost. They are what we have to pay for the imports. The larger the volume of imports we can get for each unit of exports the better" (Friedman [1978b] 1983, 362). One senses the specter of Cold

War competition in his addendum that free trade would not only help others economically but would be a powerful tool to promote freedom abroad (Friedman 1962a, 74).

In *Free to Choose*, Friedman—echoing a litany of classical liberals that came before him—added a number of other economic and political arguments for free trade while countering standard arguments against it. First, he argued that free trade increases economic well-being while protectionist measures benefit concentrated interests at the expense of consumers. It is an economic fallacy that we are harmed by an unfavorable balance of trade; and the same is true of "unfair" competition, as the law of comparative advantage readily demonstrates. Second, echoing the Manchesterites again, he claimed that free trade promotes "harmonious relations" and removes "potent sources of conflict" among different nations/states, just as it does so at home among people who differ in so many ways (Friedman and Friedman [1980] 1990, 51; Friedman 1953, 158). Trade restrictions, though, foster political friction in international relations. Third, Friedman thought free trade reduces the potential for domestic monopolies since it breaks cartels and exposes monopolies to power corroding competition. Lastly, he added that standard exceptions to free trade such as the "infant industries" argument are wrong.

Friedman favored one-sided free trade throughout his life but for pragmatic reasons gave qualified support for trade pacts like the North American Free Trade Agreement (NAFTA). His main problem with such agreements was that they are actually more like managed trade regimes than free trade programs. Instead, he thought "it would be better if we in the United States would simply reduce our tariffs across the board for everybody in the world." As always with one eye on what could be done, Friedman was keen to support such openings and advocated an even broader NAFTA that would encompass all of Latin America (AoA Interview 1991).

Despite being a spokesman for free trade, Friedman was not absolutely opposed to all trade restrictions. He thought that security concerns could justify interference with free trade in some cases. For example, he noted during the height of the Cold War that "deliberate inference" in the free flow of goods and services "may be justified on strictly political and military grounds; for example, banning the sale of strategic goods to communist countries" (Friedman 1962a, 71). He also thought tariffs could be used legitimately to keep alive "otherwise uneconomical productive facilities" critical to national security (Friedman and Friedman [1980] 1990, 48). However, Friedman thought such measures should only be taken after a careful comparative analysis of other means that might achieve the same ends.

Despite accepting strategic arguments for limited trade in certain circumstances, Friedman opposed using trade sanctions as a tool of statecraft. He considered sanctions "an ineffective weapon of political warfare" that tend to harm us as much as they harm their intended targets. Just as important, Friedman thought sanctions weaken the very market system that "is our greatest source of strength" (Friedman [1980d] 1983, 372).

Immigration

Consistent with his vision of a world with a relatively unhindered flow of goods and services, Friedman was a supporter of open immigration—in theory, that is. As he said in 2006, immigration is "good for freedom," and "In principle, you ought to have completely open immigration" (Wall Street Journal Interview 2006). Yet Friedman did not write very often on the subject. Indeed, immigration is basically ignored in his two major works on freedom. This may seem surprising given Friedman's family history and that of his wife (who was an immigrant born in Russia).[42] This omission is even more surprising considering that immigration policy is a key issue for a free society, not least because of the existence of the welfare state. Moreover, immigration would potentially have a major impact on the feasibility of his negative income tax proposal and his early arguments for government funding of education.

Friedman's position on immigration was that it should be relatively open in a free society under limited government. In a lecture titled "What is America?" given in 1977, Friedman discussed the positive nature of U.S. immigration policy before 1914 when it was basically an open door regime. Specifically, he argued that this system led to positive sum results for all: "If you have free immigration, in the way we had it before 1914, everybody benefited. The people who were here benefited. The people who came benefited." When immigrants "migrate to jobs," Friedman argued that "They take jobs that most residents of this country are unwilling to take. They provide employers with the kind of workers that they cannot get. They're hard workers, they're good workers, and they are clearly better off." He specifically referenced Mexican immigration as good for both those particular immigrants and the United States (Friedman 1977b).[43]

However, the presence of the welfare state complicated the issue for Friedman. Indeed, he went so far as to say on numerous occasions that "It's just obvious that you can't have free immigration and a welfare state" (Hoover Digest Interview 1998; and see ISIL Interview 1999; Wall Street Journal Interview 2006). Why? Because Friedman assumed that such a combination would become a magnet, drawing people in for the sake of a free lunch. To Friedman, this "free immigration to welfare" as opposed to "free immigration to jobs" would mean that those who are already members of a particular political community would be harmed under this regime, as they would have to pay for the welfare benefits provided to new immigrants. As he noted in his 1977 speech, "If you have a welfare state, if you have a state in which every resident is promised a certain minimal level of income, or a minimum level of subsistence, regardless of whether he works or not, produces it or not. Then it really is an impossible thing." Taken to the extreme—which he understood to be an exaggeration—it "would mean a reduction of everybody to the same, uniform level" (Friedman 1977b). So the problem for Friedman is the potential for immigration to welfare, not immigration on its own.

Therefore, without the welfare state, Friedman was fine with opening the borders. As he explained in a 1999 interview, "I would like to see a world in which you could have open immigration . . ." (ISIL Interview 1999). To Friedman, "If there were no welfare state you could have open immigration, because everybody would be responsible for himself" (Wall Street Journal Interview 2006). Friedman confirmed this in private correspondence with economist Don Boudreaux, noting he would indeed favor "a return to the pre-1920s immigration regime *if* the United States abolished its welfare state."[44] However, he was pessimistic that this scenario would ever unfold, stating that we need to "stop kidding" ourselves that this will ever happen (ISIL Interview 1999).

Perhaps most interesting, Friedman favored relatively open immigration in practice, even with our current political institutions—as long as it is and remains illegal! As stated previously, the problem for Friedman was not immigration but the welfare state. Therefore, if one could remove the potential burden that immigrants might impose on others due to welfare transfers, then he saw no reason to oppose it—and to him, maintaining the illegal status of immigration solved this particular problem. Again, in "What is America?," Friedman notes that "As long as it's illegal, the people who come in do not qualify for welfare, they don't qualify for social security, they don't qualify for the other myriad benefits that we pour out of our left pocket to our right pocket. So long as they don't qualify they migrate to jobs" (Friedman 1977b).

Unfortunately, it is unclear what Friedman thought of all of the other problems that his proposal might entail or the potential problem of the state opening, in whole or in part, welfare benefits to illegal immigrants. Furthermore, as journalist Will Wilkinson points out, it is quite clear from the 1999 interview cited above that Friedman did not consider "the logical and practical possibility of severing legal residency from welfare eligibility" other than to argue when asked about such a system—quite feebly—that he did not think it "desirable to have two classes of citizens in a society" (Wilkinson 2008; ISIL Interview 1999).

Foreign Aid

Friedman agreed with foreign aid advocates that the economic development of the poor countries of the world was both in the United States' national interest and served the general good. However, he believed foreign aid was detrimental to all of those ends in the long run, even if it might "win us some temporary allies" (Friedman [1958a] 1987, 80). Specifically, Friedman thought that, in practice, foreign aid hindered real economic growth because it was premised on flawed economic logic and tended to strengthen the government in recipient countries rather than the private sector. This would only improve the prospects of the communists. As one might expect from a classical liberal, he preferred for the United States to focus on promoting the kinds of things that led to our own success: namely, free markets and free trade (which we could assist by lowering our own barriers to trade). He argued that the people of the "underdeveloped world" needed "only a favorable environment to transform the face of their countries . . . . In short, a vigorous, free, capitalistic market" (Friedman [1958a] 1987, 86; and see Friedman [1970a] 1975, 301–03).

The Use of Military Force

In terms of U.S. military intervention abroad, Friedman did not have a set position over the course of his life. Indeed, he rightly denied that "the libertarian philosophy dictates a foreign policy" (Reason Interview 1995). Nonetheless, based on the admittedly small number of data points, one gets the impression that Friedman was relatively hawkish for most of his life.

As a younger man, Friedman was an early advocate of U.S. intervention into World War II. He may have held this position as early as the fall of 1940 and certainly by the spring of 1941, since it was while he was at the University of Wisconsin that he openly advocated "that the United States ought to go to war on the side of the Allies" (AoA Interview 1991). Rose confirmed this in their autobiography, noting that "Milton and I were strongly anti-Nazi and pro-British, very much in favor of U.S. assistance to the Allies and even of the U.S. entering the war as an active combatant" (Friedman and Friedman 1998, 94).

Friedman maintained his hawkishness during the Cold War. Lanny Ebenstein notes that Friedman "appears to have been, through the early 1960's, at least a moderate interventionist with respect to the battle against worldwide Communism." To support this contention, Ebenstein mentions a letter from Friedman to Arthur Seldon expressing great concern about the fate of Laos and that "Britain and the U.S. seem to be prepared to sell yet another country down the road" (Ebenstein 2007, 232). Regardless of his stance on any particular intervention, Friedman seemed to favor a muscular defense posture. He argued during the Vietnam War that "we must have a large military force and a strong one" (Tax 1967). Furthermore, in 1979, he hawkishly (and insecurely) argued in the context of a possible draft revival that "We need a strong military. We are endangered throughout the world by the decline in our military strength relative to that of Russia" (Friedman 1979a). In addition, he supported Nixon's foreign policy approach, noting later that "Nixon had an imaginative, and on the whole effective, foreign policy" (Friedman and Friedman 1998, 388). This all dovetails with other depictions of Friedman as belonging to the "muscular" side of the libertarian movement (Pipes 1991).

Friedman also supported the Persian Gulf War.[45] Although he did not think oil-related economic arguments justified war, Friedman supported U.S. military action on political grounds. In October 1990, the *San Francisco Chronicle* reported that Friedman "emphasized" his support for "Bush's response," despite his agreement with critics who debunked the economic rationale for using force. Specifically, Friedman argued: "Iraq is the first violator of the peace since the end of the Cold War," and "There are a lot of other tin horn dictators around who will do the same thing if you don't respond" (Marshall 1990, A14).

This fits with what Friedman privately wrote to economist David Henderson during the run-up to the war.[46] Henderson had prepared a statement on the issue of Iraqi control of oil that he was circulating to economists for their signature and which he planned to run as an ad in the *New York Times* and the *Washington Post.* On September 17, Henderson asked Friedman to sign the statement. On September 28, 1990, Friedman told Henderson he would not sign because, even though he agreed with Henderson's economic argument in the statement, he did not want to be "regarded as an opponent of the Bush policy." He went even further, arguing:

> I thoroughly agree with the actions that President Bush has taken, not for economic reasons but for geopolitical reasons. This is the first major case of aggression since the end of the cold war. There are many potential Saddam Husseins around. If we let the first one of them get away with it, there will be repeated episodes of the same sort. That is not healthy for the United States or more generally for the peace of the world. I believe that it is desirable to demonstrate that the Iraqi tactics will not be permitted to work. I believe that if we can satisfactorily resolve this case it will be a very worthwhile investment for the long-term peace of the world as well as for the ability of the U.S. to limit its own external interventionist activities.

After Henderson wrote a long reply on October 3 imploring the famous economist to sign, on October 18 Friedman again denied the request and reiterated his support for Bush's policy as well as the president's general approach to foreign policy.

Friedman tried to backtrack from his support of the war several years later. He noted in a 1995 interview: "I always had misgivings about the Gulf War, but I never came to a firm decision. It was more nearly justified than other recent foreign interventions, and yet I was persuaded that the major arguments used to support it was [*sic*] fallacious" (Reason Interview 1995). Ebenstein goes even further in his biography of Friedman, stating that "He opposed the Gulf war in 1991" (Ebenstein 2007, 232). There is no evidence to support either Friedman's or Ebenstein's statements.[47] More tellingly, they do not jibe with what Friedman told the *Chronicle* or his fellow economist David Henderson. As Henderson notes in a 2006 report, he himself "tried, in vain, to persuade him [Friedman] to be against the first Gulf War" (Henderson 2006).[48]

Despite his support for the Gulf War, Friedman had become fairly sympathetic to a less active approach to U.S. foreign policy. Indeed, he confessed such sentiments in his correspondence with Henderson in 1990. In one letter, he noted, "I have a good deal of sympathy with the non-interventionist policy approach yet, taken all in all, I nonetheless approve in this case of what President Bush has done." In another, Friedman explained that such sympathy "derives simply from the fact that I have no confidence in government's ability to do the right thing abroad any more than I have in its ability to do the right thing at home. Hence, it seems to me the presumption has to be overwhelming before one approves of intervention abroad."[49] Later, in 1995, Friedman asserted: "I'm an anti-interventionist," but he was quick to add, "but I'm not an isolationist." Furthermore, Friedman seemed defensive about being seen as too soft, given that he added: "I don't believe we ought to go without armaments. I'm sure we spend more money on armaments than we need to; that's a different question. I don't believe that you can derive from libertarian views the notion that a nation has to bare itself to the outside without defense, or that a strong volunteer force would arise and defend the nation" (Reason Interview 1995).

Friedman continued moving toward a less aggressive position as time went on. In the early 2000's, Friedman, without equivocation—and on more than one occasion—asserted his view that "war is an enemy of freedom" and that in a time of war, "we invariably reduce our freedom" (Fox Interview 2004; Mont Pelerin Society Interview 2002). Yet he thought that such reductions do not have to be permanent if we "keep in mind what we're doing."

Friedman very much opposed the decision to go to war in Iraq. As he noted in numerous interviews at the end of his life, he thought that "We should not have gone into Iraq" (New Perspective Quarterly Interview 2006; Wall Street Journal 2006). He saw it as aggression and thus opposed the war, later telling the *Wall Street Journal* (2006): "I was opposed to going into Iraq from the beginning. I think it was a mistake, for the simple reason that I do not believe the United States of America ought to be involved in aggression." Moreover, Friedman was not entirely convinced that U.S. attempts to bring about change in the Middle East would be best accomplished using military force. He also thought this war was eroding American stature, though he held out the possibility that if Iraq became "a self-governing country that is not a threat to anybody," then U.S. prestige would rebound (New Perspectives Quarterly Interview 2006). Indeed, Friedman thought that our Iraq policy was misguided well before the Iraq War began, noting in 1998 that "Our Iraq policy has been stupid from the beginning. We ought to declare defeat. Give up. Say we're not going to be a policeman for the Europeans. Call it isolationist if you will, but I don't see any other way out" (Hoover Digest 1998). Yet once we had gone to war, he emphasized the need to stay the course even if the decision to go to war in the first place was a mistake: "Where I do feel strongly, is that having gone into it, whether we should have or not, we must see it through" (Fox Interview 2004; Wall Street Journal Interview 2006).

Free Expression: Free Speech, Drugs, and Discrimination Policy

Friedman was a consistent classical liberal in his positions on the wide realm of personal expression. In the area of free speech, he was practically an absolutist who thought there should be almost no government-imposed limitations on speech.

Friedman even thought speech expressing racial or ethnic hatred should be legally tolerated and that the government should not prevent suicide (AoA Interview 1991; Friedman [1972c] 1975). He also bemoaned the rise of political correctness on campus and thought this phenomenon restricted people's "freedom to listen" (AoA Interview 1991). Of course, he understood that some speech could be harmful. However, he thought free speech was so important to the preservation of a free society that we should have a very high presumption against restricting it even in the case of significant negative externalities (Friedman [1978a] 1987, 16). He regarded speech as so important to a free society that we should avoid creating institutions that might chill free speech. This was one of the reasons he opposed the draft (Tax 1967). Friedman's position on speech was rooted firmly in intellectual humility, namely, the idea that we could be wrong and therefore we should be free to persuade others and to hear other views that might change our own minds (AoA Interview 1991).

Unlike many free speech advocates, Friedman extended his argument beyond political speech into the realm of commercial speech. He thought economic speech should be just as robustly protected as other forms of speech; any distinction was essentially arbitrary (Friedman [1978a] 1987, 13). Moreover, he argued that economic freedom itself was a crucial condition of free speech since "in order for men to advocate anything, they must in the first place be able to earn a living" (Friedman 1962a, 16).[50] Friedman also opposed government speech (even state-mandated speech such as warning labels on cigarette cartons) designed to push particular causes, even ones with which he agreed. He considered this propaganda and a misuse of the state's power (Friedman [1969a] 1975, 218–19). Friedman had particular disdain for the speech-limiting actions of the Federal Communications Commission (FCC) and opposed campaign finance laws due to their speech reducing effects (Roberts Interview 2006).

Friedman's views on discrimination resembled his views on speech. Although personally opposed to discriminating on the basis of race or religion, he thought the government should not forbid private discrimination. Reminiscent of the recent controversy surrounding Kentucky Senate candidate Rand Paul's view of the Civil Rights Act of 1964, Friedman opposed using the coercive power of the state in order to avoid what he argued were negative but noncoercive harms such as discrimination in employment. He thought such government action "reduces freedom and limits voluntary co-operation" (Friedman 1962a, 113). Thus, he was against legislation that presaged the Civil Rights Act of 1964. It is worth noting that many libertarians today do not agree with Friedman on this matter (see Bernstein 2010 for one of many examples). Instead of using the state, Friedman favored employing persuasion to push for social change and, like his student Gary Becker, he thought markets would break down private discrimination given the economic costs of such behavior (Friedman 1962a, 109–10). Friedman was at least consistent on the issue of freedom of association. He also opposed right to work laws and yellow-dog contracts (Friedman 1962a, 115).

Despite his opposition to government antidiscrimination efforts, Friedman vigorously supported the elimination of official discrimination. He was against Jim Crow, comparing it to Hitler's Nuremberg laws, and endorsed racial desegregation of public schools (Friedman 1962a, 113 and 117). Friedman also opposed the minimum wage and urban renewal in part because he considered them especially harmful to African-Americans (Friedman [1967d] 1975).

Finally, Friedman was an early and staunch opponent of the "War on Drugs." Unlike William F. Buckley and many others on the so-called American Right, Friedman never supported the drug war and did not base his opposition on a narrowly consequentialist footing. Instead, he argued on deontological grounds that the state does not have the right to restrict an individual's use of any kind of drugs. As he explained in an interview just before his death:

> The major basis for my opposition has not been how badly it's [the drug war] worked. It has not been the fact that it has produced a lot more harm than good. It has been primarily a moral reason. . . . I do not think the state has any more right to tell me what to put in my mouth than it has to tell me what can come out of my mouth. (Marijuana Policy Project Interview; and see Friedman [1972c] 1975)

Although relying primarily on a rights-based argument, Friedman also opposed the drug war due to its negative consequences. In particular, he argued that the drug war is ineffective at reducing the number of addicts, extremely expensive in terms of budgetary costs and the attention of law enforcement personnel, promotes crime and corruption while benefiting drug lords, creates many innocent victims (especially in poor segments of the populace), hurts drug addicts themselves, and packs our jails (see Friedman [1972c] 1975, 1988b, 1989, 1991, 1992a; Marijuana Policy Project Interview; Paige Interview 1991). Friedman also stressed that the drug war compromises U.S. foreign policy and unnecessarily harms other countries such as Columbia where many drugs originate (Friedman 1988b). At the end of his life, he was even willing to question whether drug use itself was bad, asking "Who are we to say whether they [drug users] are doing the right thing or not by using the drug?" (Marijuana Policy Project Interview).

Friedman thought prohibition would never work since demand for drugs will always exist. Therefore, he believed we should completely legalize all drugs. Friedman's policy preference was quite radical, since he wanted to keep the state almost completely out of the area except for restrictions related to children. Indeed, he thought it would be perfectly acceptable to have drugs "sold through ordinary retail outlets"—though he was a bit squeamish about allowing advertising (Friedman 1988b). Friedman advocated for full legalization despite admitting that it would increase use (though not that much) and that there would still be innocent victims due to drugs (Friedman 1991; Paige Interview 1991). Ever the pragmatist, Friedman was willing to support the compromise of legalizing drugs but treating them in the same way we treat alcohol and tobacco (thus allowing significant restrictions on their sale and promotion) (Friedman 1988b, 1992a). He thought this was at least a step in the right direction.

Social Responsibility of Business (and Labor)

Friedman made an enduring contribution to the study of business ethics known as stockholder theory (Friedman 1962a; Friedman [1970c] 1987; Business and Society Review Interview 1972; Hasnas 1998). The Classical or stockholder theory holds that the social responsibilities or ethical duties of businessmen are very limited, perhaps even that their only social obligation is to increase profits. Friedman first articulated this argument briefly in a few pages of *Capitalism and Freedom* and then at a slightly greater length in a widely read and cited article in *The New York Times Magazine.* This latter work is so popular—often appearing even today in business ethics textbooks—because it so starkly and unflinchingly lays out a possible pole in the debate about corporate social responsibility (for example, see Ciulla, Martin, and Solomon 2010).

Friedman's basic argument is that business agents in their corporate role have a solitary social responsibility to stockholders rather than to other potential stakeholders. As philosophers Tibor Machan and Douglas Den Uyl explain, "The practical import of this is that management organizes the firm, including the work force, in a way most efficient (but lawful) for purposes of the longterm well-being of the company (owners)" (Machan and Den Uyl 1987, 114). However, the exact formulation of Friedman's position has changed slightly over time.

In *Capitalism and Freedom*, Friedman offers the purest and most stringent form of stockholder theory, arguing that in a free society, the only social responsibility of business leaders is to increase profits, plain and simple. Specifically, he argued, "there is one and only one social responsibility of business—to use its resources and engage in activities designed to increase its profits so long as it stays within the rules of the game, which is to say, engages in open and free competition, without deception or fraud" (Friedman 1962a, 133).

Yet in his later *New York Times Magazine* piece, Friedman relaxes his view that profit should be the sole or even primary social responsibility of business. Instead, executives should do what their employers want them to do, which will usually be maximizing profits, but could include meeting other ends or goals. Specifically, Friedman claims that managers have a direct responsibility to their employers and "That responsibility is to conduct the business in accordance with their desires, which generally will be to make as much money as possible while conforming to the basic rules of the society, both those embodied in law and those embodied in ethical custom" (Friedman [1970c] 1987, 37). The key difference from his earlier statement is Friedman's acknowledgment that different institutions could have different purposes. Therefore, corporate executives can legitimately focus on fulfilling other ends, as long as they are specifically directed by their employers. Although this formulation allows for a more expansive range of acceptable activities by business leaders, it is still quite different from competing arguments in business ethics such as stakeholder theory and social contract theory.

By the end of his life, Friedman seemed to circle back to the more pure profit model. In 1995, he engaged in a debate on corporate social responsibility with John Mackey, the philanthropist CEO of Whole Foods, which appeared in *Reason* magazine. Instead of reiterating his argument from 1970 that business leaders should run their companies as their employers see fit—

and thus having to accede to many of Mackey's points about the acceptability of corporate philanthropy as long as it is explicitly part of a corporation's mission as laid out by its founders—Friedman focuses on profits and the problems of corporate philanthropy (Friedman et al., 2005). In response, Mackey fails to reference Friedman's 1970 position but does criticize him for ignoring his critical point that corporate missions matter. Giving credence to the above claim that Friedman returns to his 1962 position (which he may never have whole-heartedly abandoned anyway given that by 1972 his rhetoric was largely back to the pure view, though he is inconsistent since he also talks about the responsibility of executives to do "whatever the shareholders would like to see done" (see Business and Society Review Interview 1972, 7), Mackey boils Friedman's position down to the following: "maximizing profits for the investors is the only acceptable justification for all corporate actions" (Friedman et al., 2005).

Of course, given that doing good is frequently an aid to doing well, Friedman does not criticize much of what business does under the banner of social responsibility.[51] He understood clearly that "in practice the doctrine of social responsibility is frequently a cloak for actions that are justified on other grounds rather than a reason for those actions" (Friedman [1970c] 1987, 40). For example, as Friedman notes, "It may well be in the long-run interest of a corporation that is a major employer in a small community to devote resources to providing amenities to that community or to improving its government. That may make it easier to attract desirable employees, it may reduce the wage bill or lessen losses from pilferage and sabotage or have other worthwhile effects" (Friedman [1970c] 1987, 40–41). The key is recognizing the difference between actions taken ultimately to improve the bottom-line for investors and those grounded in a belief that businesses have a philanthropic or social responsibility to third parties. Otherwise, we might end up believing the mantra of social responsibility when, to Friedman, nothing of the sort exists. Even worse, we may suffer from the consequences of those pernicious beliefs, including growing collectivism and reduced freedom.

Friedman, in both his pure and relaxed formulations, accepts that there are legitimate constraints on business and that executives have key nonsocial responsibilities. As John Hasnas notes, "stockholder theory does not instruct managers to do anything at all to increase the profitability of the business" (Hasnas 1998, 22). For Friedman, businesses have a duty to obey applicable law and thus cannot engage in potentially profitable but illegal activities. He also claims that business should conform to "the basic rules of society, both those embodied in law and those embodied in ethical custom" (Friedman [1970c] 1987, 37). However, he is not clear about what this specific point entails, other than perhaps avoiding deceptive or essentially fraudulent (but legal) practices. Business ethicist Bill Shaw interprets it as, at minimum, "truth-telling and promise-keeping, fidelity, fairness, and doing no harm" (Shaw, 1988, 542). However, Hasnas claims such a broad injunction "becomes a triviality asserting nothing more than that one should pursue profits ethically" (Hasnas 1998, 37). Potentially more problematic, it could be an almost entirely empty concept entailing nothing other than following those customs ensconced in the positive law, as Sean McAleer claims. In McAleer's view, this interpretation is strongly suggested by Friedman's dismissal of the duty to reduce pollution below legal requirements, even though this could be consistent with the customary ethical extra-legal negative duty not to harm or injure (Friedman, [1970c] 1987; McAleer 2002, 440).

Friedman's general position on corporate social responsibility is rooted in both deontological and consequentialist concerns. In terms of the former, Friedman argues that it is simply wrong for executives, without direction from their principals, to spend money that is not theirs even if doing so would produce social benefits. He equates this with a tax on stockholders, customers, and employees aimed at fulfilling the executives' visions of the good (Friedman [1970c] 1987). Given Friedman's belief that taxes are properly a governmental function, he thinks it improper to impose these costs without anyone's consent and without the proper checks and balances we have created in the political realm. In the name of social responsibility, executives thus are able to operate unchecked as "legislator, executive, and jurist" (Friedman [1970c] 1987, 38).

Friedman holds that such activities are unethical for consequentialist reasons as well. First, he alleges that business leaders face a substantial knowledge problem in determining how to discharge any other-regarding social responsibilities. Since executives are experts in running a company, not political actors or social service providers, they are not well suited to perform such tasks. Friedman thus asks how a business leader is to know how to spend money to provide social goods. Even if he could successfully answer this question, it will also be difficult for him to determine "how much cost he is justified in imposing on his stockholders, customers, and employees for this social purpose" (Friedman [1970c] 1987, 39).

Second, Friedman argues that corporate giving has negative effects on individuals. In particular, he claims that "it prevents the individual stockholder from himself deciding how he should dispose of his funds" (Friedman 1962a: 135). Although he does not provide any further discussion on this point, one could infer that this destroys an individual's ability to fulfill his own preferences or ends. This could include his ability to give to charities of his own, rather than his agent's, choosing. Thus, this limitation on the individual stockholder's freedom amounts to reducing his ability to be virtuous, since true virtue requires free choice.

Third, Friedman believes that businesses produce much social good from simply focusing on profits. In fact, the businessman might do more good from doing well than from trying to do good. In the *Reason* debate with Mackey, Friedman questions whether Whole Foods' policy of giving away 5 percent of net profits is actually a good one. He goes on to ask, "what reason is there to suppose that the stream of profit distributed in this way would do more good for society than investing that stream of profit in the enterprise itself or paying it out as dividends and letting the stockholders dispose of it?" (Friedman et al., 2005). He explicitly borrows this argument from Adam Smith, who long ago noted that an individual, "by pursuing his own interest he frequently promotes that of the society more effectually than when he really intends to promote it" (Smith 1776 [1976], 456; Friedman 1962a, 133; Friedman et al., 2005).

Indeed, Friedman goes further than Smith. He asserts more broadly that "Mackey's flat statement that 'corporate philanthropy is a good thing' is flatly wrong" (Friedman et al., 2005). To Friedman, a market system in which individual businessmen focus on profits will produce better outcomes than one in which business leaders think about their so-called social responsibilities. As he notes in his debate with Mackey, "But with all its defects, the current largely free-market, private-property world seems to me vastly preferable to a world in which a large fraction of resources is used and distributed by 501c(3)s and their corporate counterparts" (Friedman et al., 2005).

Fourth, and most importantly, Friedman worries that the doctrine of social responsibility will lead to the replacement of the cooperative, voluntary market with collectivist, government control. He argues that businesses promoting or trying to fulfill so-called socially beneficial functions—such as efforts to rein in prices and wages—harm a free society. As he argued bluntly in *Capitalism and Freedom*, "Few trends could so thoroughly undermine the very foundations of our free society as the acceptance by corporate officials of a social responsibility other than to make as much money for their stockholders as possible" (Friedman 1962a, 133). Especially damaging is that a businessman who talks of his social responsibility "strengthens the already prevalent view that the pursuit of profits is wicked and immoral and must be curbed and controlled by external forces," leading ultimately to the rule of "the iron fist of government bureaucrats" (Friedman [1970c]: 1987, 41–42).

Although Friedman concentrated his attention on business, he thought the same arguments applied to labor organizations as well (but importantly, not to individual proprietors). He argued that "the 'social responsibility' of labor leaders is to serve the interests of the members of their unions" (Friedman 1962a, 133). For these agents to do otherwise would be to violate their duty to their principals: in this case, the membership of the unions they represent.

Of course, if the same caveats that apply to businesses also apply to unions (which Friedman does not make explicit) in terms of playing by the rules—including engaging in open and free competition—much of the political behavior of union leaders to serve their members' interests would be unethical in Friedman's schema. For example, lobbying to enact or maintain prevailing wage laws (such as the Davis-Bacon Act of 1931) would be an unethical practice given that it artificially inhibits free competition among union and nonunion employees.[52] However, it also follows from Friedman's caveats that antiunion collusion by businesses or government actions in the service of business against peaceable union collective action would also be unethical.

Notably, in applying his overall argument to labor, Friedman's pronouncements could be interpreted as being at odds with some of his more utilitarian sensibilities. In *Capitalism and Freedom*, he notes that unions, by increasing wages for their members, have "not only harmed the public at large and workers as a whole by distorting the use of labor; they have also made the incomes of the working class more unequal by reducing the opportunities available to the most disadvantaged group" (Friedman 1962a, 124). However, Friedman would have to conclude that union leaders were acting "socially responsible" by doing so, given it was in their members' interests and assuming the unions played by the rules. Of course, Friedman would probably argue that, without special government treatment that violates his fair play caveat, unions would have a tougher time gaining these generally harmful concentrated benefits. This inference is supported by Friedman's discussion of unions, particularly the Teamsters, benefiting greatly from their exemption from the Sherman Anti-Trust Act (Friedman 1962a, 125).

Notes

1 This is a highly problematic contention and something that not even his wife, Rose, was willing to accept. Indeed, she thought nearly the opposite: "I have always been impressed by the ability to predict an economist's positive views from my knowledge of his political orientation" (Friedman and Friedman 1998, 217). It is my view that values and interests, not scientific understanding, are at the root of political differences—and this holds for economists as much as the rest of us. Indeed, even when economists are in agreement on policy despite different political views, this is often because of a commonly shared fundamental agreement on values, namely a generally consequentialist—even utilitarian—ethical framework that itself is exogenous to economics as a science. It is worth noting that Milton wavered later in life in his confidence in his earlier view, noting "I am much less confident now that I am right and she is wrong than I was more than four decades ago when I wrote the methodology article . . ." (Friedman and Friedman 1998, 219).

2 Wible (1987) argues that Friedman did not have an actual philosophy of science but merely "a methodology of economic science."

3 Friedman provided glimpses into his methodological views in a number of earlier pieces, especially a 1946 book review of Oskar Lange's *Price Flexibility and Employment* (see Friedman [1946] 1953).

4 Many scholars have argued that the data used to construct a theory should not be used to test that theory. However, not all scholars agree. See Van Evera (1996, 22–23) for more on this.

5 The problem with this argument, as Blaug (2009, 353) points out, is that "After all, Friedman gave no prescriptive advice in F53 on how best to validate economic theories. Should we use econometric evidence or historical evidence?"

6 It is worth noting that Brumberg was one of Friedman's former students.

7 Some, however, would claim that Friedman was working, at least in part, within the Keynesian tradition and thus was not making an assault on it. See Burton 1981.

[8] Those wishing more specific scholarly discussion of the quantity theory of money would be well served by Gordon (1974).

[9] For earlier examples where he challenged Keynes, see Friedman [1948] 1953, 136; [1951c] 1953.

[10] The last of the three volumes with Schwartz also looked at Great Britain.

[11] Friedman later changed his mind about the importance of individuals such as Strong (Friedman [1984] 1987).

[12] Josh Hendrickson suggested this important distinction.

[13] On "free banking," see Selgin 1988.

[14] Friedman, however, did recognize that a commodity standard—especially a gold standard –did have many positive features: "The only basically attractive features of any commodity standard are the restraints it can impose on unwise political intervention and the possibilities it offers of an international currency." For his discussion of the pros and cons of commodity standards, see Friedman [1951b] 1953, 205ff, and 248.

[15] He later, in 1984, changed his mind about how much personality was a factor in actually determining Federal Reserve policies and inducing instability into the system. He claimed that he was "impressed with the continuity of Fed policy, despite the wide differences in the personalities and backgrounds of the persons supposedly in charge" (Friedman [1984b] 1987, 417).

[16] Friedman argues that discretion can be used outside of "ordinary" times in the "current emergency", "pending long-run reform" (see Friedman [1951a] 1953, 265, 267, and 273). However, he was careful to note that this "does not imply its indorsement [*sic*] as a permanent instrument of stabilization policy. Under more usual circumstances such a policy is likely to be undesirable; it may well increase rather than decrease instability." Of course, one could criticize him here for giving an opening to those who favor discretion since current problems are frequently considered "emergencies" that require changes from the norm!

[17] Though one wonders if that result occurred despite there not being "an independent bank in this fullest sense of the term"—and thus it could have been worse—or because it was not fully independent. See Friedman [1962c] 1987, 434).

[18] This should not be confused with the so-called Friedman Rule that is related to interest rates (namely, that nominal interest rates should be zero percent).

[19] His preferred definition of money was "currency held by the public plus adjusted demand deposits plus time deposits in commercial banks but exclude[ing] time deposits in mutual savings banks, shares

in savings and loan associations, and the like" (Friedman 1960, 90–91).

[20] For more on Friedman's view of competitive currencies and free banking, see Selgin 2008.

[21] Friedman defined political freedom as "the absence of coercion of a man by his fellow men" (Friedman 1962a, 15).

[22] Ebenstein (2007, 140ff) stresses the influence of Mill. However, Smith was a more powerful influence than even Mill (and not just in terms of economics) as seen in Friedman 1955; Friedman 1962; Friedman [1976a] 1978; and Friedman and Friedman [1980] 1990. For example, Friedman's discussion of the role of government is essentially constructed upon Smith's three duties for a sovereign. See Smith 1976. Friedman seems to have been influenced by Spencer, directly or indirectly, in terms of the latter's "law of equal freedom" though not in terms of any theory of Social Darwinism (which is dubiously attributed to Spencer anyway). Long after making this connection, I discovered that Wood and Woods (1990, xx) and Macpherson (1968) also see Spencer in Friedman.

[23] See the section on his philosophical development in Chapter 1 for more specifics and for citations regarding these influences.

[24] Earlier in his career, he also stressed "substantial equality of economic power." However, over time, this largely dropped out as one of his stated political objectives. See Friedman [1948] 1953, 134; and Friedman and Stigler 1946.

[25] Such a limited role was not only consistent with his vision of justice but flowed from Friedman's concern that having the government do anything more imperiled its ability to successfully do even traditional state functions (Friedman and Samuelson 1980, 7).

[26] As for children, Friedman was careful to point out that the parents are primarily responsible for their own children. Likewise, he did not imply that a government role in providing relief for those in distress meant that it should be the primary or even lead player in fulfilling such a task. See Friedman and Friedman [1980] 1990, 33; Friedman 1951d.

[27] Something, as Andrew Farrant relayed to me, Friedman shared with Frank Knight.

[28] This is not to suggest that Friedman was even in that early stage something other than a thorough going classical liberal. But he was far less extreme in his "neoliberal" days. See Friedman 1951d.

[29] He did discuss methodology in an interview with Daniel Hammond. See Hammond 1992.

[30] On the notion of rights, for example, as "trumps" in liberal thought, see Dworkin 1978.

[31] Moreover, while potentially quite inconvenient and inefficient, monopoly does not really threaten our individual freedom except in the most severe cases of a possible monopoly supplier of basic necessities such as food or water.

[32] It is also worth noting that Friedman did not think individual rights are natural—just really important despite his never telling us exactly why! (AoA Interview 1991; Friedman 1962a, 162).

[33] Later in life, Friedman pointed out that what is often called political freedom should actually be divided into civic freedom and political freedom. Civic freedom to him included things like freedom of speech and assembly while political freedom related to the freedom to participate in aspects of democratic political life such as voting. See Liberty Fund Interview 2003.

[34] It is appropriately titled, "Why I Am Not a Conservative."

[35] Ebenstein has a very different read of Friedman's explanation for the piece's genesis. He argues that Friedman's "larger interest in liberty springs largely from the vouchers idea" (Ebenstein 2007, 223). I do not think this follows at all from Friedman's explanation or from Friedman's earlier activities, including his relationship with FEE and Hayek and his participation in the Mont Pelerin Society meeting in 1947 (not to mention his early enthusiasm for the society and its mission) (see Friedman and Friedman 1998, 333; Hartwell 1995). Friedman claims in his autobiography that he did not attend another MPS meeting after the first one in 1947 until 1957. However, Hartwell notes that Friedman gave a paper at the Bloomendaal, Holland, meeting in 1950. Regardless, it is nearly certain that Friedman's interest in educational choice sprang from his blossoming interest in liberty rather than the other way around. Indeed, that is what Friedman seems to be saying himself in the 2005 piece Ebenstein refers to where he notes (and repeats in 2006) that "The original article was not a reaction to a perceived deficiency in schooling. . . . My interest was in the philosophy of a free society. Education was the area that I happened to write on early. I then went on to consider other areas as well. The end result was *Capitalism and Freedom* . . ." (Friedman [2005a, b] 2006).

[36] My argument that the Friedmans' view in 1980 is essentially what they admitted in 1998 seems to be supported by Tooley's (2006) similar interpretation.

[37] The personal allowance would allow his negative income tax proposal to be part of the plan.

38 Importantly, Friedman did not believe there was a "right" to basic goods. See Friedman [1972b] 1975.

39 Unfortunately, Doherty discusses this debate between Friedman and people like Rand—as well as other arguments involving Chicago School "types" and the Randians and Rothbardians—as pitting efficiency against "morality" (Doherty 2007, 192). This plays into the hands of those making the efficiency argument and does them a disservice at the same time. In the former case, it allows people, especially economists, to argue they are not making a moral or ideological argument but just focusing on "what works" or "the consequences" of any course of action—thus appealing to the lay pragmatism of regular voters and elites distrustful of ideology and moralizing in politics. In the latter case, it does not properly account for the deep moral argument at the heart of concerns for efficiency, as well as not recognizing the utilitarian ethics at the core of many so-called economic arguments in public policy debates.

40 By the time *Capitalism and Freedom* was published in 1962, Friedman seemed to be less enamored with equality of results than might have been the case in 1946. See Friedman 1962a, Chapter 10. The specific passage that was so controversial was Friedman and Stigler's assertion that "The fact that, under free market conditions, better quarters go to those who have larger incomes or more wealth is, if anything, simply a reason for taking long-term measures to reduce the inequality of income and wealth. For those, like us, who would like even more equality than there is at present, not alone for housing but for all products, it is surely better to attack directly existing inequalities in income and wealth at their source than to ration each of the hundreds of commodities and services that compose our standard of living. It is the height of folly to permit individuals to receive unequal money incomes and then to take elaborate and costly measures to prevent them from using their incomes" (emphasis added).

41 In 1966, he restricted this to manning the officer corps. In 1980, he made no distinction.

42 Her birthplace is actually in present-day Ukraine, though it was part of Russia at the time of her birth. See Friedman and Friedman 1998, 2.

43 Transcribed and reported in "What Milton Friedman Really Said About Immigration" February 5, 2008 at http://freestudents.blogspot.com/2008/02/what-milton-friedman-really-said.html.

44 Referenced at www.cafehayek.com/2007/09/a-note-on-my-an.html.

45 Ebenstein mistakenly argues that Friedman opposed the Gulf War in 1991. See Ebenstein 2007, 232. Others do as well, see Bandow 2006.

For evidence against this position, see Marshall 1990; Henderson 2006; and private correspondence between Friedman and Henderson. Furthermore, Friedman clearly did not oppose the war since even the most kind (to Ebenstein) interpretation of the evidence would only have Friedman neither supporting nor opposing the war. See Reason Interview 1995.

[46] I would like to thank Professor David Henderson for giving me access to and permission to publish from this correspondence. The dates of the letters are September 12, 1990; September 28, 1990; October 3, 1990; and October 18, 1990.

[47] It is, of course, possible that Friedman changed his mind between October and when the United States began to directly use force against Iraq on January 17, 1991.

[48] Even if one argues that Friedman is referencing Operation Desert Shield as opposed to Operation Desert Storm (in terms of his support for Bush's actions), the logic of his argument about preventing other would-be aggressors strongly suggests support for more hostile action than sitting in the Saudi desert and not removing the Iraqi military from Kuwait by force.

[49] What is so frustrating about Friedman's support for the First Gulf War is that he followed this statement by admitting that "Needless to say, I am far from certain that I am right on this occasion that the presumption is overwhelming, yet that is the way I feel about it."

[50] This is a potentially dangerous argument for a supporter of free markets and limited government to make since it veers very closely to the Left's argument that anyone without economic means cannot truly be politically free (and thus freedom requires positive government action to insure a minimal income).

[51] In fact, Friedman cleverly notes that criticizing such behavior would be inconsistent with his overarching views. As he states in *Capitalism and Freedom*, "It would be inconsistent of me to call on corporate executives to refrain from this hypocritical window-dressing because it harms the foundations of a free society. That would be to call on them to exercise a 'social responsibility'!" However, it might be argued that Friedman is asking the executive to be stirred by something more than mere profit, indeed a social responsibility, when he asks them to play by the rules and engage in open and fair competition (unless by that he only means legal responsibilities).

[52] As Congressman Ron Paul argued in 1999, "The Davis-Bacon Act of 1931 forces contractors on all federally-funded contraction projects to pay the `local prevailing wage,' defined as 'the wage paid to the majority of the laborers or mechanics in the classification on similar

projects in the area.' In practice, this usually means the wages paid by unionized contractors. For more than sixty years, this congressionally-created monstrosity has penalized taxpayers and the most efficient companies while crushing the dreams of the most willing workers." http://www.house.gov/paul/congrec/congrec99/cr021199.htm.

Chapter 3

Reception and Influence

In a sense, Friedman is like a Paris designer whose haute couture is bought by a select few, but who nonetheless influences almost all popular fashions.

— *Time (1969b)*

At least among economists, it is common when discussing the influence of ideas to hear references to either John Maynard Keynes's or George Stigler's (or Arthur Pigou's before that) nearly polar opposite pronouncements on the subject. Keynes famously argued that ideas matter a great deal. In particular, he claimed at the end of his opus *The General Theory* that

> The ideas of economists and political philosophers, both when they are right and when they are wrong, are more powerful than is commonly understood. Indeed the world is ruled by little else. Practical men, who believe themselves to be quite exempt from any intellectual influences, are usually the slaves of some defunct economist. Madmen in authority, who hear voices in the air, are distilling their frenzy from some academic scribbler of a few years back. (Keynes 1936, 383)

Stigler and Pigou, on the other hand, were far more skeptical about the role of ideas in society. Pigou lamented, "The hope that an advance in economic knowledge will appreciably affect actual happenings is, I fear, a slender one" (quoted in Dillard 1957, 85). Stigler was even more pessimistic, arguing that "economists exert a minor and scarcely detectable influence on the societies in which they live" (Stigler [1976] 1982, 63). Instead, larger macro forces move the world.

So who is right? Friedman lends some insight into the matter. He agreed with Marx (and Stigler) that "inevitable forces of history" are the prime causes of change (Yergin and Stanislaw 2002, 131). However, perhaps taking a position in between the two poles of the debate, Friedman thought that ideas matter at particular moments when the world is in need of and looking around for a solution to a pressing problem. It is then that the ideas of scholars and intellectuals—who develop them or keep them "alive"—are pulled off even dusty shelves and deployed into battle (Yergin and Stanislaw 2002, 131). Specifically, Friedman argued, "I have long believed that we do not influence the course of events by persuading people that we are right when we make what they regard as radical proposals. Rather, we exert influence by keeping options available when something has to be done at a time of crisis" (Friedman and Friedman 1998, 220).

Friedman is closer to the truth than either Keynes or Stigler in terms of the direct effect of ideas, though it is admittedly difficult to isolate the independent influence of ideas from the use of ideas as a veneer for other causes or as part of a complicated set of causes. However, even if ideas have little direct influence, there is also the indirect effect ideas may have in changing, if only as a contributing cause, the minds of men. Moreover, Stigler recognized that ideas matter to other scholars, who then determine what ideas are transmitted in our educational system.

Emulating Dillard (1957) in his assessment of Keynes's ideas, the following discussion of Friedman's reception and influence is divided into two categories. First, I describe the reception and impact of Friedman's work as a scientist within the discipline of economics. Second, I look at how Friedman directly and indirectly influenced the broader world in terms of specific public policies as well as general ideological values or sensibilities.

In summary, Friedman was as influential a figure in economics and in the wider world as any economist in the twentieth century, save Keynes. His academic scholarship influenced our scientific understanding of economics and, combined with his more normative policy-oriented work, also had an impact on official policy. Friedman revived the study of money and the classical emphasis on free markets. Indeed, as Nicholas Kaldor noted, "The 'new monetarism' is a 'Friedman Revolution' more truly than Keynes was the sole fount of the 'Keynesian Revolution'" (Kaldor 1970, 1). Friedman also stimulated new approaches to policy aimed at improving human welfare and expanding individual freedom. Some of the proposals he put on the shelf, so to speak, have been utilized by policy makers around the world—particularly during moments of crisis. Finally, in addition to other thinkers such as Hayek, Friedman's free-market ideas had a diffuse, but no doubt important, influence on the general mindsets of people across the globe. This was in no small measure due to Friedman's skillful and tireless efforts to communicate his views to a general audience that, especially by the late 1970s, was ready to listen. Two caveats are in order. First, while it is important not to downplay Friedman's role in the changes that the world witnessed in the twentieth century, it is also key to avoid overstating the causal effect of any single individual on some of the larger changes of that era—something that Friedman's conservative and classical liberal fans, not to mention certain historians, might be tempted to do at the expense of both other individuals and more macro variables.[1] Second, we should temper how much we credit Friedman with influencing the world, given that many of his libertarian proposals were rejected. More importantly, his general classical liberal approach, while popular amongst a small band of libertarians and free-marketeers, has not been widely accepted in a world where active government is still the dominant force. It is perhaps more fruitful to consider how much Friedman was able to accomplish despite his radical and largely unpopular vision.

As for his reception, Friedman was an incredibly controversial figure throughout his career and even in death. This is true in economics but especially in the wider public policy arena. He attracted controversy from an early age, even leaving aside the Friedman Affair at Wisconsin. For example, one of his first forays into public policy—the piece on rent control he wrote with Stigler—inspired attacks from both modern liberals *and* fellow classical liberals. More importantly, his leadership of the monetarist counterrevolution against Keynesianism inspired decades of sharp debate within and beyond economics. Most notoriously, Friedman's admittedly limited contact with foreign governments, especially Pinochet's Chile, inspired large protests that dogged him for years wherever he spoke, including during the Nobel ceremonies in Sweden. Finally, in the years following his death, Friedman's notoriety has lived on, with Naomi Klein's attack on him as the intellectual fountainhead of our recent economic problems, Paul Krugman's recent critical pieces, and controversy over the naming of an economics research center in his honor at the University of Chicago.

Reception and Influence Within Economics

Friedman's reception in economics is a mixed tale. Many of his ideas, especially those for which he is most known in the discipline, sparked controversy right out of the gate. Indeed, Friedman provoked an enormous outpouring of scholarship that sought to confirm, build upon, or debunk his views [a small sample of which are contained in Wood and Woods' (1990) four-volume collection of critical assessments, which runs approximately 2,000 pages!]. When he was a young scholar, many of Friedman's peers had a negative view of him. According to economist Edward Herman, "Friedman was considered an extremist and something of a nut in the early post war years" (quoted in Overtveldt 91). Some never wavered from this view. Yet it is undeniably true that Friedman was widely respected by most of his colleagues even when they did not agree with him. For some, though, this respect took time to grow. Larry Summers, for example, was probably not unique in terms of how he viewed Friedman through the years: "As for Milton Friedman, he was the devil figure in my youth. Only with time have I come to have large amounts of grudging respect. And with time, increasingly ungrudging respect" (Yergin and Stanislaw 1998, 113).

Friedman's early technical work was certainly appreciated in the wider discipline, given that he was awarded, in 1951, the John Bates Clark Medal. This honor, as the American Economic Association (AEA) website notes, is conferred on an "American economist under the age of forty who is judged to have made the most significant contribution to economic thought and knowledge." Clearly Friedman would not have been given this award had he been viewed as a crank rather than a serious scholar of the first rank. However, not all of his early work was received well by the profession, as one might guess from the above Herman quotation. For example, one of his first serious forays into advocacy work—his 1946 piece against rent control with George Stigler—was attacked in the *American Economics Review* as "a political tract" and in another publication as "drivel" (Bangs 1947, 482; Friedman and Friedman 1998, 150).[2] Moreover, Friedman's 1953 book *Essays in Positive Economics,* while widely reviewed, contained a number of highly controversial essays that sparked a litany of critiques. Foremost among these was his essay on methodology. Another essay in that book advocating flexible exchange rates was also divisive, though it—like many of Friedman's contributions—ultimately won the regard of much of the profession (Friedman and Friedman 1998, 219). However, nothing compared to the furor that erupted over the assortment of pieces he wrote on money and monetary policy. This work marked him as a hero to a few but a heretic to the larger community of adherents to the Keynesian religion that dominated the period between World War II and the late 1970s. In fact, Friedman came to be viewed as a pariah in some parts of the profession, especially as he turned more and more aggressive in the 1960s in terms of both his monetarism and his political advocacy of classical liberalism and the Republican Party. However, given the Clark medal and his election as president of the AEA in 1967, it is an overstatement to say—as some have argued—that "Until the 1970s, the economics profession overwhelmingly greeted Friedman's ideas with hostility" (Hetzel 2007, 2). Indeed, by the time of his death, Friedman was widely revered in the profession even though he was a leading advocate of very polarizing ideas, many of which were not always accepted by his colleagues.

* * *

Friedman's influence in the field of economics is arguably unparalleled by any other economist in the post-World War II era. Indeed, a case could be made that only Keynes beats out Friedman as the most important economist of the twentieth century.[3] The respect Friedman garnered for his scientific contributions came from all sides of the discipline, as evidenced by Paul Krugman's recent claim that "Friedman's theoretical work is universally admired by professional economists" (2007).

In terms of his general influence, Friedman is frequently credited with reviving classical economics, rehabilitating respect for free markets, and leading the monetarist counterrevolution. As Breit and Hirsch (2004, 347) note, "Friedman made it respectable for economists to question the efficacy of Keynesian policy; he resurrected the quantity theory of money and placed it on a secure footing; and he championed the private market economy at a time when intellectuals who did so were often subjected to ostracism in respectable academic circles. Few would doubt that we are all richer for his having become an economist" (Breit and Hirsch 2004, 347). Indeed, Friedman was so influential that a number of his ideas have simply become part of "textbook economics" and have lost their identification with his name or his particular school of thought.[4] Economist Bradford DeLong suggested just this in 2000, when he claimed that many of the monetarist insights have survived under other banners and that "perhaps the extent to which they are simply part of the air that modern macroeconomists today believe is a good index of their intellectual hegemony" (DeLong 2000b, 92). Indeed, Friedman has had a big impact on two key research programs in economics that have emerged recently: New Classical Economics and New Keynesianism (DeLong 2000b). Economists have likewise internalized many other Friedmanite views outside the area of money and banking, particularly his methodological perspective. Not to be forgotten is Friedman's personal influence on his students and colleagues, as well as on the development and flourishing of the Chicago School itself during what Overveldt (2007, 27) calls "the Friedman era."

Another measure of Friedman's impact in academia is the number of times he has been cited by other scholars.[5] Of course, rough empirical numbers like this have their limitations for assessing scholarly influence/reputation and should be interpreted cautiously, but they do tell us something.[6] According to Justin Wolfers of the *New York Times*' *Freakonomics* blog, Friedman is cited by 8,924 articles in JSTOR (an online compendium of prominent journals) journals compared to 4,945 for Keynes, and 1,745 for Hayek (Smith and Marx beat everyone by a wide margin). A more careful analysis reveals a similar story about Friedman's high level of relative influence versus other economists.[7]

A study of the influence of then-living economists by Breit and Huston (1997) that utilizes economic textbook references confirms Friedman's status as one of the leading influences within and beyond the discipline. Specifically, Breit and Huston (1997, 453–54) report that Friedman is "the most influential economist" as he is mentioned in the greatest number of textbooks (100 percent) and is the top-ranked living economist in terms of both percentage of texts in which he is mentioned and total references. Friedman's importance among economists outside of the United States is revealed by a recent poll finding that 85 percent of German economists think Friedman's research is very important or somewhat important to contemporary

Economist	Overall JSTOR Count	JSTOR Count—Economics Only
Milton Friedman	9,118	5,587
Kenneth Arrow	8,752	4,943
Gary Becker	5,978	3,815
George Stigler	5,632	3,998
Robert Solow	5,465	3,762
James Tobin	5,463	3,336
John Maynard Keynes	5,313	2,991
Paul Samuelson	4,857	3,621
Friedrich Hayek	4,389	2,082
John Kenneth Galbraith	3,790	1,614
Alvin Hansen	2,919	2,193
John Hicks	2,779	1,498
Arthur Pigou	2,511	1,889
Abba Lerner	1,856	1,604
Robert Lucas	1,696	1,235
Don Patinkin	1,537	1,347
Ludwig von Mises	1,183	722
Bill Phillips[8]	619	386

understanding of economics (Fricke 2010). Qualitative indicators lend more confidence that Friedman's influence, as indicated by the citation counts, is accurate. Excluding the many tributes given to Friedman through the years by his former students, Chicago colleagues, and ideological allies, Friedman is mentioned frequently by other prominent economists when discussing economics and the discipline. Whether they agree or disagree, most seem to feel a need to reckon with Friedman (see Klamer 1983; Breit and Hirsch 2004).

Friedman was influential as a unifying force and leader of economists on the Right. Economist Scott Sumner argues that Friedman held together a very diverse set of scholars and practitioners in the field in the same way Reagan held together his governing coalition. With both groups, when these big figures departed, the movements they led "cracked up." To Sumner, the paucity of leadership among these economists following

Friedman's death has led to suboptimal policy results, namely, their failure to recognize that low interest rates during the recent economic crisis are a sign of "too little inflation" and the need to speak with a unified voice in favor of greater liquidity (Money Illusion 2010).

Friedman's influence is also indicated by the number of his specific contributions that have changed the way economists and other social scientists think. One of the most important of these is his seminal essay on methodology (Friedman 1953). Despite economist Barkley Rosser's correct contention that Friedman's identification with the instrumentalist approach to economics is fading, Friedman's view of how to do economics looms large over the discipline.[9] Moreover, the piece has provoked discussion and debate that has ranged widely since its publication and is still ongoing today. One of his primary critics was Paul Samuelson, author of an important response that coined the term "F-twist" to describe one of Friedman's arguments (Samuelson 1963). Proof of its lingering importance lies in the fact that Cambridge University Press just published an entire book of excellent original essays focused on the 1953 piece (Mäki 2009). In addition, the piece traveled far from economics. For example, Friedman's methodological approach was harnessed by Kenneth Waltz (1979) in his field-defining book laying out the "neorealist" theory of international politics.

Friedman's ultimately less controversial but equally influential contributions were his permanent income hypothesis (PIH) and his argument against the long-run negatively sloping Phillips Curve (which included his postulate about a natural rate of unemployment). One scholar, Josh Hendrickson, has gone so far as to call the PIH "the best theoretical construction proposed and supported by empirical evidence of the 20th century." Only a bit less positive, Krugman (2007) notes that it, along with Ando and Modligano's similar work, "remain the foundations of how economists think about spending and saving to this day." As for Friedman's claims about the Phillips Curve and the relationship between unemployment and inflation, Krugman called Friedman's advance prediction of stagflation one of the "great triumphs of postwar economics" that "has stood the test of time."

Friedman's corpus of monetarist writing has also been incredibly influential, though in some particulars he failed to win over his critics. In general, Friedman successfully brought back money to business cycle analysis; this cannot be overemphasized. As for specific contributions, many would consider his work with Anna Schwartz on the monetary history of the United States to be his most influential (for example, see Hetzel 2007, 14). Among other things, it has largely reshaped our understanding of the causes of the Great Depression. There is now widespread acceptance of their thesis that the Federal Reserve's deflationary policies severely exacerbated the economic crises of the 1930s (see Bernanke 2000). More importantly, none other than the chairman of the U.S. Federal Reserve Ben Bernanke is a disciple of Friedman's analysis. He argued that Friedman's work on the Depression "has become the leading and most persuasive explanation of the worst economic disaster in American history, the onset of the Great Depression" (Bernanke 2002). Indeed, the long shadow of this research may extend into the current economic crisis where Bernanke, according to some, has attempted to put Friedman's advice into action (Bullock 2009; Williamson 2009; Cowen 2009a, 2009b). This would not be surprising, given that Bernanke apologized in 2002 for the Fed's role in the Depression and addressed Friedman in saying, "We're very sorry. But thanks to you, we won't do it again" (Bernanke 2002).

Other aspects of the monetary counterrevolution have also had an important impact on the profession. Many nonmonetarists now accept the limits of fiscal policy and acknowledge the problem that lags present for stabilization policies (see DeLong 2000b). Furthermore, as Thygesen (1977, 83) notes, Friedman at the least "generated a fundamental debate about the scope for discretionary action in monetary and fiscal policy." As Bernanke (2004, 214) concluded, "one can hardly overstate the influence of Friedman's monetary framework on contemporary monetary theory and practice."

However, Friedman's belief that we should in essence scrap central banks and replace them with automatic rules (focused on a stable increase in the money supply) has met with more mixed success. It is true, as Anna Schwartz has pointed out, that central bankers "have accepted responsibility for inflation control"—something we have seen most dramatically in the United States and the United Kingdom (Schwartz 2008b). Additionally, even the New Keynesians have accepted monetary rules as important, and central bank policy in a number of states has been influenced by the notion that rules are useful. Indeed, the U.S. Federal Reserve has operated somewhat on the basis of a rule (with notable exceptions) over the last three decades. However, since a short experiment with it in the late 1970s and early 1980s in both the United States and the United Kingdom, neither country has focused directly on money stock as Friedman counseled. Instead, the U.S. Fed relied somewhat on the Taylor Rule, which aims to target interest rates [Some see this as recognition of the importance of rules and thus a partial success of monetarist prescriptions—what political economist Jason Sorens has called "monetarism mugged by reality"; others like Krugman (2007) believe the Fed has been engaged in "discretionary fine-tuning" rather than Friedmanesque rule following]. More importantly, the 1980s and 1990s are widely thought to have infirmed part of Friedman's teachings on money, especially the notions that velocity is stable (or easily measured for use in policy making aimed at monetary targets) and that interest rates are relatively unimportant to monetary policy (see DeLong 2000b, 2000a).

Reception and Influence on Policy and Ideology

Friedman was—and remains—an extremely controversial figure in public life, especially in the United States. His early work on policy matters marked him as a classical liberal and instantly put him at odds with the dominant modern liberal ideology of his era.

This translated into no shortage of contempt from the intelligentsia. As *Time* noted in 1969, "For years, the maverick views of Milton Friedman, the towering iconoclast of U.S. economics, attracted just about as much ridicule as respect." He remained a polarizing figure among intellectuals and activists for the rest of his career. Indeed, after his notorious visit to Chile in 1975, Friedman inspired protests wherever he spoke, and these continued for years. One of the largest occurred during the Nobel ceremonies in Sweden in 1976, and the award ceremony itself was interrupted by a noisy protestor in the gallery. Friedman has also provoked pieces lambasting him and his political views, including an entire book titled *Not So Free to Choose* (Rayack 1987), not to mention Naomi Klein's scathing 2007 book *The Shock Doctrine* (more on this in Chapter 4). One scholar, Andre Gunder Frank, went so far as to accuse Friedman of supporting "economic genocide" in Chile (quoted in Burton 1981, 66).

Despite these attacks, Friedman eventually became a fairly popular academic among the broader American public. He was the face of free markets for many people, friends and enemies alike, and was widely respected around the globe. Indeed, as the *New York Times* later noted, Friedman "became something of a celebrity" (Noble 2006). Friedman wrote a prominent column for *Newsweek*, was interviewed frequently (including on general audience television programs like the *Phil Donahue Show*), and was invited to speak all over the world. One report noted that during his trips to Hong Kong, Friedman was "mobbed like a rock star" (Ebenstein 2007, 214). He even appeared on the cover of *Time* and the *New York Times Magazine*—something fairly remarkable for a radical economist without any official office. Friedman's fame only grew after his documentary *Free to Choose* aired on television in the United States, the United Kingdom, and other countries. As Brian Doherty (2007, 14) accurately concludes, "As economist and polemicist, he has been the most widely respected libertarian of the twentieth century."

Another sign of his reception and influence is that foreign leaders sought Friedman out for advice on economic policy.

This included his infamous meeting with General Pinochet of Chile as well as visits with Margaret Thatcher of the United Kingdom, Zhao Ziyang and Jiang Zemin of China, and heads of state, central bankers, and key officials of numerous other countries.

Friedman's popular books met with a mixed reception by critics but sold well. *Capitalism and Freedom* was reviewed in many academic outlets, but often negatively. Beyond the ivory tower, it was essentially ignored rather than attacked—something odd, as Friedman himself later noted with some bitterness, for a serious work by a well-known scholar (Friedman and Friedman 1998, 340). An exception was a relatively positive review in the *Economist* (1963). In contrast, Friedman's later general audience book, *Free to Choose*, was widely and more often positively reviewed. Moreover, it was a bestseller with more than a million copies ultimately sold, and the book was translated into numerous other languages (*Capitalism and Freedom* sold more than a half million copies).

Friedman was warmly welcomed and eventually quite adored by both the conservative and libertarian camps that emerged out of the Old Right in the postwar era. This was not as obvious an outcome as one might think, given the hostility of many traditional conservatives to libertarianism, not to mention the Republican Party's accommodating "me-tooism" during much of Friedman's life. Indeed, William F. Buckley, Friedman's "skiing buddy," and his coterie at *National Review* had read more than a few people out of respectable circles for extremism—and Friedman's views were pretty radical even by that magazine's standards (Buckley 2006). Moreover, Friedman vehemently rebuffed efforts by his friends and opponents to brand him as a conservative.[10]

The Right's warm reception started very early in Friedman's career. In 1945, Hayek enlisted Friedman's support for the Free Market Study that he and the libertarian Volker Fund had been plotting with Henry Simons (Van Horn and Mirowski 2009; Overtveldt 2007). Over the next decade, Friedman was invited to participate in a number of other normatively oriented activities, including the founding Mont Pelerin Society meeting and the Volker Fund's summer programs. He was also a founding member of the conservative Philadelphia Society and a member of the American Enterprise Institute's Academic Advisory Board. Friedman was invited into Republican Party politics as well, eventually serving as a counselor for Barry Goldwater, Richard Nixon, and Ronald Reagan. By the 1960s, Friedman was essentially the voice of laissez-faire on the so-called American "Right" and was embraced—even lionized—as their champion for free-market economics. Thus, it was no surprise that Ronald Reagan ultimately bestowed upon Friedman the Presidential Medal of Freedom in 1988.

However, Friedman was not universally loved in these circles. He was attacked by Ayn Rand and not-so-subtly criticized by the Foundation for Economic Education for his excessive concern for equality and efficiency in his rent control piece with George Stigler (Doherty 2007; Friedman and Friedman 1998, 151). Additionally, Austrian School economists and natural-rights libertarians/anarcho-capitalists such as Murray Rothbard were vocally critical of Friedman throughout his career. They were especially hostile to numerous aspects of the Chicago approach to economics that Friedman represented. Austrians criticized Friedman for everything from his methodological views, to his understanding of the Great Depression, to his negative income tax plan, to his opposition to the gold standard and free banking (Skousen 2005). Rothbard, in particular, was quite nasty toward Friedman. Rothbard called him "the Establishment's Court Libertarian" and an "unofficial apologist for Nixonite policy" (Rothbard [1971] 2002, 37). Worse, he described Friedman as a "technician advising the State on how to be efficient in going about its evil work" (40).[11] Libertarians in general, though, loved and cherished the man they affectionately referred to as "Uncle Miltie." Friedman is still frequently cited as one of their heroes. Doherty (2007, 456) notes, however, that he "is still judged skeptically among radical segments of the libertarian movement."

* * *

As for Friedman's influence on public policy and ideology, it too has been mixed. There is little doubt he has had an important, diffuse effect on how many people around the globe, especially Americans, have come to think about economics and the government's role in society and the market. Indeed, this was probably the greatest source of his influence. As the *Los Angeles Times* noted in its obituary of Friedman, he "almost single-handedly altered the boundaries of public debate on an array of national issues" (Peterson 2006). Friedman also counseled presidents (Nixon and Reagan) and central bankers—though his influence was very limited with Nixon and uncertain with Reagan, especially since the Gipper already shared many of his views (Friedman and Friedman 1998, 390).[12] Gary Becker suggested Friedman also exerted a big influence by improving economic literacy via his popular works, like his *Newsweek* column and *Free to Choose* (Liberty Fund Interview 2003). Friedman had a particularly large effect on the tiny world of classical liberalism since he offered an appealing "scientific" consequentialist alternative to the moral doctrines of natural rights thinkers. This expanded the pool of adherents and likely converted many a conservative to his more radical vision.

Any discussion of influence must acknowledge that impacting the thoughts of *some* of the public and having influence on the general course of social and political change are two different things, especially in an age which, in many ways, stands as a rebuke to much of the classical liberal view Friedman espoused. As Albert Kraus asked in the *New York Times* in 1968, "What role is there for an intellectual radical in a politics of consensus?" (Kraus 1968). Nonetheless, *Time* (1969b) probably put it best when it elegantly noted that "In a sense, Friedman is like a Paris designer whose haute couture is bought by a select few, but who nonetheless influences almost all popular fashions."

Friedman's influence on specific policies is a bit harder to measure and is certainly a more complicated story. However, it is not an exaggeration to state that his influence in politics was as large as that of any American public intellectual in his era and certainly of any economist in the entire twentieth century (other than Keynes). *The New York Times* (Noble 2006) went even further, describing Friedman as "the grandmaster of free-market economic theory in the postwar era and a prime force in the movement of nations toward less government and greater reliance on individual responsibility." Although such encomiums to his influence were common, especially following his death, Friedman's batting average was not as good as they would suggest in terms of his more direct influence. Instead, Friedman's record was mixed, with important examples of his influencing policy but many cases where his proposals fell on deaf ears. Moreover, as Krugman noted, the swing back toward laissez-faire policies starting in the 1970s would have happened without Friedman, though the Chicago economist certainly "helped accelerate the process, both in the United States and around the world" (Krugman 2007). Yet Friedman's overall record is still pretty remarkable given that he, as Allan Meltzer notes, swam against such a strong current of thought (Meltzer 2004).

In the policy arena, Friedman had the most success with his proposal to move from a fixed to a floating exchange rate system (Friedman 1953). This was one of the ideas Friedman put on the shelf only to have it ignored, even mocked, by policy makers for nearly two decades (Friedman and Friedman 1998, 220). As his wife, Rose, noted, Friedman's "recommendation was disregarded but the consequences he predicted occurred" (Rose Friedman 1976d, 24). Then very quickly, when the United States and the world faced balance of payments problems that could not be resolved within the Bretton Woods system, Friedman's idea was among those considered by the Nixon administration and eventually won the day in 1973. Economist Barkley Rosser calls it "one of his [Friedman's] big policy triumphs, maybe his biggest influence"—though there has been some drift back due to pegging and the realization that speculation has not been as positive as Friedman claimed.[13] Friedman—and later Allan Meltzer—explained that one of the reasons it (and other seemingly dormant free-market proposals) succeeded is that there was a long gestation period during which the idea was thoroughly vetted and became familiar to a broader audience who thought it might work (Friedman and Friedman 1998, 220; Meltzer 2004).

Friedman was also on the winning side of the fight against the military draft in the United States. Gates Commission member Alan Greenspan and many others have argued that Friedman played a key role in the decision to end conscription (*Power of Choice*). Moreover, Bernard Rostker (2006, 749), in his comprehensive RAND study of the all-volunteer force (AVF), claims that Friedman "was the intellectual father" of it. Friedman's advocates usually make the case for Friedman's influence by referring to his early writings against conscription and his participation in the 1966 Chicago conference on the draft as well as the Gates Commission, which recommended its end (Henderson 2005, 2006; Doherty 2007, 372). However, Friedman gets more credit than he probably deserves in this case. He undoubtedly played an important role in the process by which conscription was terminated, especially as one of the most eloquent voices preparing the intellectual battle space for the ultimate decision (see Tax 1967). Moreover, Friedman, as is frequently noted, helped move the Gates Commission from being evenly divided among advocates, opponents, and fence-sitters to its eventual, unanimous support for ending the draft. Nonetheless, one could argue that the draft's demise was practically inevitable for a number of reasons. First, Nixon was committed to ending the draft and had favored an AVF before he even won the presidency. In fact, he made a commitment to end the draft during the 1968 campaign (Anderson 1982). Moreover, Nixon formed the Gates Commission in the first place to provide support for his preestablished goal of abolishing the draft (see Nixon statement of March 27, 1969 quoted in Henderson 2005). Second, even if ideas were critical to the policy shift, Friedman was not the only nor even the most important intellectual proponent of the AVF. In terms of economists, Walter Oi and others were important voices who had already done a lot of the legwork by the time Friedman became actively involved in the fight (Anderson 1982; Henderson 2006). Third, Martin Anderson was a critical figure who deserves at least as much, if not more, credit for the demise of the draft. He was the first person to raise the idea with the Nixon team in 1967 and was the point man for the AVF in the administration. He both determined the membership of the Gates Commission and made sure the commission's recommendations made it through the decision-making process (Rostker 2006, 748). Fourth, given the post-Tet Offensive political climate as well as changes in military technology, the economics of defense, demographic shifts, and how the Vietnam-era military came to see draftees, one could argue that the policy shift would have happened regardless of the players involved (see Rostker 2006, 746). This is supported by the fact that macro variables like these ultimately led other developed countries to end conscription without Friedman's assistance (though the work done in the United States no doubt played a factor). Even Ebenstein (2007, 179) in his largely reverential biography downplays Friedman's role in this area.

Friedman had a number of other partially successful policy proposals, including vouchers and the negative income tax. Friedman put the idea of educational choice and vouchers on the map, generating a great deal of heated debate since he first wrote on the subject in 1955 (not least because educational choice threatens the interests of teachers' unions). There have been some limited and partial attempts to put Friedman's ideas into practice, most notably in Milwaukee, Cleveland, and now New Orleans. However, as Eric Hanushek (2006, 70) accurately concludes, "the voucher idea has yet to be met with much policy success in the United States."

Friedman's negative income tax (NIT) idea bolstered his reputation as someone concerned about the poor and met with some success in the form of the Earned Income Tax Credit (EITC) (see Frank 2006). Robert Moffitt notes that the NIT "proposal has been a major influence both in policy circles and in the academic literature," and the "growth of the Earned Income Tax Credit in the 1990's has introduced a type of negative income tax on a vaster scale that Friedman ever imagined"

(Moffitt 2003, 120). However, as one might guess from Friedman's opposition to its precursor, the Family Assistance Program, the EITC did not live up to his original hopes. In particular, it has not replaced other welfare programs and the vast bureaucracies overseeing them. Indeed, as Moffitt notes, "U.S. policy has moved in the diametrically opposite direction" (Moffitt 2003, 135). This has not stopped Charles Murray from explicitly building off Friedman's plan and proposing an equally bold revision of the welfare system (see Murray 2006; Borders Interview). According to Meltzer (2004, 197–98), Friedman was also influential in ending the ceilings on interest rates. His views on corporate social responsibility have had a long life, not least as a common fixture in business ethics textbooks.

In some areas, Friedman's views prevailed, but it is not all that clear he had much to do with the results. For example, wage and price controls are relatively unpopular policy levers today. However, it is hard to believe that Friedman had very much to do with this, especially since Nixon imposed them in the early 1970s over Friedman's vehement objections, both directly and in his *Newsweek* column. What turned policy makers against them were the negative experiences in the 1970s and what they learned from these episodes. Likewise, one could argue that Friedman's tireless efforts spreading the virtues of markets and trade helped spur the greater trade liberalization the world has enjoyed since the trough of the pre-World War II era. However, this movement started before Friedman took up its cudgel, and he was only one of many voices and interests pushing such an agenda. Moreover, the Unites States has not pursued the unilateral free trade he advocated. Nonetheless, it is hard to argue that Friedman's authority and consistent appeal for freeing global trade had zero impact. As for rent control, although Friedman was an early critic of it, the near unanimity of economists against rent control suggests that the policy would have died for the most part eventually, regardless of his efforts. The same might have been said on the flip side in terms of Friedman's efforts to introduce tax withholding at the source. Although he played a key role in its genesis, Friedman himself noted that it would have been adopted whether or not he was involved. He did, however, accept responsibility (to him, this meant "blame") for "helping to make it more efficient than it otherwise might have been" (Friedman and Friedman 1998, 123).

Fortunately or not, depending on your view, most of Friedman's other policy proposals were either dead on arrival or have failed to gain any substantial support even when actually considered in the public realm. For example Meltzer (2004, 194) notes, in his own discussion of Friedman's policy import, how many of the proposals in *Capitalism and Freedom* and *Free to Choose* were never seriously considered and are unlikely to be in the near future. National parks, public housing, minimum wage laws, agricultural supports, the FCC and other "alphabet" agencies and departments, Social Security, occupational licensing, corporate income taxes, and progressive personal income taxes are only some of the things Friedman wanted to eliminate that seem unlikely to disappear anytime soon. Additionally, Friedman's opposition to the drug war was valiant, but this expansive complex of efforts is still going strong despite some movement to free up marijuana laws in a few states. Lastly, Friedman's fight for tax and spending limits achieved some legislative success before ultimately failing, while deregulation gained some momentum in the late 1970s and early 1980s but largely stalled (in some cases going in the other direction).

Friedman's influence also extended beyond the United States. His ideas found especially fertile ground in the United Kingdom during the rise and reign of Margaret Thatcher.[14] Economist Andrew Farrant has noted that while Hayek provided Thatcherism with vision, Friedman supplied it with concrete ideas for change.[15] The primary transmission belt for Friedman's views was the Institute of Economic Affairs (IEA) in London. This think tank pushed his monetarism with great vigor starting in the early 1970s, giving him a prominent speaking and publishing outlet in the United Kingdom. Friedman's work quickly gained attention inside and out of the British government. For example, a Friedman pamphlet on unemployment and inflation was said, by one official in the summer of 1975, to have "excited considerable interest in Government circles" (quoted in Cockett [1994] 1995, 156). The IEA kept rising star Margaret Thatcher informed on monetarist scholarship and ultimately arranged a private dinner between Friedman and the future prime minister in 1978. Additionally, the IEA worked to have the *Free to Choose* documentary aired on public television, which historian Richard Cockett notes "had an enormous impact on British public opinion" (Cockett [1994] 1995, 152). Key figures in the press who were converted to monetarism by Friedman's work also helped disseminate his ideas. These included Samuel Brittan of the *Financial Times,* whose writing kept Friedman and Hayek in the public eye. Friedman even had an influence on the Tory's opponents, as evidenced by James Callaghan's 1976 Labor Party Conference speech in which he rebuked Keynesian policies (Cockett [1994] 1995, 185–87).[16]

Friedman is credited with influencing policies in other states as well. For example, many argue he played a role—for good or for bad—in the economic and political reforms of Pinochet's Chile (see Lewis 1975; Wald and Pauling 1976; Baltimore and Luria 1976; Letelier 1976; Klein 2007; Stephens 2010). However, as pointed out in Chapter 1, the reality is that while free-market ideas influenced Chilean reformers under Pinochet, Friedman's direct influence was rather limited. Indeed, giving Friedman the main share of praise or blame for free-market reforms around the world in the late twentieth century does a great disservice (or too great a service as the case may be!) to other thinkers of the era, not to mention the classical liberal tradition which stretches back well before Friedman's time and which was kept alive by a number of institutions and actors, indigenous and external to reforming countries.

Nonetheless, Friedman was certainly a key member of that group of liberal thinkers who helped free-market ideas briefly occupy—or at least share—the "commanding heights" at the end of the twentieth century (Yergin and Stanislaw [1998] 2002).

Peter Boettke (2004, 141ff), in his look at Friedman's impact during the period after 1979, argues the Chicago economist did have an important influence around the globe. In particular, Friedman had a hefty indirect impact "as the leading intellectual spokesman for economic liberalism." Boettke also claims that Friedman's ideas had a more direct impact in helping shape the transition policies of eastern European states emerging from the communist era, especially in Poland and the Czech Republic (where Vaclav Klaus has acknowledged a deep debt to Friedman). Estonia also stands out as a place where Friedman had a profound impact. Former prime minister Mart Laar has consistently argued that his free-market reforms were influenced by Friedman:

> I had read only one book on economics—Milton Friedman's *Free to Choose.* I was so ignorant at the time that I thought that what Friedman wrote about the benefits of privatization, the flat tax and the abolition of all customs rights, was the result of economic reforms that had been put into practice in the West. It seemed common sense to me and, as I thought it had already been done everywhere, I simply introduced it in Estonia, despite warnings from Estonian economists that it could not be done. They said it was as impossible as walking on water. We did it: we just walked on the water because we did not know that it was impossible.[17]

Indeed, the number of cases in which one could argue Friedman had some influence is too great to chronicle. However, the extent of Friedman's perceived influence is best captured by a Danziger political cartoon from 1990 in which a Milton Friedman statue is erected in Poland in place of Lenin (Friedman and Friedman 1998, 513)!

Although Friedman undoubtedly influenced governments around the world, including in the United States, it is often difficult to say with any precision how much influence he had in any particular case compared to other, larger forces. Friedman himself, as Cockett notes, argued in his Nobel lecture that policy changes were a response "almost entirely to the force of events; brute experience proved far more potent than the strongest of political or ideological preferences." However, this is perhaps too modest, given that he and his fellow free-marketeers developed and popularized a set of ideas to which governments around the world could turn during troubled times (Cockett [1994] 1995, 198–99). Coming full circle to the beginning of this chapter, Friedman—not his friend Stigler nor his opponent Keynes—was right about the power of ideas. Yet even Friedman's ideological compadres would no doubt question the extent of his actual impact, given that the world, especially looking at it in 2010, is still very friendly to the mixed economy and paternalist government that Friedman fought for decades. Indeed, many latter-day Friedmanites would say the state of freedom is even worse today than when Clive Crook (2006), in the *Atlantic*, expressed grave doubt about Friedman's lasting impact:

> Enormously influential as he was, and triumph as he invariably did in debate with his intellectual opponents, I don't know if you could say that Friedman was on the winning side in the 20th century's great battle of ideas. Communism collapsed, to be sure, but in Europe and the United States, economists like Friedman saw a lot of ground surrendered to higher taxes and public spending, and to an ever-proliferating web of economic regulation. There were interruptions now and then (notably Ronald Reagan in the United States and Margaret Thatcher in the United Kingdom), but interruptions is all they were. Over recent decades the trend in America has been toward gradually diminishing economic freedom.

Perhaps, echoing Zhou Enlai on the French Revolution, it is still too soon to tell. Friedman played a key role by keeping alive certain ideas that, as both their proponents and detractors will acknowledge, will certainly ride again.

Notes

[1] One possible example of many might be Yergin and Stanislaw's comment that "Indeed, the fundamental shift in the global attitude towards markets might never have happened, at least in the form it did, had it not been for several decades worth of highly unfashionable academic 'scribbling' by Friedman and his colleagues at the University of Chicago" (2002, 127).

[2] What is interesting is that by 1979, 98 percent of economists surveyed agreed that "A ceiling on rents reduces the quantity and quality of housing available" (Kearl et al., 1979, 30). I am not sure what percentage of economists thought that way in 1946.

[3] Of course, a claim for Friedman's influence is not the same as a claim that he was right. Napoleon's invasion of Russia was a monstrous error—and yet there is no doubt he was an incredibly influential figure in the early eighteenth century!

[4] This line of thinking (to which I return in Chapter 4) flowed from a conversation I had with economist Barkley Rosser.

[5] For an earlier attempt to quantify "intellectual debtors and creditors" in economics, see Stigler 1982. He also provides some nice caveats of such an approach. His numbers confirm the relatively high importance of Friedman in the discipline.

[6] On the differences between reputation and influence, see Breit and Huston 1997.

[7] Google Scholar citations substantiate these numbers (based on "Publish or Perish") with Friedman earning 51,628 total citations compared to 27,583 for Keynes; 42,943 for Samuelson; 72,750 for Arrow; 31,493 for Hayek; 55,619 for Lucas, and everyone else on the list above had far fewer citations. I would like to thank Andy Knauer for his help compiling these numbers. For additional information on the methodology used, please contact the author at wr16@txstate.edu.

[8] The citation counts for Phillips and Keynes show the downside of using such data to measure influence or reputation. In both cases, the counts artificially deflate the importance of these figures since there are many, many uncited references to the Phillips Curve (approximately 5,000!) and Keynes or Keynesianism in the economics literature.

[9] Personal interview with Rosser in 2010. For more on the influence of this piece, see Meyer 2009.

[10] This raises the question of why he was so fully embraced on the Right and did not suffer attacks from traditionalist conservatives. A big

part of the story has to be that Friedman's obvious brilliance and impeccable scientific bona fides bulletproofed him from much criticism, especially from a movement thin on supporters from the academic ranks. Friedman's willingness to compromise, institutional service (helping found big-tent organizations such as the Philadelphia Society), and friendly (but tough) personality must have contributed as well.

[11] Friedman could dish it out in return. He was very critical of the Austrians and was dismissive toward the "utopian strand in libertarianism" despite his own idealism (Skousen 2005, 246).

[12] Friedman quipped on *The Donahue Show* that most of the time his advice to presidential aspirants had not been taken!

[13] Personal interview with Rosser in 2010.

[14] This section is based on Richard Cockett's excellent work on the role of think-tanks in the United Kingdom

[15] Personal correspondence with Farrant in July 2010.

[16] This speech was first called to my attention by economist Andrew Farrant.

[17] This quotation appears in multiple places. I accessed it from http://www.cato.org/special/friedman/laar/.

Chapter 4

Contemporary Relevance

Milton Friedman was an intellectual giant, and his voice is dearly missed.

— *Scott Sumner* (Money Illusion *2010*)

It has been years since Milton Friedman died and more than three decades since he retired. Yet he is still a relevant figure in current economic and political debates. Indeed, the shadow of his ideas has loomed large over the discussion of how to respond to the financial crisis that began in 2007 and the economic recession that followed.[1] His relevance extends even beyond this economic realm (and the discipline of economics) into broader policy debates and political battles. However, just as in life, Friedman remains a controversial, polarizing figure in death. He is missed by many (as evidenced by the quotation heading this chapter) and inspires in terms of both his great intellectual bequest to economics and his great love for freedom. To others, Friedman is a notorious figure with noxious ideas that need burying.

Since the 1970s, Friedman has been a popular target of the Left, especially in the United States. However, it is a bit surprising how much animosity and attention Friedman still generates among this group today, years after he ceased being active in public life. To many of those on the Left, Friedman is a "devil figure" (as Larry Summers once thought) who advised murderous dictators and helped create a world less friendly to cries for social justice. For example, Naomi Klein places Friedman front and center in her recent book *The Shock Doctrine: The Rise of Disaster Capitalism.* To Klein and others like her, Friedman was the "grand guru of the movement for unfettered capitalism and the man credited with writing the rulebook for the contemporary, hypermobile global economy" (Klein 2007, 4)—and this is not meant as a compliment. Instead, the world she largely credits Friedman with creating is one of corporatism and exploitation of the poor. In the words of Eduardo Galeano, "The theories of Milton Friedman gave him the Nobel Prize; they gave Chile General Pinochet" (quoted in Klein 2007, 73).[2]

Klein is not Friedman's only assailant today. For example, Congressman Bernie Sanders—wearing an anti-Friedman lapel pin—took the time to deliver an entire speech attacking him during which the House member argued, "Friedman's ideology caused enormous damage to the American middle class and to working families here and around the world . . . . his economic program is nothing more than a wish list for the greediest, the most monied interests in our society" (Sanders 2009). Similar rhetoric can be found commonly on the Left, especially among academics. Indeed, there has been a large recent kerfuffle at the University of Chicago over the decision to name an economics research center the Milton Friedman Institute. Opponents of the decision have gathered 170 faculty signatures on a petition claiming Friedman's "relentless championing of a free-market fundamentalism [is] now largely discredited" and that he provided services "rendered to brutally repressive regimes in Chile, China, and elsewhere" (Schmidt 2010). Lastly, in 2009, Friedman's opponents went so far as to plaster large stickers all over Washington and other places, showing a smiling Friedman with the caption "Milton Friedman/Proud Father of Global Misery" (Root 2009).

On the other hand, conservatives and libertarians continue to treat Friedman as a hero and inspiration. This was seen in the vast outpouring of pieces praising Friedman following his death (for examples, see Cole 2007; Henderson 2006; Crook 2006). Adoration in the public sphere has continued up to the present. Stephen Moore of the *Wall Street Journal,* for example, wrote a piece in 2009 titled, "Missing Milton: Who Will Speak for Free Markets?" in which he ranked Friedman, next to Reagan, as "the greatest apostle for freedom and free markets in the second half of the twentieth century" (Moore 2009). Bret Stephens (2010), also in the *Wall Street Journal*, went so far as to claim Friedman helped save Chile from its recent earthquake! On television, Fox Business's John Stossel aired an entire program in the summer of 2010 dedicated to feting Friedman and his free-market vision. Even Republican politicians have found time to praise Friedman. Mitch Daniels, governor of Indiana and possible future presidential candidate, recently noted Friedman had a deep influence on him and listed *Free to Choose* as one of the five best conservative books (*Five Books* 2010).[3] Similarly, Representative Jeff Flake claimed that "His influence on those of us who believe in the power of free markets cannot be measured."[4] Every two years, the Cato Institute gives an award to someone who has advanced liberty called the Milton Friedman Prize. Additionally, since 2008, a variety of conservative and libertarian groups and individuals have held "Milton Friedman Day" gatherings on his birthday to celebrate the man and his ideas. In 2010, there was one such gathering in each of 43 different American states and 5 other countries.[5] Even a quick perusal of conservative and libertarian magazines and blogs will show consistent positive references to Friedman and his ideas. Moreover, a Google search for "Milton Friedman" yields 1.4 million hits!

The regular media has also kept Friedman in the news. For example, apropos of nothing, the *New York Times* ran a piece on Friedman in 2008 titled "A Fresh Look at the Apostle of Free Markets" (Goodman 2008). In 2007, PBS aired a largely hagiographical documentary on Friedman titled *The Power of Choice.*

Academics and policy makers, too, continue to discuss Friedman's ideas and legacy. This is most obvious in economics. Indeed, Harvard economist Andrei Shleifer (2009) recently published a piece on the relationship between free-market policies and increased global welfare titled "The Age of Milton Friedman." Of course, Friedman's explanation of the Depression still holds wide sway in the discipline, as does his permanent income hypothesis and other theoretical innovations discussed in Chapter 3. Friedman's relevance is also seen in areas outside economics. For example, political theorist Jerry Muller recently published a book on capitalism and Jews that takes as one of its departure points Friedman's nearly 40-year-old thoughts on the matter (Friedman 1984a [1987]; Muller 2010). Likewise, Friedman's arguments about corporate social responsibility, school choice, the draft, and the negative income tax still draw scholarly and public attention.

Of course, the biggest claim for Friedman's continued relevance is found in the area of monetary policy. His views on the Depression and how central banks should operate have been critical in informing the debate over the best response to the financial crisis that started in 2007. Indeed, some claim that Friedman has played a huge role in how the Federal Reserve itself has behaved since the crisis started. The transmission belt for Friedman's ideas has been Fed Chairman Ben Bernanke, a self-admitted disciple of Friedman's monetary theories. According to one account, "Bernanke is following a monetarist depression-prevention model laid out by Nobel laureate and libertarian patron saint Milton Friedman" (Bullock 2009). In particular, the Fed Chairman cut interest rates and engaged in "quantitative easing"—something Friedman recommended to Japan when it faced economic crisis in the 1990s. The article goes on to quote Bernanke's 2009 congressional testimony, in which the Fed Chairman specifically referenced Friedman and Schwartz's study of the Depression and then claimed, "With that lesson in mind, the Federal Reserve has reacted very aggressively to cut interest rates in this current crisis. Moreover, we've tried to avoid the collapse of the banking system." Likewise, Congressman Ron Paul, Bernanke's hostile interrogator during that testimony and a Friedman critic, also thought the Fed Chairman was channeling Friedman. He later argued that "In essence, Bernanke is following Friedman's advice. He's a Friedmanite when it comes to massively inflating. Bernanke was able to justify [his policies] by using Friedman" (quoted in Bullock 2009). Finally, *New York Times* columnist and economist Tyler Cowen has made the case that Bernanke was guided by Milton Friedman and followed a roughly Friedmanite approach to the crisis.[6]

This argument tightly linking Bernanke's policies to Friedman has not gone unchallenged. For example, economist David Henderson and economic historian Jeff Hummel have argued Bernanke's approach was inconsistent with Friedman's past guidance. In particular, Bernanke, worried by the possibility of the whole financial system collapsing, targeted funds to bail out financial intermediaries that were "too big to fail." Yet at the same time, as Henderson notes, Bernanke "sterilized" (using open-market operations—buying or selling government bonds—to offset other monetary changes in the opposite direction) the impact of these bailouts on the money supply. These scholars claim Friedman would have opposed such a bank bailout, favoring instead a general increase in the money supply rather than Bernanke's targeted approach that propped up insolvent banks while—at least at first—avoiding money stock growth.[7]

Both sides in this debate make good points. However, it seems as if Bernanke *was* acting in the spirit of Friedman's view of how monetary policy could prevent events such as the Great Depression emerging from economic crises and recessions.[8] More importantly perhaps when discussing relevance, Bernanke certainly saw himself as being guided by Friedman's monetarist approach and the lessons learned from Friedman and Schwartz's work on monetary history. This is clearly seen in his response to Ron Paul's 2009 congressional interrogation.[9] However, it is very likely that Bernanke did not intervene exactly the way Friedman would have since Friedman's intervention would have been more general and less targeted (though he may have bailed out some banks, as Cowen notes, because of his praise for Bagehot's view that the central bank should do what is necessary to avoid a bank crisis). Nonetheless, even if Friedman bailed out insolvent banks for the reasons Bernanke-Cowen give, he would have allowed the money stock to increase rather than sterilizing it (especially given that sterilization, to Friedman, was a big mistake made by the Depression-era Federal Reserve System). However, it is important to remember that Friedman would have intervened one way or the other, thus making the distinction between the Bernanke-Cowen view and the Henderson-Hummel approach less critical. There is also a caveat to this discussion: it is not easy to say exactly what Friedman would have done given, as Brad DeLong notes, there are "many Friedmans."[10] Perhaps surprisingly, Friedman's co-author Anna Schwartz has been critical of increasing liquidity during the current crisis (saying the Fed is "fighting the last war" rather than dealing with the bad asset problem we actually face) and has favored allowing insolvent firms to fail (Willoughby 2008; Schwartz 2008a).

In the midst of the debate about how monetary authorities should respond to the financial crisis, there has also been renewed interest in the discretion vs. rules debate that Friedman provoked long ago. John Taylor of "Taylor Rule" fame, for example, argued in May 2010 that there has been a "Great Deviation" since 2003: the Federal Reserve has diverged from the rules-based (one might say, Friedmanite) approach it had followed the previous two decades to one characterized by discretionary intervention to fine-tune the economy. Taylor claims—echoing Friedman—that it has done so with poor results: "The Great Deviation killed the Great Moderation, gave birth to the Great Recession, and left a troublesome legacy for the future" (Taylor 2010). Such discussion is another sign of Friedman's continued relevance. On the other hand, some think the financial crisis will bury Friedman. According to James Galbraith of the University of Texas, "The inability of Friedman's successors to say anything useful about what's happening in financial markets today means their influence is finished" (quoted in Moore 2009).

* * *

Milton Friedman was a great economist and a spirited defender of a free society. But will he be long remembered? Does Friedman have much staying power compared to other big thinkers of the twentieth century? Of course, it is much too early to tell.

However, a recent article in *Prospect* claims Friedman is fading and Hayek is overtaking him, arguing that the Austrian economist's "insights go much deeper and offer a better framework for the research programmes [*sic*] of the 21st century" (Ormerod 2006). This is likely an overstatement, especially given the continued influence and relevance of many of Friedman's contributions to economics and public policy. However, when discussing future relevance, one has to separate this into his relevance to economics as a science, to the realm of public policy, and to classical liberalism (both its members and its thought). In economics, Friedman's enduring arguments will become part of the general textbook approach and less and less tied to him as an individual, especially given that the field has little use for intellectual history and the origins of ideas. But he will always remain a key iconic figure with the likes of Fisher, Keynes, and Samuelson. As one economist put it, Friedman "is still 'the man'" and "will still be discussed in fifty years."[11] Friedman will also remain in the classical liberal pantheon (but decline as a target of modern liberal wrath), though his popular books will likely become less accessible to future generations as the specific examples and policy debates he engaged recede from public concern and the public memory. Lastly, one could argue that the area hardest to predict his future relevance is in the realm of public policy. The radicalism of Friedman's freedom agenda may not give him much purchase on the minds of a twenty-first century looking more and more committed to an expansive role for government.[12] However, that itself may provide Friedman with an enduring legacy—for his voice may be regarded in the future as, in the words of one of the presidential candidates he worked for, "a choice not an echo."[13]

Notes

1 For a useful timeline of the crisis, see the Federal Reserve Bank of St. Louis's website: http://timeline.stlouisfed.org/index.cfm?p=timeline.

[2] Klein's attack on Friedman has been roundly criticized, including in the *New York Times* (see Redburn 2007). Also see Norberg 2008.

[3] Oddly, the website changed the title from "Mitch Daniels on American Conservatism" to "Mitch Daniels on How Libertarians Can Govern."

[4] This and other tributes to Friedman can be found at http://www.edchoice.org/friedmans/statementworld.jsp.

[5] For a list, see http://www.edchoice.org/friedmanday/.

[6] Personal correspondence with Cowen, 2010. See Cowen's articles on the popular economics blog *Marginal Revolution* at www.marginalrevolution.com, including Tyler Cowen, "Were the Bailouts a Good Idea?" *Marginal Revolution* (August 25, 2009); Tyler Cowen, "What Did Milton Friedman Favor?" *Marginal Revolution* (August 27, 2009); Tyler Cowen, "Views on What the Fed Should Have Done," *Marginal Revolution* (September 2, 2009).

[7] See the following blog posts from Henderson at http://econlog.econlib.org/: David Henderson, "Tyler Cowen on Pretense," *Econlog* (August 25, 2009); David Henderson, "Tyler Cowen, Milton Friedman, and Bailouts," *Econlog* (August 31, 2009); David Henderson, "Friedman vs. Bernanke," *Econlog* (September 4, 2009); David Henderson, "Friedman vs. Bernanke, II." *Econlog* (September 9, 2009). Also see Jeffrey Rogers Hummel, "Article by Hetzel on the 2008–2009 Recession," *Liberty and Power* (August 9, 2009), http://hnn.us/blogs/entries/112015.html.

[8] Though, as Jeff Hummel reminded me in personal correspondence on this matter, Bernanke and Friedman were not in specific agreement about the causes of the Depression (especially as regards the relative importance of nonmonetary factors). Interestingly, Bernanke only saw his work as an "embellishment" on Friedman and Schwartz rather than a competing argument. See Bernanke 2002.

[9] An alternative interpretation is that Bernanke was using Friedman as cover from conservative or libertarian critics of his move. However, Bernanke's history of praise for Friedman and his work, as well as Bernanke's own Friedman-inspired research, suggest that Bernanke was making an honest argument here.

[10] See Brad DeLong, "Tyler Cowen's Ultimate Milton Friedman Post," *Grasping Reality with Both Hands* (September 5, 2009), http://delong.typepad.com/sdj/2009/09/tyler-cowens-ultimate-milton-friedman-post.html.

[11] Personal interview with Barkley Rosser.

[12] The same, though, could be said for Hayek.

[13] Barry Goldwater.

Bibliography

Works by Milton Friedman

Friedman, Milton. (1935), "Professor Pigou's Method for Measuring Elasticities of Demand from Budgetary Data." *Quarterly Journal of Economics* 50:1 (November): 151–63.

—. (with A. C. Pigou and N. Georgescu-Roegen). (1936), "Marginal Utility of Money and Elasticities of Demand." *Quarterly Journal of Economics* 50:3 (May): 532–39.

—. (1937), "The Use of Ranks to Avoid the Assumption of Normality Implicit in the Analysis of Variance." *Journal of the American Statistical Association* 32 (December): 675–701.

—. (1940), "A Comparison of Alternative Tests of Significance for the Problem of m Rankings." *Annals of Mathematical Statistics* 11 (March): 86–92.

—. (1943), "The Spendings Tax as a Wartime Fiscal Measure." *American Economic Review* 33 (March): 50–62.

—. ([1946] 1953), "Lange on Price Flexibility and Employment: A Methodological Criticism." *American Economic Review* 36 (September): 613–31. Reprinted in Milton Friedman. *Essays in Positive Economics.* Chicago: University of Chicago Press, 277–300.

—. ([1947a] 1953), "Lerner on the Economics of Control." Journal of Political Economy 55 (October): 405–16. Reprinted in Milton Friedman. *Essays in Positive Economics.* Chicago: University of Chicago Press, 301–19.

—. (1947b), "Utilization of Limited Experimental Facilities When the Cost of Each Measurement Depends on Its Magnitude." In *Techniques and Statistical Analysis,* ed. C. Eisenhart, M. W. Hastay, and W. A. Wallis, 319–28. New York: McGraw-Hill.

—. ([1948] 1953), "A Monetary and Fiscal Framework for Economic Stability." *American Economic Review* 38 (June): 245–64. Reprinted in Milton Friedman. *Essays in Positive Economics.* Chicago: University of Chicago Press, 133–56.

—. ([1949] 1953), "The Marshallian Demand Curve." *Journal of Political Economy* 57 (December): 463–95. Reprinted in Milton Friedman.

Essays in Positive Economics. Chicago: University of Chicago Press, 47–99.

—. ([1951a] 1953), "Comments on Monetary Policy." *Review of Economics and Statistics* 33 (August): 186–91. Reprinted in Milton Friedman. *Essays in Positive Economics.* Chicago: University of Chicago Press, 263–73.

—. ([1951b] 1953), "Commodity-Reserve Currency." *Journal of Political Economy* 59 (June): 203–32. Reprinted in Milton Friedman. *Essays in Positive Economics.* Chicago: University of Chicago Press, 204–50.

—. ([1951c] 1953), "The Effects of a Full-Employment Policy on Economic Stability: A Formal Analysis." Economie Appliquee 4 (July–December): 441–56. Revised and reprinted in Reprinted in Milton Friedman. *Essays in Positive Economics.* Chicago: University of Chicago Press, 117–56.

—. (1951d), "Neo-liberalism and Its Prospects." *Farmand* (February 17): 89–93. Translation available from Milton Friedman Papers, Hoover Institution, Box 42.

—. (1953), *Essays in Positive Economics.* Chicago: University of Chicago Press.

—. ([1954] 1968b), "Why The American Economy is Depression-Proof." *Nationalekonomiska Foreningens Forhandlingar.* Reprinted in Milton Friedman. *Dollars and Deficits: Inflation, Monetary Policy, and the Balance of Payments.* Englewood Cliffs, NJ: Prentice-Hall, 72–96.

—. (1955a), "Liberalism, Old Style." In *1955 Collier's Year Book.* ed. William Couch. New York: Collier's.

—. (1955b), "The Role of Government in Education." In *Economics and the Public Interest.* ed. Robert S. Solo, 123–44. New Brunswick, N.J.: Rutgers University Press. Available at *www.friedmanfoundation.org/friedmans/writings/1955.jsp.*

—, ([1956] 1987), "The Quantity Theory of Money—A Restatement." In *Studies in the Quantity Theory of Money.* ed. Milton Friedman. Chicago: University of Chicago Press. Reprinted in Kurt R. Leube, ed. *The Essence of Friedman.* Stanford: Hoover Institution Press, 285–303.

—. (1957), *A Theory of the Consumption Function.* Princeton: Princeton University Press.

—. ([1958a] 1987), "Foreign Economic Aid: Means and Objectives." *The Yale Review* 47 (Summer). Reprinted in Kurt R. Leube, ed. *The Essence of Friedman.* Stanford: Hoover Institution Press, 79–91.

—. ([1958b] 1969b), "The Supply of Money and Changes in Prices and Output." In *The Relationship of Prices to Economic Stability and Growth.* 85th Congress, 2nd Session, Joint Economic Committee Print, Washington D.C.: Government Printing Office. Reprinted in

Milton Friedman. *The Optimum Quantity of Money and Other Essays.* Chicago: Aldine Publishing, 171–87.

—. ([1959] 1969b), "The Demand for Money: Some Theoretical and Empirical Results." *The Journal of Political Economy* 67:4 (August). Reprinted in Milton Friedman. *The Optimum Quantity of Money and Other Essays.* Chicago: Aldine Publishing, 111–39.

—. (1960), *A Program for Monetary Stability.* New York City: Fordham University Press.

—. ([1961] 1969b), "The Lag in Effect of Monetary Policy." *The Journal of Political Economy* 69:5 (October). Reprinted in Milton Friedman. *The Optimum Quantity of Money and Other Essays.* Chicago: Aldine Publishing, 237–60.

—. (1962a), *Capitalism and Freedom.* Chicago: University of Chicago Press.

—. (1962b), *Price Theory: A Provisional Text.* Chicago: Aldine Publishing.

—. ([1962c] 1987), "Should There Be An Independent Monetary Authority?" In *In Search of a Monetary Constitution,* ed. Leland B. Yeager. Cambridge: Harvard University Press. Reprinted in Kurt R. Leube, ed. *The Essence of Friedman.* Stanford: Hoover Institution Press, 429–45.

—. (1964), "The Goldwater View of Economics." *New York Times* (October 11).

—. ([1966a] 1969b), "Interest Rates and the Demand for Money." *The Journal of Law and Economics.* 9 (October). Reprinted in Milton Friedman. *The Optimum Quantity of Money and Other Essays.* Chicago: Aldine Publishing, 141–55.

—. ([1966b] 1975), "A Volunteer Army" *Newsweek* (December 19). Reprinted in Milton Friedman. *There's No Such Thing as a Free Lunch: Essays on Public Policy.* LaSalle, Illinois: Open Court, 188–90.

—. ([1967a] 1987), "The Case for Abolishing the Draft—and Substituting for It an All-Volunteer Army." *The New York Times Magazine* (May 14). Reprinted in Kurt R. Leube, ed. *The Essence of Friedman.* Stanford: Hoover Institution Press, 69–78.

—. ([1967b] 1975), "Higher Taxes? No." *Newsweek* (January 23). Reprinted in Milton Friedman. *There's No Such Thing as a Free Lunch: Essays on Public Policy.* LaSalle, Illinois: Open Court, 88–89.

—. ([1967c] 1969b), "The Monetary Theory and Policy of Henry Simons." *Journal of Law and Economics* 10 (October). Reprinted in Milton Friedman. *The Optimum Quantity of Money and Other Essays.* Chicago: Aldine Publishing, 81–94.

—. ([1967d] 1975), "The Negro in America." *Newsweek* (November 11). Reprinted in Milton Friedman. *There's No Such Thing as a Free Lunch: Essays on Public Policy.* LaSalle, Illinois: Open Court, 216–18.

—. (1967e), "Value Judgments in Economics." In *Human Values and Economic Policy.* ed. Sidney Hook, 85–93. Chicago: University of Chicago Press.

—. ([1968a] 1987), "The Case for the Negative Income Tax." In *Republican Papers,* ed. Melvin R. Laird. New York: Praeger. Reprinted in Kurt R. Leube, ed. *The Essence of Friedman.* Stanford: Hoover Institution Press, 57–68.

—. (1968b), *Dollars and Deficits: Inflation, Monetary Policy, and the Balance of Payments.* Englewood Cliffs, NJ: Prentice-Hall.

—. ([1968c] 1975), "The Draft." *Newsweek* (March 11). Reprinted in Milton Friedman. *There's No Such Thing as a Free Lunch: Essays on Public Policy.* LaSalle, Illinois: Open Court, 190–92.

—. ([1968d] 1987), "The Role of Monetary Policy." *American Economic Review* 58:1 (March): 1–17. Reprinted in Kurt R. Leube, ed. *The Essence of Friedman.* Stanford: Hoover Institution Press, 387–403.

—. ([1969a] 1975), "Book-Burning, FCC Style." *Newsweek* (June 16). Reprinted in Milton Friedman. *There's No Such Thing as a Free Lunch: Essays on Public Policy.* LaSalle, Illinois: Open Court, 218–19.

—. (1969b), *The Optimum Quantity of Money and Other Essays.* Chicago: Aldine Publishing.

—. ([1970a] 1975), "Development Fashions." *Newsweek* (December 21). Reprinted in Milton Friedman. *There's No Such Thing as a Free Lunch: Essays on Public Policy.* LaSalle, Illinois: Open Court, 301–03.

—. ([1970b] 1975), "The End of the Draft?" *Newsweek* (March 16). Reprinted in Milton Friedman. *There's No Such Thing as a Free Lunch: Essays on Public Policy.* LaSalle, Illinois: Open Court, 192–94.

—. ([1970c] 1987), "The Social Responsibility of Business." *The New York Times Magazine* (September 13). Reprinted in Kurt R. Leube, ed. *The Essence of Friedman.* Stanford: Hoover Institution Press, 36–42.

—. ([1970d] 1975), "Welfare Reform Again" *Newsweek* (September 7). Reprinted in Milton Friedman. *There's No Such Thing as a Free Lunch: Essays on Public Policy.* LaSalle, Illinois: Open Court, 201–03.

—. ([1971a] 1975), "Morality and Controls" *New York Times* (October 28 and 29). Reprinted in Milton Friedman. *There's No Such Thing as a Free Lunch: Essays on Public Policy.* LaSalle, Illinois: Open Court, 129–33.

—. ([1971b] 1975), "Roofs or Ceilings." *Newsweek* (March 22). Reprinted in Milton Friedman. *There's No Such Thing as a Free Lunch: Essays on Public Policy.* LaSalle, Illinois: Open Court, 223–25.

—. ([1971c] 1975), "'Steady as You Go' Revisited." *Newsweek* (May 14). Reprinted in Milton Friedman. *There's No Such Thing as a Free Lunch: Essays on Public Policy.* LaSalle, Illinois: Open Court, 49–51.

—. ([1972a] 1975), "Can We Halt Leviathan?" *Newsweek* (November 6). Reprinted in Milton Friedman. *There's No Such Thing as a Free Lunch: Essays on Public Policy*. LaSalle, Illinois: Open Court, 99–101.

—. ([1972b] 1975), "Is Basic Welfare a Human Right?" *Newsweek* (December 18). Reprinted in Milton Friedman. *There's No Such Thing as a Free Lunch: Essays on Public Policy*. LaSalle, Illinois: Open Court, 205–07.

—. ([1972c] 1975), "Prohibition and Drugs." *Newsweek* (May 1). Reprinted in Milton Friedman. *There's No Such Thing as a Free Lunch: Essays on Public Policy*. LaSalle, Illinois: Open Court, 227–29.

—. ([1973] 1975), "A Monumental Folly." *Newsweek* (June 25). Reprinted in Milton Friedman. *There's No Such Thing as a Free Lunch: Essays on Public Policy*. LaSalle, Illinois: Open Court, 140–41.

—. (1974a), "A Theoretical Framework for Monetary Analysis." In *Milton Friedman's Monetary Framework: A Debate with his Critics*. ed. Robert J Gordon (Chicago: University of Chicago Press): 1–62.

—. ([1974b] 1975), "Volunteer Armed Force: Failure or Victim?" *Newsweek* (February 11). Reprinted in Milton Friedman. *There's No Such Thing as a Free Lunch: Essays on Public Policy*. LaSalle, Illinois: Open Court, 194–96.

—. (1975), *There's No Such Thing as a Free Lunch: Essays on Public Policy*. LaSalle, IL: Open Court.

—. ([1976a] 1978), "Adam Smith's Relevance for 1976." Selected Papers No. 50. Chicago: Graduate School of Business, The University of Chicago. Reprinted in *Adam Smith and the Wealth of Nations: 1776–1976 Bicentennial Essays*, ed. Fred R. Glahe. Boulder, CO: Colorado Associated University Press.

—. (1976b), "Homer Jones: A Personal Reminiscence." *Journal of Monetary Economics* 2: 433–36.

—. ([1976c] 1983), "Parkinson Revisited." *Newsweek* (July 12). Reprinted in Milton Friedman. *Bright Promises, Dismal Performance: An Economist's Protest*. San Diego, New York, and London: Harcourt Brace Jovanovich, 325–27.

—. ([1977a] 1987), "Nobel Lecture: Inflation and Unemployment." *Journal of Political Economy* 85 (June): 451–72. Reprinted in Kurt R. Leube, ed. *The Essence of Friedman*. Stanford: Hoover Institution Press, 347–69.

—. (1977b), "What is America?" Lecture delivered at the University of Chicago, October 3, 1977.

—. ([1978a] 1987), "The Economics of Free Speech." Reprinted in Kurt R. Leube, ed. *The Essence of Friedman*. Stanford: Hoover Institution Press, 9–17.

—. ([1978b] 1983), "In Defense of Dumping." *Newsweek* (February 20). Reprinted in Milton Friedman. *Bright Promises, Dismal Performance: An Economist's Protest.* San Diego, New York, and London: Harcourt Brace Jovanovich, 361–63.

—. ([1978c] 1983), "Is Capitalism Humane?" Reprinted in Milton Friedman. *Bright Promises, Dismal Performance: An Economist's Protest.* San Diego, New York, and London: Harcourt Brace Jovanovich, 83–90.

—. ([1978d] 1983), "The Kemp-Roth Free Lunch." *Newsweek* (August 7). Reprinted in Milton Friedman. *Bright Promises, Dismal Performance: An Economist's Protest.* San Diego, New York, and London: Harcourt Brace Jovanovich, 322–24.

—. ([1978e] 1983), "What Belongs to Whom?" *Newsweek* (March 13). Reprinted in Milton Friedman. *Bright Promises, Dismal Performance: An Economist's Protest.* San Diego, New York, and London: Harcourt Brace Jovanovich, 99–101.

—. (1979a), "Don't Draft GI Joe." *Newsweek* (April 16).

—. (1979b), "Universal National Service." *Newsweek* (May 14).

—. ([1980a] 1983), "Balanced on Paper." *Newsweek* (June 23). Reprinted in Milton Friedman. *Bright Promises, Dismal Performance: An Economist's Protest.* San Diego, New York, and London: Harcourt Brace Jovanovich, 119–21.

—. (1980b), "The Draft Isn't the Issue." *Newsweek* (Sept 29).

—. (1980c), "Draft Registration." *Newsweek* (February 11).

—. ([1980d] 1983), "Economic Sanctions." *Newsweek* (January 21). Reprinted in Milton Friedman. *Bright Promises, Dismal Performance: An Economist's Protest.* San Diego, New York, and London: Harcourt Brace Jovanovich, 370–72.

—. ([1980e] 1983), "Our Hidden New Taxes." *Newsweek* (April 14). Reprinted in Milton Friedman. *Bright Promises, Dismal Performance: An Economist's Protest.* San Diego, New York, and London: Harcourt Brace Jovanovich, 316–18.

—. ([1981] 1983), "Whose Money Is It Anyway?" *Newsweek* (May 4). Reprinted in Milton Friedman. *Bright Promises, Dismal Performance: An Economist's Protest.* San Diego, New York, and London: Harcourt Brace Jovanovich, 303–06.

—. (1983), *Bright Promises, Dismal Performance: An Economist's Protest.* San Diego, New York, and London: Harcourt Brace Jovanovich.

—. ([1984a] 1987), "Capitalism and the Jews: Confronting a Paradox." *Encounter* 63:1 (June). Reprinted in Kurt R. Leube, ed. *The Essence of Friedman.* Stanford: Hoover Institution Press, 43–56.

—. ([1984b] 1987), "Monetary Policy for the 1980's." In *To Promote Prosperity: U.S. Domestic Policy in the Mid–1980's,* ed. John H. Moore.

Stanford: Hoover Institution Press. Reprinted in Kurt R. Leube, ed. *The Essence of Friedman.* Stanford: Hoover Institution Press, 404–28.

—. ([1986] 2004), "Milton Friedman." In *Lives of the Laureates: Eighteen Nobel Economists.* 4th ed., ed. William Breit and Barry T. Hirsch, 65–77. Cambridge: MIT Press.

—. ([1987] 1987), "Quantity Theory of Money." In *The New Palgrave: A Dictionary of Economics,* 4 vols. London: Macmillan; New York: Stockton Press. Adapted and reprinted in Kurt R. Leube, ed. *The Essence of Friedman.* Stanford: Hoover Institution Press, 370–84.

—. (1988a), "Letter to the Editor: Any Reaction to Friedman's Travels?" *Stanford Daily,* October 27, 1988.

—. (1988b), "Stop Taxing Non-Addicts." *Reason Magazine* (October).

—. (1988c), "Tribute to Arthur F. Burns by Milton Friedman." In *In Memoriam: Arthur F. Burns, 1904–1987.* Washington D.C. American Enterprise Institute for Public Policy Research, 6–11.

—. (1989), "An Open Letter to Bill Bennett." *Wall Street Journal* (September 7).

—. (1991), "The War We Are Losing." In *Searching for Alternatives: Drug-Control Policy in the United States,* ed. Melvyn B. Krauss and Edward P. Lazear, 53–67. Stanford: Hoover Institution Press.

—. (1992a), "The Drug War as a Socialist Enterprise." In *Friedman and Szasz on Liberty and Drugs.* ed. Arnold S. Trebach and Kevin B. Zeese. Washington, D.C.: The Drug Policy Foundation.

—. (1992b), "Milton Friedman: Autobiography." *In Nobel Lectures, Economics 1969–1980.* ed. Assar Lindbeck. Singapore: World Scientific Publishing Co.

—. ([1992c] 1994), *Money Mischief: Episodes in Monetary History.* Harvest Edition. San Diego, New York, and London: Harcourt Brace and Company.

—. (1993), *Why Government is the Problem.* Stanford: Hoover Institution Press.

—. (2002), "My Five Favorite Libertarian Books." *Freeman* 52:4 (April).

—. ([2005a] 2006), "Education, the Next 50 Years." *American Spectator* (November). Reprinted as "Epilogue: School Vouchers Turn 50, But the Fight Is Just Beginning." In *Liberty and Learning: Milton Friedman's Voucher Idea at Fifty,* ed. Robert C. Enlow and Lenore T. Ealy Washington, 155–58. Washington, D.C.: Cato Institute.

—. ([2005b] 2006), "Free to Choose" Wall Street Journal (June 9). Rev. and reprinted as "Prologue: A Personal Retrospective." In *Liberty and Learning: Milton Friedman's Voucher Idea at Fifty,* ed. Robert C. Enlow and Lenore T. Ealy Washington, vii–x. Washington, D.C.: Cato Institute.

—. (2009), "Final Word." In *The Methodology of Positive Economics: Reflections on the Milton Friedman Legacy,* ed. Uskali Mäki, 355. Cambridge: Cambridge University Press.

Co-authored Works by Milton Friedman

Shoup, Carl S., Milton Friedman, and Ruth P. Mack. (1943), *Taxing to Prevent Inflation: Techniques for Estimating Revenue Requirements.* New York: Columbia University Press.

Friedman, Milton and Simon Smith Kuznets. (1945), *Income from Independent Professional Practice.* New York: National Bureau of Economic Research.

Friedman, Milton, and George Stigler. (1946), *Roofs or Ceilings?: The Current Housing Problem.* Popular Essays on Current Problems, Vol. 1, No. 2. Irvington on Hudson, NY: Foundation for Economic Education. Available at http://fee.org/library/books/roofs-or-ceilings-the-current-housing-problem/.

Freeman, Harvey A., Milton Friedman, Frederick Mosteller, and W. Allen Wallis. (1948), *Sampling Inspection.* New York: McGraw-Hill.

Friedman, Milton, and L. J. Savage. (1948), "The Utility Analysis of Choices Involving Risk." *Journal of Political Economy* 56: 4 (August): 279–304.

Friedman, Milton, and L. J. Savage. (1952), "The Expected-Utility Hypothesis and the Measurability of Utility." *Journal of Political Economy* 60: 6 (December): 463–74.

Friedman, Milton, and David Meiselman. (1963), "The Relative Stability of Monetary Velocity and the Investment Multiplier in the United States, 1897–1958." In *Stabilization Policies.* Englewood Cliffs, NJ: Prentice-Hall.

Friedman, Milton, and Anna Jacobson Schwartz. (1963), *A Monetary History of the United States, 1867–1960.* Princeton: Princeton University Press.

Friedman, Milton, and Walter W. Heller. (1969), *Monetary vs. Fiscal Policy: A Dialogue.* New York: Norton and Company.

Friedman, Milton, and Anna Jacobson Schwartz. (1970), *Monetary Statistics of the United States: Estimates, Sources, Methods.* New York: Columbia University Press.

Friedman, Milton, and Rose D. Friedman. ([1980] 1990), *Free to Choose: A Personal Statement.* Harvest Edition. San Diego, New York, and London: Harcourt.

Friedman, Milton, and Paul A. Samuelson. (1980), *Milton Friedman and Paul A. Samuelson Discuss the Economic Responsibility of Government.* College Station, TX: Texas A&M University.

Friedman, Milton, and Anna Jacobson Schwartz. (1982), *Monetary Trends in the United States and the United Kingdom.* Chicago: University of Chicago Press.

Friedman, Milton, and Anna Jacobson Schwartz. ([1986] 1987), "Has Government Any Role in Money?" *Journal of Monetary Economics* 17: 37–62. Reprinted in Kurt R. Leube, ed. *The Essence of Friedman.* Stanford: Hoover Institution Press, 499–525.

Friedman, Milton, and Rose D. Friedman. (1998), *Two Lucky People: Memoirs.* Chicago: University of Chicago Press.

Friedman, Milton, John Mackey, and T. J. Rodgers. (2005), "Rethinking the Social Responsibility of Business?: A Reason Debate Featuring Milton Friedman, Whole Foods' John Mackey, and Cypress Semiconductor's T. J. Rodgers." *Reason* (October). Available at http://reason.com/archives/2005/10/01/rethinking-the-social-responsi/singlepage.

Interviews, Documentaries, and Testimony

Academy of Achievement Interview. (1991). Available at http://www.achievement.org/autodoc/page/fri0int-1.

American Prospect Interview. (2005). Robert Kuttner. "Agreeing to Disagree" *American Prospect* (December 18). Available at http://www.prospect.org/cs/articles?articleId=10764.

Booknotes Interview. (1994). Brian Lamb. "Introduction to the 50th Anniversary Edition of F. A. Hayek's Road to Serfdom." *Booknotes.* (November 20). Available at http://www.booknotes.org/Transcript/?ProgramID=1226.

Borders Interview of Charles Murray. (2006). Max Borders. "The Plan to Replace the Welfare State." (March 28). Available at http://www.aei.org/article/24127.

Business and Society Review Interview. (1972). "Milton Friedman Responds." *Business and Society Review* 1 (Spring 1972): 5–16.

Commanding Heights Interview. (2000). Available at http://www.pbs.org/wgbh/commandingheights/shared/minitext/int_milton-friedman.html#1.

Fox Interview. (2004). David Asman. "'Your World' Interview with Economist Milton Friedman." Fox News. (November 16). Available at www.foxnews.com/story/0,2933,230045,00.html.

Friedman, Milton. (1942), "Statement by Milton Friedman before the Ways and Means Committee of the House of Representatives, May 7, 1942." Milton Friedman Papers, Hoover Institution. Box 37, Folder 17.

Goldring Interview of David Friedman. (2009). Ariel Goldring, "An Interview with David Friedman." Available at http://freemarketmojo.com/?p=5539.

Hammond, J. Daniel. (1992), "An Interview with Milton Friedman on Methodology." *Research in the History of Economic Thought and Methodology, Volume 10.* Greenwich, CT: JAI Press.

Hawkins Interview. (No date). John Hawkins. "An Interview with Milton Friedman." *Right Wing News.* Available at http://www.rightwingnews.com/interviews/friedman.php.

Hoover Digest Interview. (1998). Peter Brimelow. "Milton Friedman, Soothsayer." *Hoover Digest* 2. Available at http://www.vdare.com/pb/060914_friedman.htm.

ISIL Interview. (1999). Available at http://www.vdare.com/misc/archive00/friedman.htm.

Liberty Fund Interview. 2003. *The Intellectual Portrait Series: A Conversation with Milton Friedman* (Indianapolis: Liberty Fund). Available at http://oll.libertyfund.org/index.php?option=com_staticxt&staticfile=show.php%3Ftitle=975&Itemid=29.

Marijuana Policy Project Interview. (No date - circa 2006). Available at http://tv.mpp.org/shorts/profiles-in-marijuana-reform-milton-friedman-part-1.

Mont Pelerin Society Meeting Interview. (2002). Available at http://200.0.176.35/gsm/index.php?title=Interview_with_Rose_and_Milton_Friedman.

New Perspectives Quarterly Interview. (2006). Nathan Gardels. "Free Markets and the End of History." *New Perspectives Quarterly* (Spring). Available at http://www.digitalnpq.org/archive/2006_winter/friedman.html.

Open Mind Interview. (1975). Broadcast in New York City on WPIX, Channel 11 Sunday, December 7, 1975, 10:30 – 11:00 P.M. Moderator/Host Richard D. Heffner. Available at http://www.theopenmind.tv/searcharchive_episode_transcript.asp?searchString=extreme&id=494.

Paige Interview. (1991). Randy Paige, "Interview with Milton Friedman on the Drug War." *America's Drug Forum.* Available at www.druglibrary.com/schaffer/misc/friedm1.htm.

Playboy Interview. ([1973] 1983), "Playboy Interview." *Playboy* (February). Reprinted in Milton Friedman. *Bright Promises, Dismal Performance: An Economist's Protest.* San Diego, New York, and London: Harcourt Brace Jovanovich, 9–59.

The Power of Choice: The Life and Ideas of Milton Friedman. (2006), Produced by Katherine Anderson. 90 min. Free to Choose Media. DVD.

Reason Interview. (1995). Brian Doherty. "Best of Both Worlds." *Reason* (June). Available at http://reason.com/archives/1995/06/01/best-of-both-worlds.

Roberts Interview. (2006). Russell Roberts, "An Interview with Milton Friedman." *Econlib.* (September 6). Available at http://www.econlib.org/library/Columns/y2006/Friedmantranscript.html.

Times Herald Interview. (1978). "Milton Friedman Interviewed." *The Times Herald* (Norristown, PA). (December 1). Available at http://www.cooperativeindividualism.org/friedman-milton_interview-1978.html.

Uncommon Knowledge (Hoover) Interview. (1999). Peter Robinson. "Take it to the Limits: Milton Friedman on Libertarianism." *Uncommon Knowledge.* (February 10). Available at http://www.hoover.org/multimedia/uncommon-knowledge/26936.

Wall Street Journal Interview. (2006). Tunku Varadarajan. "Rose and Milton Friedman: The Romance of Economics." *Wall Street Journal* (July 22). Available at http://online.wsj.com/article/SB115352827130914276.html.

Works by Others

Anderson, Martin. (1982), *The Military Draft: Selected Readings on Conscription.* Stanford: Hoover Institution Press.

Backhouse, Roger E. (2009), "Friedman's 1953 Essay and the Marginalist Controversy." In *The Methodology of Positive Economics: Reflections on the Milton Friedman Legacy,* ed. Uskali Mäki, 217–40. Cambridge: Cambridge University Press.

Baltimore, David, and S. E. Luria. (1976), "To the Editor." *New York Times* (October 24).

Bandow, Doug. (2006), "Losing a Giant of Liberty." *American Spectator Online* (November 20).

Bangs, Robert. (1947), "Book Review: *Roofs or Ceilings?*" *American Economic Review* 37:3 (June): 482–83.

Becker, Gary S. (1957), *The Economics of Discrimination.* Chicago: University of Chicago Press.

—. (1991), "Milton Friedman." In *Remembering the University of Chicago: Teachers, Scientists, and Scholars,* ed. Edward Shils, 138–46. Chicago: University of Chicago Press.

Bender, Marylin. (1971), "Chicago School Goes to the Head of the Class." *New York Times* (May 23).

Bernanke, Ben S. (2000), *Essays on the Great Depression.* Princeton: Princeton University Press.

—. (2002), "Remarks by Governor Ben S. Bernanke at the Conference to Honor Milton Friedman, University of Chicago, Chicago, Illinois." Available at http://www.federalreserve.gov/BOARDDOCS/SPEECHES/2002/20021108/default.htm.

—. (2004), "Friedman's Monetary Framework: Some Lessons." In *The Legacy of Milton and Rose Friedman's Free to Choose,* ed. Mark A. Wayne, Harvey Rosenblum, and Robert L. Formaini, 207–14. Dallas: Federal Reserve Bank of Dallas.

Bernstein, David. (2010), "Context Matters: A Better Libertarian Approach to Anti-Discrimination Law." *Cato Unbound.* June 16. Available at http://www.cato-unbound.org/2010/06/16/david-bernstein/context-matters-a-better-libertarian-approach-to-antidiscrimination-law/.

Blaug, Mark. (2009), "The Debate Over F53 After Fifty Years." In *The Methodology of Positive Economics: Reflections on the Milton Friedman Legacy,* ed. Uskali Mäki, 349–54. Cambridge: Cambridge University Press.

Boaz, David. (1997), *Libertarianism: A Primer.* New York: The Free Press.

Boettke, Peter J. (2004), "Milton and Rose Friedman's 'Free to Choose' and Its Impact in the Global Movement Toward Free Market Policy: 1979–2003." In *The Legacy of Milton and Rose Friedman's Free to Choose,* ed. Mark A. Wayne, Harvey Rosenblum, and Robert L. Formaini, 137–52. Dallas: Federal Reserve Bank of Dallas.

Boland, Lawrence A. (1979), "A Critique of Friedman's Critics." *Journal of Economic Literature* 17:2 (June): 503–22.

Brandl, John E. (2006), "Choice, Religion, Community, and Educational Quality." In *Liberty and Learning: Milton Friedman's Voucher Idea at Fifty,* ed. Robert C. Enlow and Lenore T. Ealy, 25–34. Washington D.C.: Cato Institute.

Breit, William, and Barry T. Hirsch, eds. (2004), *Lives of the Laureates: Eighteen Nobel Economists.* 4th ed. Cambridge: MIT Press.

Breit, William, and John H. Huston. (1997), "Reputation versus Influence: The Evidence from Textbook References." *Eastern Economic Journal* 23:4 (Fall): 451–56.

Breit, William, and Roger L. Ransom. (1971), *The Academic Scribblers: American Economists in Collision.* New York: Holt, Rinehart, and Winston.

Bronfenbrenner, M. (1962), "Observations on the 'Chicago School(s)' " *Journal of Political Economy* 70:1 (February): 72–75.

Buckley, William F. (2006), "Milton Friedman, R.I.P." *National Review Online.* (November 21). Available at http://article.nationalreview.com/299173/milton-friedman-rip/william-f-buckley-jr.

Bullock, Penn. (2009), "Friedman Economics: Is Fed chairman Ben Bernanke a follower of John Maynard Keynes or Milton Friedman?"

Reason (September 1). Available at http://reason.com/archives/2009/09/01/friedman-economics/print.

Bureau of Economic Analysis, U.S. Department of Commerce. National Economic Accounts. National Income and Products Accounts Table. Table 1.1.6. Real Gross Domestic Product, Chained Dollars.

Burton, John. (1981), "Positively Milton Friedman." In *Twelve Contemporary Economists*, ed. J. R. Shackleton and Gareth Locksley, 53–71. New York: John Wiley and Sons.

Business Week. (1967), "Maverick in the Fed System." *Business Week*. (November 18).

Caldwell, Bruce J. (1980), "Critique of Friedman's Methodological Instrumentalism." *Southern Economic Journal* 47:2 (October): 366–74.

Capaldi, Nicholas. (2004), *John Stuart Mill: A Biography*. Cambridge: Cambridge University Press.

Cherrier, Beatrice. (n.d.), "The Lucky Consistency of Milton Friedman's Science and Politics, 1933–1963."

Christ, Carl F. (1994), "The Cowles Commission's Contributions to Econometrics at Chicago 1939–1955." *Journal of Economic Literature* 32:1 (March): 30–59.

Ciulla, Joanne, and Clancy Martin and Robert Solomon, eds. (2010), *Honest Work: A Business Ethics Reader*. Oxford: Oxford University Press.

Cockett, Richard. ([1994] 1995), *Thinking the Unthinkable: Think-Tanks and the Economic Counter-Revolution, 1931–1983*. London: Fontana Press. HarperCollins did first one.

Cole, Julio H. (2007), "Milton Friedman, 1912–2006." *Independent Review* 12:1 (Summer): 115–28.

Cowen, Tyler. (2009a), "Were the Bailouts a Good Idea?" *Marginal Revolution Blog*. Available online at http://www.marginalrevolution.com/marginalrevolution/2009/08/were-the-bailouts-a-good-idea.html.

—. (2009b), "What Did Milton Friedman Favor?" *Marginal Revolution Blog*. Available online at http://www.marginalrevolution.com/marginalrevolution/2009/08/what-did-milton-friedman-favor.html.

Crook, Clive. (2006), "On Milton Friedman's Unfinished *Work" Atlantic Unbound* (December). Available at http://www.theatlantic.com/magazine/archive/2006/12/on-milton-friedman-apos-s-unfinished-work/5498/.

DeLong, J. Bradford. (2000a), "Correspondence" *The Journal of Economic Perspectives* 14:4 (Fall): 227.

—. (2000b), "The Triumph of Monetarism?" *The Journal of Economic Perspectives* 14:1 (Winter): 82–94.

De Vroey, Michel. (2009), "On the Right Side for the Wrong Reason: Friedman on the Marshall-Walras Divide." In *The Methodology of*

Positive Economics: Reflections on the Milton Friedman Legacy, ed. Uskali Mäki, 321–46. Cambridge: Cambridge University Press.

Dillard, Dudley. (1957), "The Influence of Keynesian Economics on Contemporary Thought." *American Economic Review* 47:2 (May): 77–87.

Doherty, Brian. (2007), *Radicals for Capitalism: A Freewheeling History of the Modern Libertarian Movement.* New York: Public Affairs.

Dworkin, Ronald. (1978), *Taking Rights Seriously.* Cambridge: Harvard University Press.

Dwyer, Gerald P. (1999), "How Was Milton Friedman Distinctive as a Teacher?" In *The Legacy of Milton Friedman as Teacher,* ed. J. Daniel Hammond, 3–8. Cheltenham, UK: Edward Elgar.

Ebenstein, Lanny. (2007), *Milton Friedman: A Biography.* New York: Palgrave Macmillan.

Elliott, Alan C., and Wayne A. Woodward. (2007), *Statistical Analysis Quick Reference Guidebook: With SPSS Examples.* Thousand Oaks, CA; Sage.

Enlow, Robert C., and Lenore T. Ealy. (2006), *Liberty and Learning: Milton Friedman's Voucher Idea at Fifty.* Washington D.C.: Cato Institute.

Fand, David I. (1999), "Friedman's Price Theory: Economics 300 at the University of Chicago in 1947–1951." In *The Legacy of Milton Friedman as Teacher,* ed. J. Daniel Hammond, 9–21. Cheltenham, UK: Edward Elgar.

Five Books (2010), "Mitch Daniels on American Conservatism." http://fivebooks.com/interviews/mitch-daniels-on-how-libertarians-can-govern.

Frängsmyr, Tore, ed. (1996), The Nobel Prize 1995. Stockholm: Nobel Foundation. Available at http://nobelprize.org/nobel_prizes/economics/laureates/1995/lucas.html.

—, ed. (2001), *The Nobel Prizes 2000.* Stockholm: Nobel Foundation. Available at http://nobelprize.org/nobel_prizes/economics/laureates/2000/heckman-autobio.html.

Frank, Robert. (2006), "The Other Milton Friedman: A Conservative With a Social Welfare Program." *New York Times* November 23, 2006.

Frazer, William. (1988), *Power and Ideas: Milton Friedman and the Big U-Turn.* 2 vols. Gainesville, FL: Gulf/Atlantic Publishing.

Frazer, William J, Jr., and Lawrence A. Boland. (1983), "An Essay on the Foundations of Friedman's Methodology." *American Economic Review* 73:1 (March): 129–44.

Fricke, Thomas. (2010), "Okonomenumfrage 2010." *Financial Times Deutschland* (25 June). Available at http://www.Ftd.de/wirtschafts wunder/index.php?op=ViewArticle&articleId=2448&blogId=10.

Friedman, David. (1973), *The Machinery of Freedom.* New York: Harper and Row.

Friedman, Patri. "Beyond Folk Activism." Cato Unbound. April 6, 2009. Available at http://www.cato-unbound.org/2009/04/06/patri-friedman/beyond-folk-activism/.

Friedman, Rose D. (1976a), "Milton Friedman: Husband and Colleague—(1) Early Years." *Oriental Economist* (May): 28–32.

—. (1976b), "Milton Friedman: Husband and Colleague—(2) The Beginning of a Career." *Oriental Economist* (June): 18–22.

—. (1976c), "Milton Friedman: Husband and Colleague—(3) The Beginning of a Teaching Career." *Oriental Economist* (July): 18–23.

—. (1976d), "Milton Friedman: Husband and Colleague—(4) The Years 1946–1953." *Oriental Economist* (August): 21–26.

—. (1976e), "Milton Friedman: Husband and Colleague—(5) A Spokesman for Libertarianism." *Oriental Economist* (September): 22–27.

—. (1976f), "Milton Friedman: Husband and Colleague—(6) Milton Friedman and Monetarism." *Oriental Economist* (October): 22–26.

—. (1976g), "Milton Friedman: Husband and Colleague—(7) Journalist and Lecturer." *Oriental Economist* (November): 16–21.

Garraty, John A. (1987), *The Great Depression.* Garden City, NJ: Anchor Books.

Goodman, Peter S. (2008), "A Fresh Look at the Apostle of Free Markets." *New York Times* (April13).

Gordon, Robert J., ed. (1974), *Milton Friedman's Monetary Framework: A Debate with His Critics.* Chicago: University of Chicago Press.

Hammond, J. Daniel. "Columbia Roots of the Chicago School: The Case of Milton Friedman." December 2000. Unpublished Paper.

Hammond, J. Daniel, ed. (1999), *The Legacy of Milton Friedman as Teacher.* Cheltenham, UK: Edward Elgar.

Hansen, Alvin H. (1938), *Full Recovery or Stagnation?* New York: Norton.

—. (1941), *Fiscal Policy and Business Cycles.* New York: Norton.

Hanushek, Eric A. (2006), "Is There Hope for Expanded School Choice." In *Liberty and Learning: Milton Friedman's Voucher Idea at Fifty,* ed. Robert C. Enlow and Lenore T. Ealy Washington, 67–80. Washington, D.C.: Cato Institute .

Harberger, Arnold. (1976), "Setting the Record Straight on Chile." *Wall Street Journal* (December 10). Reprinted in Friedman, Milton, and Rose D. Friedman. (1998), *Two Lucky People: Memoirs.* Chicago: University of Chicago Press.

Hartwell, R. M. (1995), *A History of the Mont Pelerin Society.* Indianapolis: Liberty Fund.

Hasnas, John. (1998), "The Normative Theories of Business Ethics: A Guide for the Perplexed." *Business Ethics Quarterly* 8:1 (January): 19–42.

Hayek, Friedrich A. (1960), *The Constitution of Liberty.* Chicago: University of Chicago Press.

Heinemann, H. Erich. (1968), "Friedman-Heller Debate Proves an Even Match." *New York Times* (November 15): 65, 76.

Henderson, David. (2005), "The Role of Economists in Ending the Draft." *Econ Journal Watch* 2:2 (August): 362–76.

—. (2006), "Milton Friedman: A Tribute." *Antiwar.com* (November 20). Available at http://www.antiwar.com/henderson/?articleid=10042.

Henderson, David, ed. (2008), *The Concise Encyclopedia of Economics.* Indianapolis, IN: Liberty Fund. Hetzel, Robert L. (2007), "The Contributions of Milton Friedman to Economics." *Economic Quarterly* 93:1 (Winter): 1–30.

Hirsch, Abraham and Neil De Marchi. (1984), "Methodology: A Comment on Frazer and Boland, I." *American Economics Review* 74:4 (September): 782–88.

—. (1990), *Milton Friedman: Economics in Theory and Practice.* Ann Arbor: University of Michigan Press.

Hoover, Kevin. (2009), "Milton Friedman's Stance: The Methodology of Causal Realism." In *The Methodology of Positive Economics: Reflections on the Milton Friedman Legacy,* ed. Uskali Mäki, 285–302. Cambridge: Cambridge University Press.

Johnson, Harry G. (1976), "A Tribute to Homer Jones." *Journal of Monetary Economics* 2: 437–38.

Johnson, Paul. (1997), *A History of the American People.* New York: Harper Collins.

Kaldor, N. (1970), "The New Monetarism." *Lloyds Bank Review* (March): 1–17.

Kandell, Jonathan. (1975), "Chilean Junta Resisting Critics." *New York Times.* (September 21).

Kearl, J. R., Clayne Pope, Gordon C. Whiting, and Larry T. Wimmer. (1979), "A Confusion of Economists?" *American Economic Review* 69:2 (May): 28–37.

Keyes, Ralph. (2006), *The Quote Verifier: Who Said What, Where, and When.* New York: St. Martin's Griffin.

Keynes, John Maynard. (1936), *The General Theory of Employment Interest and Money.* New York: Harcourt, Brace, and Company.

Kirzner, Israel M. (1967), "Divergent Approaches in Libertarian Economic Thought." *Intercollegiate Review* 3 (January–February): 101–08.

Klamer, Arjo. (1983), *Conversations with Economists: New Classical Economists and Opponents Speak Out on the Current Controversy in Macroeconomics.* Totowa, NJ: Rowman and Allanheld.

Klein, Naomi. (2007), *The Shock Doctrine: The Rise of Disaster Capitalism.* New York: Metropolitan Books.

Kraus, Albert L. (1968), "Friedman: A Challenger." *New York Times* (November 13): 61, 63.

Krugman, Paul. (2007), "Who Was Milton Friedman?" *The New York Review of Books* 54:2 (February 15). Available at http://www.nybooks.com/articles/archives/2007/feb/15/who-was-milton-friedman/?pagination=false.

Laird, Melvin R., ed. (1964), *The Conservative Papers.* New York: Doubleday Anchor.

—. ed. (1968), *Republican Papers.* New York: Praeger.

Lampman, Robert J., ed. (1993), *Economists at Wisconsin, 1892–1992.* Madison: University of Wisconsin Press.

Lebergott, Stanley. (1964), *Manpower in Economic Growth: The American Record since 1800.* New York: McGraw-Hill.

Leeson, Robert. (2000), "Patinkin, Johnson, and the Shadow of Friedman." *History of Political Economy* 32:4 (Winter): 733–63.

Leeson, Robert, ed. (2003), *Keynes, Chicago, and Friedman.* London: Pickering and Chatto.

Letelier, Orlando. (1976), "The Chicago Boys in Chile: Economic Freedom's Awful Toll." *The Nation* (August 28).

Lewis, Anthony. (1975), "For Which We Stand: II." *New York Times* (October 2).

Lindbeck, Assar, ed. (1992), *Nobel Lectures, Economics 1969–1980.* Singapore: World Scientific Publishing Co. Available at http://nobelprize.org/nobel_prizes/economics/laureates/1976/friedman.html.

Machan, Tibor R., and Douglas J. Den Uyl. (1987), "Recent Works in Business Ethics: A Survey and Critique." *American Philosophical Quarterly* 24:2 (April): 107–24.

Macpherson, C. B. (1968), "Elegant Tombstones: A Note On Friedman's Freedom." *Canadian Journal of Political Science* 1 (March): 95–106.

Mäki, Uskali. (1986), "Rhetoric at the Expense of Coherence: A Reinterpretation of Milton Friedman's Methodology." *Research in the History of Economic Thought and Methodology* 4: 127–43.

—. (1992), "Friedman and Realism." *Research in the History of Economic Thought and Methodology* 10: 171–95.

—. (2009), *The Methodology of Positive Economics: Reflections on the Milton Friedman Legacy.* Cambridge: Cambridge University Press.

Marshall, Jonathan. (1990), "Economists Say Iraq's Threat to U.S. Oil Supply is Exaggerated." *San Francisco Chronicle* (October 29): A14.

Mayer, Thomas. (2009), "The Influence of Friedman's Methodological Essay." In *The Methodology of Positive Economics: Reflections on the Milton Friedman Legacy*, ed. Uskali Mäki, 119–42. Cambridge: Cambridge University Press.

McAleer, Sean. (2003), "Friedman's Stockholder Theory of Corporate Moral Responsibility." *Teaching Business Ethics* 7:4 (November): 437–51.

McArdle, Megan. "Milton Friedman and Chile." *The Atlantic Online*. July 15, 2008. Available at http://www.theatlantic.com/business/archive/2008/07/milton-friedman-and-chile/3841/FirefoxHTML%5CShell%5COpen%5CCommand.

Meltzer, Allan H. (2004), "Choosing Freely: The Friedmans' Influence on Economic and Social Policy." In *The Legacy of Milton and Rose Friedman's Free to Choose*, ed. Mark A. Wayne, Harvey Rosenblum, and Robert L. Formaini, 191–205. Dallas: Federal Reserve Bank of Dallas.

Mill, John Stuart. ([1859] 1879), *On Liberty and the Subjection of Women*. New York: Henry Holt.

Mirowski, Philip. (2002), *Machine Dreams. Economics Becomes Cyborg Science*. Cambridge: Cambridge University Press.

Mirowski, Philip, and D. Wade Hands. (1998), "A Paradox of Budgets." In *From Interwar Pluralism to Postwar Neoclassicism*. Supplement to vol. 30 of *History of Political Economy*, ed. M. Morgan and M. Rutherford, 260–92. Durham, NC: Duke University Press.

Modigliani, Franco, and Richard H. Brumberg. (1954), "Utility Analysis and the Consumption Function: An Interpretation of Cross-Section Data." In *Post-Keynesian Economics*, ed. Kenneth K. Kurihara, 388–436. New Brunswick, NJ: Rutgers University Press.

Moffitt, Robert A. (2003), "The Negative Income Tax and the Evolution of U.S. Welfare Policy." *The Journal of Economic Perspectives* 17:3 (Summer): 119–40.

Moore, Stephen. (2009), "Missing Milton: Who Will Speak for Free Markets?" *The Wall Street Journal* (May 29): W13.

Muller, Jerry Z. (2010), *Capitalism and the Jews*. Princeton: Princeton University Press.

Murray, Charles. (2006), *In Our Hands : A Plan To Replace The Welfare State*. Washington, D.C.: AEI Press.

Nagel, Ernest. (1963), "Assumptions in Economic Theory." *American Economic Review* 53:2 (May): 211–19.

Noble, Holcomb B. (2006), "Milton Friedman, Free Market Theorist, Dies at 94." *New York Times* (November 16).

Norberg, Johan. (2008), "Defaming Milton Friedman." *Reason* (October). Available at http://reason.com/archives/2008/09/26/defaming-milton-friedman.

Ormerod, Paul. (2006), "The Fading of Friedman." *Prospect* 129 (December 16). Available at http://www.prospectmagazine.co.uk/2006/12/thefadingoffriedman/.

Overtveldt, Johan Van. (2007), *The Chicago School: How the University of Chicago Assembled the Thinkers Who Revolutionized Economics and Business.* Chicago: Agate Publishing.

Paine, Thomas. ([1791] 1955), *Rights of Man. In Collected Writings.* New York: The Library of America.

Patinkin, Don. (1969), "The Chicago Tradition, The Quantity Theory and Friedman." *Money, Credit, and Banking* 1:1 (February): 46–70.

Peterson, Jonathan. (2006), "Nobel Winner Milton Friedman Dies at 94." *Los Angeles Times* (November 16).

Phelps, Edmund. (1967), "Phillips Curves, Expectations of Inflation and Optimal Employment over Time." *Economica* 34:3 (August): 254–81.

Phillips, A. W. (1958), "The Relation Between Unemployment and the Rate of Change of Money Wage Rates in the United Kingdom, 1861–1957." *Economica,* 25:100 (November): 283–99.

Pipes, Daniel. (1991), "Book Review of *America Entangled* (and exchange with William Niskanan)" *Orbis* (Fall). Available at http://www.danielpipes.org/529/america-entangled-the-persian-gulf-crisis-and-its.

Rayack, Elton. (1987), *Not So Free to Choose: The Political Economy of Milton Friedman and Ronald Reagan.* New York: Praeger.

Redburn, Tom. (2007), "It's All a Grand Capitalist Conspiracy." *New York Times* (September 25).

Reder, Melvin W. (1982), "Chicago Economics: Permanence and Change." *Journal of Economic Literature* 20 (March): 1–38.

Report of the President's Commission on an All-Volunteer Armed Force. (1970), Washington, D.C.: U.S. Government Printing Office.

Richman, Sheldon. (2000), "Annotated Bibliography of Frédéric Bastiat." Available at http://www.econlib.org/library/Bastiat/BastiatBib.html.

Root, Damon W. (2009), "Hating Milton Friedman: A Proud Father of Global Prosperity." *Reason* (May).

Rossant, M. J. (1964), "A Talk With a Goldwater Man." *New York Times* (October 8).

Rostker, Bernard. (2006), *I Want You! The Evolution of the All-Volunteer Force.* Santa Monica: RAND Corporation.

Rothbard, Murray N. ([1971] 2002), "Milton Friedman Unraveled" *Journal of Libertarian Studies* 16:4 (Fall): 37–53. Originally in The Individualist 1971.

Rotwein, Eugene. (1983), "Jacob Viner and the Chicago Tradition." *History of Political Economy* 15:2 (Summer): 265–80.

Samuelson, Paul. (1963), "Discussion." *American Economic Review* 53:3 (May): 231–36.

Sanders, Bernie. (2009), "The Failed Prophet: As Wall Street Collapses, So Does Milton Friedman's Legacy." *In These Times* (February). Available at http://inthesetimes.com/article/4193/the_failed_prophet.

Schivelbusch, Wolfgang. (2006), *Three New Deals: Reflections on Roosevelt's America, Mussolini's Italy, and Hitler's Germany, 1933–1939.* New York: Picador.

Schmidt, Peter. (2010), "U. of Chicago Plans for Milton Friedman Institute Stir Outrage on the Faculty." *The Chronicle of Higher Education* (June 1) Available at http://chronicle.com/article/U-of-Chicagos-Plans-for/65737/.

Schwartz, Anna J. (2008a), "Bernanke is Fighting the Last War." *Wall Street Journal.* October 18, 2008.

—. (2008b), "Monetary Policy and the Legacy of Milton Friedman." *Cato Journal* 28:2 (Spring/Summer): 255–62.

Schwartz, Maralee. (1989), "Talking Points." *Washington Post* (September 19).

Selgin, George. (1988), *The Theory of Free Banking: Money Supply under Competitive Note Issue.* Totowa, N.J.: Rowman & Littlefield.

—. (2008), "Milton Friedman and the Case Against Currency Monopoly." *Cato Journal* 28:2 (Spring/Summer): 287–301.

Shaw, Bill. (1988), "A Reply to Thomas Mulligan's 'Critique of Milton Friedman's Essay 'The Social Responsibility of Business to Increase Its Profits." *Journal of Business Ethics* 7:7 (July): 537–43.

Shlaes, Amity. ([2007] 2008), *The Forgotten Man: A New History of the Great Depression.* Harper Perennial Edition. New York: Harper.

Shleifer, Andrei. (2009), "The Age of Milton Friedman." *Journal of Economic Literature* 47:1: 123–35.

Silk, Leonard. (1976), *The Economists.* New York: Basic Books.

Simons, Henry C. (1936), "Rules versus Authorities in Monetary Policy." *Journal of Political Economy* 44:1 (February): 1–30.

—. (1948), *Economic Policy for a Free Society.* Chicago: University of Chicago Press.

Skousen, Mark. (2001), *The Making of Modern Economics: The Lives and Ideas of the Great Thinkers.* Armonk, NY: M.E. Sharpe.

—. (2005), *Vienna & Chicago Friends or Foes?: A Tale of Two Schools of Free-Market Economics.* Washington, D.C.: Capital Press.

Smith, Adam. ([1776] 1976), *An Inquiry into the Nature and Causes of the Wealth of Nations.* 2 Vols. Oxford: Oxford University Press.

Stephens, Bret. (2010), "How Milton Friedman Saved Chile." *The Wall Street Journal* (March 1). Available at http://online.wsj.com/article/

NA_WSJ_PUB:SB10001424052748703411304575093572032665414.html#printMode.

Stigler, George J. ([1976] 1982), "Do Economists Matter?" In *The Economist as Preacher and Other Essays,* 57–67. Chicago: University of Chicago Press.

Sumner, Scott. (2010), "Two Untimely Deaths" *The Money Illusion Blog.* July 12. Available at http://www.themoneyillusion.com/?p=6061.

Tax, Sol, ed. (1967), *The Draft: A Handbook of Facts and Alternatives.* Chicago: Chicago University Press.

Taylor, John B. (2010), "Macroeconomic Lessons from the Great Deviation." Written and updated version of after dinner remarks at the 25th Macroeconomics Annual Conference, National Bureau of Economic Research, April 19, 2010. [May 2010]. Available at http://www.stanford.edu/~johntayl/NBERMacroAnnualTalkFinal.pdf.

Thygesen, Niels. (1977), "The Scientific Contributions of Milton Friedman." *Scandinavian Journal of Economics* 79:1:56–98.

Timberlake, Richard H. (1999), "Observations on a Constant Teacher by a Graduate Student Emeritus." In *The Legacy of Milton Friedman as Teacher,* ed. J. Daniel Hammond, 22–29. Cheltenham, UK: Edward Elgar.

Tooley, James. (2006), "From Universal to Targeted Vouchers: The Relevance of the Friedmans' Proposals for Developing Countries."In *Liberty and Learning: Milton Friedman's Voucher Idea at Fifty,* ed. Robert C. Enlow and Lenore T. Ealy Washington, 139–54. Washington, D.C.: Cato Institute.

Ulmer, Melville J. (1976), "Friedman's Currency." *New Republic* 175:19 (November 6): 8–9.

Van Giezen, Robert, and Albert E. Schwenk. "Compensation from before World War I through the Great Depression." *Compensation and Working Conditions* (Fall 2001).

Van Horn, Rob, and Philip Mirowski. (2009), "The Rise of the Chicago School of Economics and the Birth of Neoliberalism." In *The Road from Mont Pelerin: The Making of the Neoliberal Thought Collective,* ed. Philip Mirowski and Dieter Plehwe, 139–78. Cambridge: Harvard University Press.

Wald, George, and Linus Pauling. (1976), "To the Editor." *New York Times* (October 24).

Wallis, W. Allen. (1980), "The Statistical Research Group, 1942–1945." *Journal of the American Statistical Association* 75:370 (June): 320–30.

Waltz, Kenneth N. (1979), *Theory of International Politics.* New York: McGraw-Hill.

Wible, James R. (1984), "The Instrumentalisms of Dewey and Friedman." *Journal of Economic Issues* 18:4 (December): 1049–70.

Wilkinson, Will. (2008), "Milton Friedman's Argument for Illegal Immigration." Available at http://www.willwilkinson.net/flybottle/2008/06/11/milton-friedmans-argument-for-illegal-immigration/.

Williamson, Kevin D. (2009), "Blame Milton Friedman: Or, How I Learned to Stop Worrying and Love the Bailout." *National Review* (September 21). Available at http://nrd.nationalreview.com/article/?q=NThkZTQ0ZGFlN2FhOWRmNWE4NTY4NmU5Y2Y0NDVkMTk=.

Willoughby, Jack. (2008), "Tearing into the Fed and Treasury Plans." *Barron's* (October 27).

Wood, John Cunningham, and Ronald N. Woods. (1990), *Milton Friedman: Critical Assessments*. 4 vols. London: Routledge.

Yergin, Daniel, and Joseph Stanislaw. ([1998] 2002), *The Commanding Heights: The Battle for the World Economy*. New York: Touchstone.

No author. (1963), "A Tract for the Times." *Economist* (February 16).

No author. (1969a), "Business: The Intellectual Provocateur" *Time* (December 19).

No author. (1969b), "The New Attack on Keynesian Economics." *Time* (January 10): 74.

No author. (1982), "Milton Friedman Claims Welfare's Our Top Threat." *Spokane Chronicle* (March 3): 6.

Index